THRILLING AND HEROIC STORY . . .
UNIQUE IN WORLD HISTORY . . .

Never before in the history of the world has an army been trained to *save* lives. In ten action-filled years, the men of the Air Rescue Service of the U.S. Air Force have piled up a truly wonderful record for themselves, through floods in Holland and Japan, avalanches in Austria, typhoons in Okinawa, and around the world on all the seven seas. Famed novelist and war reporter Elliott Arnold tells the exciting, human story of the men behind the headlines—

RESCUE!—

a record of victories over overwhelming odds, hair-raising adventures, dramatic and amazing escapes from the very jaws of death —a wealth of unforgettable tales about a group of Americans known in the far corners of the world for their courage, ingenuity and self-sacrifice and for their magnificent slogan "THAT OTHERS MAY LIVE!"

Books by Elliott Arnold

- BLOOD BROTHER
- EVERYBODY SLEPT HERE
- WALK WITH THE DEVIL
- THE TIME OF THE GRINGO

Published by Bantam Books

RESCUE!

Elliott Arnold

AUTHORIZED ABRIDGMENT

Bantam Books • New York

RESCUE!

A BANTAM BOOK published by arrangement with
Duell, Sloan & Pearce, Inc.

PRINTING HISTORY

Duell, Sloan & Pearce edition published October 1956
2nd printing November 1956
Serialized in *Magazine Management* February 1958
Bantam edition published May 1958

Library of Congress Catalog Card Number: 58-7190

PRINTED IN THE UNITED STATES OF AMERICA

BANTAM BOOKS, 25 West 45th Street, New York 36, New York

A Dedication

Never before in history was a military force devoted to the saving of lives—not only military lives, but the lives of civilians in distress—those of its own nation and those of foreign lands as well.

It is my belief that in all the world no group of men is doing more to make the name of the United States sound like music than the men of the Air Rescue Service of the United States Air Force.

These men have received the blessings of many persons, renowned and unknown, in all parts of the world. They should be similarly graced at home.

I have traveled more than fifty thousand miles to talk with them. These are some of the things they told me they did ". . . that others may live."

I apologize to them for the rescue missions that space forced me to omit. And I hope and pray that I have put down the truth at least half as well as they told it to me and that I have not let the Rescue boys down.

I dedicate this book to all of them, the living and the dead.

ELLIOTT ARNOLD

Contents

See p 173

ALASKA

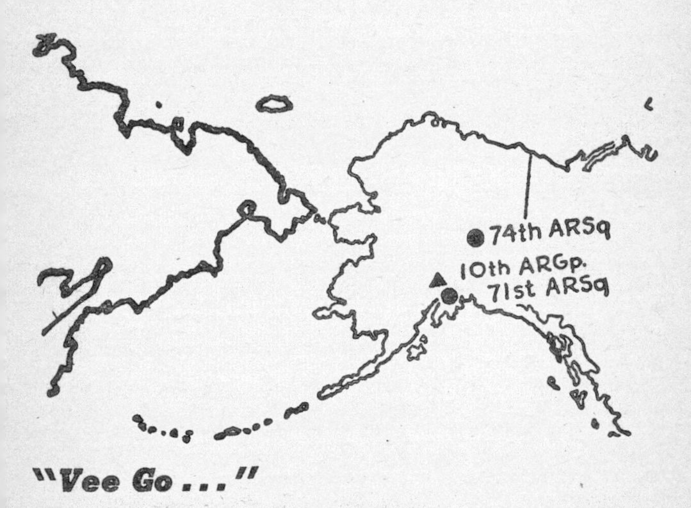

"Vee Go . . ."

If the Wright brothers had never invented the airplane somebody up in Alaska would have had to dream one up.

The flying machine and Alaska were meant for each other. There never was an automobile age in that barren, frozen land and there are almost no roads up there even today. You can count the parking lots on the fingers of one hand, but almost every village—even if only a couple of dozen Eskimos live there—has a landing strip. Alaska jumped from dog sleds to airplanes, and there are thousands of Eskimos who never saw a Ford but who can tell from a mile away whether it's a Stinson or a Piper Cub.

The bush pilots of Alaska are a breed apart and the legends of their exploits—their achievements, near misses, fatal crashes—would put to shame those of our national folk hero, the cowboy of the West. The sides of Alaskan mountain ranges look like pincushions with the tails of crashed planes sticking out, and you can't fly for an hour in any direction from anywhere without looking down and seeing where somebody had it. And it still happens because everything moves by air: the bread you eat in Nome, the paper you read in Fort Yukon, the liquor you drink up at Point Barrow.

The thing is that it is special air these planes plow through, air that is funneled through passes, bellied up from valleys, twisted over mountains, blown in from inlets, often reaching speeds almost as fast as the speed of the airplanes trying to get through it, and all the time, in one way or another, it is trying to pull down the little thing with the propeller. And these planes have to be kept light and small because they have to land and take off from those little strips or maybe from the bank of a river or just a stretch of frozen tundra with a moose standing there and the pilot somehow has to miss him.

From the beginning the Air Rescue gang in Alaska were right at home, right where they belonged. The tone was set by the fabulous Bernt Balchen when he ran the show there. When there was trouble, the only two words in the English language that Colonel Balchen could remember were: "We go." The way it came out, in his Norwegian accent, was "Vee go," and although Rescue has a fine motto, the official one, in Alaska the private slogan is still "Vee go." They still say up there that all hell could be blowing outside and Balchen would grunt his grunt and things would get moving, and that's the way they want to keep it.

"You Are Alone in Your Own World..."

Why would a man want to spend his life jumping out of airplanes? What is there about falling through space that gives some men something they can find doing nothing else?

The jumpers—paramedics—in Rescue are a breed apart. They belong to Rescue but they belong more to jumping and to each other. They are clannish and removed from other men who do not jump and they follow each other's doings all over the world, and when they get together they have their own words for each other.

I have talked to jumpers and I have listened to some hairy stories but there was this thing beyond that—the thing that comes into their faces, their eyes, the timbre of their voices, when they come to the telling of the moment of the plunge out of the plane.

It is said of a matador that he has his "moment of truth" when he finishes his passes and faces the bull with his muleta and sword for the kill. It is said that at that moment he is in a secret, personal world, a world of death that belongs to him and the animal before him, that the huge audience for whom he has been performing, for whose cheers he has been risking his life, no longer exists. I believe jumpers must have their own moments of truth—that moment when they leave the airplane and step into nothing. For a little while they are separated from life and the living, until they touch down again and become as other men. Nothing is the same until the next time.

And when is the next time? As soon as possible, always as soon as possible. It is a compulsion. That is the basic difference between men who have to jump in an emergency and men who jump from choice, what they get from it. When they cannot jump for real, on true missions, then they jump for practice, or they call it practice, only it's really because they cannot not jump. Like mountain climbers who have to climb a mountain simply because it is there. For the jumper an airplane is only a machine to take him up into the air to make a platform from which he can leap.

I tried to find a physical pattern, but there is none. Jumpers are all in the finest condition, of course, boned and muscled to perfection to take the shock of the fall, the violent jerk when the chute pops, the slamming on the ground that can be like jumping off a speeding train. But they are all sizes, big and small, wiry, stringy, beefy, compact. There are many heavy men among them, although heavy men fall faster and hit harder and are more liable to break bones.

I tried to isolate a philosophy but there is no real philosophy either, nothing that can be put down in words that would explain it wholly. Major Rufus Hessberg, a Rescue doctor and jumper who has leaped scores of times—on many real missions and in a long and patient career of testing new types of parachutes, trying to improve them—said to me, "I can't explain it, not to you or to myself. All I can say is that during those moments of falling I get a fulfillment—a peculiar, unique fulfillment. Nothing else gives it to me quite the same way." And Doc Hessberg, a small, shy, spectacled, spectacularly courageous man, whose jumps included a magnificent plunge into the mountains of Italy where an Air Force plane clobbered in, got that look on his face when he said it.

There was the one thing: in the time of falling these men are isolated, removed from the world of other living beings, as though they take respite from their membership in the human race. They all own that, that part of themselves they do not give to their ordinary living, that they award only to those interludes when the plane has gone on and they are dangling under the canopy surrounded by nothing but air.

There is that mystique, and they alone possess it and they know it.

It would be interesting, I think, for a matador, a mountain climber, and a jumper to get together and try to explain themselves to each other.

When I was at Air Rescue Headquarters at Orlando, Florida, I questioned Major Hamilton H. Blackshear, the Air surgeon, top doctor in Rescue. He told me of a strange event in his own life. It was a time when he was a very sick man. He had a crippling attack of arthritis that had his fingers paralyzed and he also had asthma and a severe case of hives. All at the same time and quite properly so, according to the school of medicine that holds that these three ailments are related and psychosomatic in origin.

He was taking a course in jumping at the time—it was when he was just beginning the business of leaping out of airplanes—and everybody said the jumping would have to be postponed until the arthritis and the asthma and the hives went away. But Blackshear said no, he wanted to jump on schedule. "I was under medication, including adrenalin, which gave no help at all," he said. "I could do nothing for myself. I had to be dressed. I had to have my shoes tied on. I had to be carried into the airplane."

The plane took off and reached jumping altitude and then a very strange thing happened to him. "Just before I jumped I felt a sudden relief. I could breathe. The arthritis left me. The hives didn't itch, not at all. And then I jumped. And I stayed relieved for a little while after I landed. But then everything returned with such force that I was in the hospital for five days and I had to be hand-fed for the first three of them. I had had only five jumps before that one so it was still a threat."

I asked another doctor in the Air Force, a nonjumping doctor, and he had his explanation: just before Blackshear jumped his body flooded with adrenalin. Blackshear agreed with that, but he pointed out that he had been taking adrenalin with a needle before that, with no effect. "Either the natural adrenalin has qualities that don't come out of the needle or it's something else," he said.

Major Blackshear is a young, extremely handsome man who looks as though he might have been cast in his role by a Hollywood director. Like Doc Hessberg, he, too, has been working for a long time on new parachutes with improved falling and guiding characteristics and in each stage of development he has insisted on taking the untried chute out first himself.

He is a sober, clear-thinking man of science and yet he, too, is aware of the mystique of the jump, and when he tries to explain it his words shuttle between psychiatry and poetry and he himself is hardly aware when ones leaves off and the other begins. He told me, "Somebody wrote a long and detailed article in a medical magazine on jumping and why people jump and what kind of people jump. The writer started out by saying, 'It is not normal for men to jump out of airplanes.' I don't doubt that is true.

"Why do men jump? There are many reasons, I would think, from what I have seen. For one thing, it sets a man apart. As a jumper he needs to say nothing more about himself. He has a label. He does not have to explain himself to anyone, his friends, his girl friend, his wife, no one. He is a jumper, and that means by definition that he is a brave man. There are men who have groped around for a long time for some kind of distinction and this is a ready-made distinction.

"The ballooned pants tucked into the jumping boots, that is their badge of courage. I just received a letter the other day from an airman who wants to get into jumping. He wrote that he was ashamed of being called 'straight legs'—that's what jumpers call other soldiers whose trousers hang free."

That made sense, as far as it went. But then I asked him why he, a doctor, of an age and position in life that did not require him to prove anything, why had he become a jumper? Why did he jump every chance he got—and when the chance didn't come along naturally go out of his way to make it? He thought for a little while and when he spoke there was another quality in his voice, the same special tone that used to come into the voice of the French poet and pilot, Antoine de St. Exupéry, when he spoke about flying. During World War II St. Exupéry and I worked out of the headquarters of the Mediterranean Allied Air Forces in Caserta, Italy, before he vanished in flight, and I was reminded of the Frenchman and his mysticism as I listened to Blackshear.

". . . You are in this big airplane and it is so noisy, metal all around you and people all around you, and then you go out and there is the little pop and the little jerk and then suddenly you are alone, completely alone. You are a little deafened by the noise of the plane so it is even more silent all around you, and by then the plane has disappeared, you'd be amazed how fast it gets away. And you are even more alone at night, all black, you cannot see the ground. You are alone in your own world." And then he said a revealing thing. "And then after a long while it ends and you get back."

He came back, from wherever it was he had gone while he was speaking. "I say simply that I enjoy it." He smiled.

"If anyone says that I'm crazy to feel this way, I'll go along."

I don't think Blackshear realized he had said "you get *back*." Not that you get *down*, but *back*. Even in talking about it he had slipped over to where he was alone, in his own world.

Why jumpers? There is a reason for these specialists. Airplanes often can't get in where other planes have crashed. Helicopters generally can, and when they can't they can hover, low, and let other men down, but helicopters are relatively slow and their range is limited and when people are hurt and need help fast it is the conventional airplane that can get there quickest and that, often, is when men have to jump.

These jumpers are medical technicians. Except for a few officers such as Hessberg and Blackshear, they are not doctors, but they have gone through a thorough training in emergency first aid: they can set broken bones, give blood transfusions, plasma, sedatives, and do a dozen other things that will keep an injured human being this side of death until a doctor can arrive.

Rescue calls upon its jumpers frequently in Alaska, perhaps more often than anywhere else. There, as has been pointed out, the airplane is practically the only thing that moves, and too often it moves down, hard. And when that happens it is the jumpers who may be the only ones who can get in to what is left.

Let us look for a little while at Staff Sergeant Charles Richard Chapman. Sixty-three jumps to his credit when I spoke to him at Ladd Field at Fairbanks, six of them on real missions in Alaska during which three or four of the victims quite probably would have died if they had had to wait even a few more hours for help.

Chapman is one of the physically big jumpers. He is six feet tall and weighs one hundred and ninety-five pounds and is the heaviest man on his jumping team. He comes from West Virginia and right after he was graduated from high school in 1946 he enlisted in the Marines. He was fifteen years old then and he had to forge his birth certificate to get in.

He became a crack Marine, good enough to travel with a drill team on a good-will tour of South America and Africa. When he returned he found the corps was toying with the idea of creating a force of para-Marines—Marines who would jump—and he volunteered. He was sent to jump school at Quantico and the first time he went out of a plane and the chute cracked open above him he knew that he had found something.

But the program was scrubbed and he was put back in the ground troops and that wasn't good enough any more. When his hitch was up he got out and three weeks later enlisted in the Air Force. "My first idea was to get into a testing outfit like at Wright-Patterson Field so I could test chutes. I put in again and again to get to Korea so I could jump there but they never sent me."

For a while it seemed that he was going to be confined to the ground even in the Air Force, but in August of 1952 he was assigned to Rescue and he went through the regular para-rescue school and the following June he was sent to Ladd. He made a few practice jumps while he waited for the real thing. He didn't have to wait long.

That was when Bud Branaham crash-landed with three passengers on a rocky shale ledge in a canyon in the Brooks Range, one hundred and fifty miles north of the Arctic Circle. Chapman and his team-mate, Sergeant Walter F. Atkins, jumped that day, with Bud on the radio down below pleading with them not to, he was afraid the rocks like glass on the ground would tear them to pieces, pleading with them even though two of the men in the crash had broken backs and his own jaw was broken and hanging down the side of his face.

Bud Branaham has lived in Alaska for more than twenty years and he is one of the best-known pilots and guides up there. He runs the Rainy Pass Lodge and other camps that cater to men who hunt big game. It was fitting that Rescue should come to his aid when he needed it because in 1942 he was commissioned a lieutenant (JG) in the Navy and was given the task of setting up a rescue service in Alaska. "We did utility work, the same function the Air Rescue Service does now, except on a much smaller scale."

In 1944 he was assigned to guide President Roosevelt on a fishing trip and he received a citation for efficiency. After the war he went into the hunting business in a big way.

Bud moves around a lot, especially in the hunting season, but I was fortunate enough to catch him one August evening when he came down from one of his camps to Fairbanks to pick up a client. What made it even luckier was that the client happened to be one of the men who had been in the crash with him: William Guse, an industrialist of Detroit. Bud, who still shows the scars of the accident on his face, and Bill Guse, a large, hearty man of fifty-eight who has hunted big game all over the world, sat down and told me what happened to them that other August day.

Bud and one of his guides, a man named Fred Wieler, started out one morning with Gus and another hunter, Albert LeClerc, another Detroit businessman who also has done a great deal of big-game hunting all over, including Africa.

Branaham: "I guess it was about 10 A.M. when we took off for the camp. The airplane we were using was a Grumman Widgeon. The two hunters and the guide and I had a considerable amount of gear and full tanks of gas. The weather was beautiful—partly cloudy. We were flying about five thousand as we approached Loon Lake where we would land. The lake itself lies in a fold in the mountains. There is one canyon and then four others that lie like fingers. The wind was from the southeast and a landing was indicated from the far end. I elected to fly through the canyon to the left and fly around the mountain and come in that way.

"I told the hunters maybe we'd see some sheep. Then I started to climb. I was well aware that the saddle was around five thousand feet. As we went up the canyon, which was on both sides about fifteen hundred feet above us, I climbed to an altitude that I considered safe before I crossed the saddle. We were about halfway up the canyon, a matter of flying two miles against the canyon walls, where you can no longer turn around. Well, we could see through the saddle, see the valley on the far side. There were three rams and some sheep below. Just as we passed the point of no return I felt the aircraft start to descend although we were still in a climbing position. I immediately applied power and then full throttle and then flaps, ten degrees, before saying anything to the passengers, not wanting to alarm them."

Guse: "I had no idea at all that we were in any kind of trouble. I was sitting in the back seat on the left-hand side of the plane. I saw some sheep and rams and I motioned to Wieler who was sitting next to me and he looked through the window. Then I seemed to see Bud pulling full throttle and I kept looking at the sheep and then I heard LeClerc, who was in the copilot's seat, saying, 'I don't think you're going to make it.' And Bud said, 'No, we're not.' "

Branaham: "This time we were below the rim and we hit a considerable downdraft. I said to the passengers, in a very loud voice I imagine, 'Fasten your safety belts, we may not make it.' Then I put on more flap and more flap until when we crashed, which I did deliberately, there was no point in trying to turn. I had forty degrees of flap, which is full flap on that airplane. I flew the aircraft to a stalling point and it bounced once about twenty feet and then hit a gravel shoulder and we came to rest."

Guse: "We hit and I said, 'Golly, what happened!' And

then I thought of what you think of first at a time like that, about the airplane catching fire, and I thought, *We got to get out, we all got to get out*. I tried to get up. We all had on safety belts and the belts had held all right but I had torn the seat loose from the plane and it was stuck on my back. Here I was moving around with the seat on me.

"I heard Fred Wieler moaning, 'My back, my back.' He couldn't move and he was lying there. I fumbled around trying to unsnap the safety-belt catch and then I opened the door and Wieler managed to get out by himself. I finally got the safety-belt unbuckled and I climbed out, and then I called out to Bud to get out. I kept thinking about fire. The gasoline was dripping from the wings. Then I saw that the port-side engine was still running and I told Bud to throw the switch. He was banged up. His jaw was hanging broken open and he was in a daze. I helped Bud out and then I called out to Al. I saw he could not move, and Bud and I dragged him out feet first.

"We took Fred and Al about thirty feet away from the plane to a flat spot. The gasoline was still dripping from the wing. I went back and started to drag out some food and equipment and gear. Bud was bleeding all over his jaw and face and there was a bone sticking out and I got some bandage and tried to tie his face together.

"Then we covered Wieler up with some sleeping bags. We saw that he and Al were lying there shivering, shaking with the cold, and we blew up some air mattresses. That was the worst time of all for me. We knew they had hurt their backs and we didn't know how bad, and I thought maybe if we moved them the wrong way it might kill them instantly. I asked them if they were able to move, and at first they could move only their arms and then they were able to pull up their legs a little and that made me feel better because I realized they were not paralyzed.

"I had had some teeth removed before I came on this trip and I still had some codeine tablets with me. I gave them the pills and then I said, 'Bud, we need some water.' Only there wasn't any water. Then I said, 'We got some whisky, where is it?' He told me it was in the back of the plane, and I went up to it again and poked around and I found the whisky and there it was in an open box and not a single bottle broken.

"We all had a little whisky and then I said to Bud, 'Where is the camp?' He said it was only a few miles away and I said I thought I could make it. All that was the matter with me was something to the back of my knee. It hurt when I moved but I thought I could make it. Bud said I couldn't make it, that it was up and down the hills, and he said, 'Let's try the radio in the airplane.' The thing I remember was how well he talked. With that jaw broken in all those places he was able to talk. When he tried to drink the whisky it poured out on his neck from the broken jaw."

Branaham: "I went back into the aircraft and turned on the radio—and it worked. I called Bettles CAA station and realized I was in the middle of her weather broadcast, making the time one forty-five. I used the word 'Mayday' twice, which is the first time I have ever had to use that word. She immediately interrupted her broadcast. I told her we had crash-landed and needed immediate assistance. I gave her our location and the fact that I thought two of the passengers were seriously injured and we needed a doctor and medical help.

"Then Bill and I proceeded to make the two injured men as comfortable as possible. After this was accomplished Bill told me we better do something about my face, as he was afraid I was bleeding to death. It was the first time I knew I had been injured. Actually, I suppose, I was in a state of shock all the time."

Guse: "There wasn't much we could do for his face. At two-fifteen he got on the radio and spoke to Bettles again. They told him right away that Air Rescue had been notified and that a plane was taking off, and then I began to feel a little better. Somebody knew about us and that was something. Then Bud said he would talk every half-hour on the radio, no more than that, to save the battery as long as he could. Then Bud told me Bettles told him a Wien Airline plane was scheduled to pass overhead any minute and, sure enough, a few minutes later the plane came over and dipped its wings to show it had seen us and I was feeling better all the time."

Now it happened that earlier that same day Chapman and his pal, Atkins, had managed to wangle themselves a training mission and they had both made jumps. They had just returned to Ladd when the report came in about Branaham crashing. The message was slightly garbled and indicated that only one person was involved in the accident. Chapman and Atkins volunteered immediately to go out again and jump into the wreck.

They were told they had just had themselves a jump, to give somebody else a chance. "It'll save time if we go," Chapman said. "We still got on our gear." "We got off," Chapman told me. "And after we reached there we didn't think there was much chance for jumping." The Rescue plane, a Grumman SA-16, a kind of big sister to the Widgeon that was smashed up below, was at 6,200 feet, and the terrain was 5,200. That made just 1,000 feet of space. The regulations say that the minimum for an operational jump is 800 feet, but that is generally considered in terms of sea level. At more than a mile high the air is thinner and the rate of descent is faster.

But it was more than that. The crashed plane was lying on a narrow saddle, a kind of land bridge between two mountain peaks, with a sharp ridge running down its length. The saddle dropped off to the north and the south. The southern face was a steep slope. The northern face slanted into a sheer cliff with a 2,000-foot drop.

Captain Max Jorgensen, the pilot on the SA-16, spoke to Branaham on the radio and asked him about the ground situation and whether he knew of a place where paramedics could jump. Jorgensen listened to Branaham and then he called Chapman on the interphone. "He says the country is too rough. He says not to jump. He says he's sure you'll both be banged up."

Chapman and Atkins looked down again. The boulders were there, big ones, big as houses, and little ones that were sharp and pointed and stuck up like spikes, and nothing soft anywhere, no cushion of any kind, no earth, just shale and rocks and stone splinters. Jorgensen called them again on the interphone. "Branaham again. He says not to jump. He says you'll rip yourselves to pieces."

"What kind of shape is he in?" Chapman asked.

"Them. There are four of them. Two of them are pretty bad."

Fred Wieler, in his own agony, lifted his head from the air mattress as Branaham pleaded. "Don't let them do it, Bud," he whispered. "They'll kill themselves. Tell them we'll make out someway. Don't let them jump."

"What do you want to do?" Jorgensen asked. The pilot cannot order jumpers to go out. He can forbid it but he can't make them do it.

"Two of them bad," Chapman said. He looked out again. He saw the drop off on the north side. He saw the rocks. Then he saw the red airplane plowed into the earth and he saw the injured men, clearly now. He looked at Atkins. He nodded. Atkins nodded. "We're going to jump," Chapman said to Jorgensen.

The pilot set up a drop pattern and after a low pass, to evaluate the terrain as much as possible, Chapman and Atkins selected the only place that was remotely level. It was a quarter mile to the west of the crash site and on the other side of the spine. It was also a few hundred feet higher than where the Widgeon had crashed, which cut down the jump space even more, but it was the only possible place.

On the second run a spotter chute was dropped to the selected zone. The wind was calm. On the third pass Chapman and Atkins went out. It seemed that the static line had just popped open the chutes when they were on the ground—just fifty yards from where the spotter chute had touched down—and just 200 yards from the edge of the cliff with the 2,000-foot drop. "I made it all right," Chapman said to me. "Atkins got banged up pretty bad on the rocks. He landed between two boulders and bruised his legs. Nothing was broken, though."

From where they had landed they could not see the crash although it was only a little more than a thousand feet from them, so pitted and uneven was the terrain. They had turned around several times coming down so it took a few moments for them to orient themselves and figure out in which direction to head.

"The first one we met was Bud Branaham," Chapman said. "His jaw was offset. One side was hanging down. The bone was completely broken. He had trouble talking. He said he was surprised we had jumped but how glad he was to see us. He took us to the others. He refused to let us take care of his injuries until we took care of the passengers. We treated the men with the back injuries first. We supported their backs with blanket rolls and we administered narcotics and made them as comfortable as possible. The third fellow, Mr. Guse, seemed just in a state of shock. We got him stretched out and treated him for that."

Because the initial report of the accident had stated that there was only one person injured, Chapman and Atkins had left their large medical kit back at Ladd and had jumped with a small kit. Now Chapman got on the radio that was strapped to him and called to Jorgensen for more medical kits and more blankets and a litter.

"All kinds of gear came tumbling out of the plane," Bill Guse said. "It was something to watch. I said to one of the boys we had whisky, did they know where we could get a little water to go with it. I said it in a kind of joke, I guess, but he said, 'Sure,' and he got on the walkie-talkie and calls up and the next time the plane comes around it dropped off a five-gallon can of water, all nicely wrapped up, just like that. Fastest chaser I ever got!

"I said to Chapman, 'I didn't want you to jump.' He said, 'We're here now. Why don't you just take it easy?' He opened up the sleeping bag and I took my shoes off and crawled into it and from then on I watched everything lying down."

Chapman: "We still didn't have enough blankets. We used chutes to wrap them with. Then I went back to treat Branaham. He was still bleeding. I put three stitches on his chin. Without any anesthetic. He had a big triangular cut and I put a stitch in each corner and I set the broken jaw as best I could, judging from the line of teeth. I put the jaw back together and bandaged it. There was still some bleeding in the mouth. I couldn't lay him down. I had to sit him up so he wouldn't strangle in his own blood.

"Then it was a matter of waiting for the helicopter. We fed them and made hot drinks. There was nothing in that altitude that would burn for a fire, so we salvaged some gasoline down from the airplane. We put the gas in a can and put in some sand and made a fire that way. When the sun went down, the water froze in the canteens."

Captain David Gardner brought in his helicopter at thirteen minutes after eight that evening, exactly twenty-one minutes before sunset. Gardner looked over the area and checked the wind and then he set his chopper down on a hillside about three hundred yards west of the crash. Gardner brought Dr. Charles Blackwell, Jr., from the base hospital at Ladd and the two men hurried across the slippery shale to where the injured were lying. As Captain Blackwell examined the men Chapman told him what he had found done for each.

"You did very well," Blackwell said. "Very well." Blackwell gave Bud a shot to put him to sleep.

Bud grabbed Gardner and said, "Don't take off where I came in—the down draft," and then passed out. Gardner looked around him. He decided that despite the rapidly approaching darkness he could bring his helicopter closer. He went back and lifted it up and set it down again just a few feet from where the men were stretched out.

The helicopter was an H-5 and at that altitude and with its gas load it could take out only one person at a time. LeClerc, the most seriously injured, was carried aboard and Gardner flew him to Loon Lake, landing there by the light of lanterns. At nine-fifteen he returned to the crash and landed in the black night and took Bud out. At ten o'clock he returned for the third time, and again he set down his helicopter in the total darkness and loaded Fred Wieler aboard.

Captain Blackwell was needed at Loon Lake to care for the injured until they could be moved, and by then the gas load had been lightened sufficiently for him to get into the helicopter as well. Since Bill Guse's injuries were minor he was asked whether he would mind remaining where he was for the balance of the night with Chapman and Atkins to keep him company.

"Sure," Guse grunted. "Get that egg beater off the mountains."

LeClerc, at the Loon Lake camp, appeared to be worsening. Another Rescue SA-16, flown by Major Joe Walker, which had flown escort for Gardner, was orbiting over the lake but could not land because the lake was too small. A Wien Airlines float plane, piloted by a bush pilot named Dave Anderson, landed on the tiny body of water and LeClerc was carried aboard. Then Anderson took off, guided only by railroad flares lit at the far end of the lake.

He flew eighty miles down a river canyon to Bettles, with Walker flying overhead, and when Anderson landed at Bettles Walker was already on the ground waiting for him. LeClerc was transferred to the SA-16 and was taken to Fairbanks. He was in a bed in St. Joseph's Hospital less than twelve hours after the crash.

Blackwell remained with Branaham and Wieler in a cabin at Loon Lake, and Chapman and Atkins stood vigil with Bill Guse, taking turns at catching a few minutes' sleep. "I woke a little after three in the morning," Guse said. "It was light again and I looked up and there the helicopter was, hovering over me, getting ready to come down, and when he came down I said to him, 'I don't know how near I'm going to get to heaven but the angels will never look better to me than you do.' Gardner grinned at me and said, 'It's nothing.' Chapman and Atkins started gathering up their gear and our guns and stuff. I asked them if they could get on until they were picked up and they said sure. As Gardner took me off they started making a big breakfast."

Branaham, Wieler, and Guse were moved from Loon Lake to Bettles and a Rescue plane took them to Fairbanks. Wieler and Guse joined LeClerc in St. Joseph's and Bud, a reserve officer, was put in the base hospital at Ladd. Wieler had a broken back, multiple contusions and abrasions, and shock; LeClerc had a broken back, severe head injuries, and shock. Despite the severity of their injuries both men recovered. Bud's jaw was found to be broken in four places and he lacked a lot of teeth. Bill Guse got off easy—a torn ligament in the right knee.

"I never could be more grateful," Guse said to me. "They had a job and they did it. While I was in the hospital they visited me and we talked about hunting. What kids!"

Bud's thoughts were still at that moment when Chapman and Atkins bailed out. "Despite all my advice they jumped anyway." He shook his head. Then he said, "Their invaluable assistance and cheerfulness and fortitude are a matter of record. I have never in all my experience seen a rescue performed so efficiently and so rapidly. We felt so keenly about it as individuals that without any prior getting together Mr. Guse and Mr. LeClerc wrote to the Secretary of Defense and I wrote to General Twining about this particular operation."

Facing Staff Sergeant Charles Chapman across the long table in Rescue Operations at Ladd, I asked, "Why do you like to jump?"

He rubbed his chin. "Ah, you train and you take all this guff, school is really rough, and if you never use it you feel left out, that it was all for nothing, so much static for nothing."

"All right. Why?"

He took a long time to answer. "Well, your big reward is when you look at Bud Branaham or Lieutenant Howell—when people are really hurt and wanting help, they're really happy to see you. I thought Lieutenant Howell was going to kiss me or something. He didn't have a stitch of clothing on him. He was so glad to see us."

What about Lieutenant Howell? Who was he and what happened to him? "Ask LaCasse," Chapman said. He stood up and started for the door, and then he stopped and turned and looked at me. "I think everybody is happy to help somebody."

"There Are More Things in Life . . ."

LaCasse is a taut man. As he spoke, he was only half seated in the chair, coiled, as though he were ready to spring. As though he were crouched at the door of a plane, latched on to the static line, waiting for the moment to go. And when he couldn't stay put any longer he bounded out of the chair and paced back and forth and the tight springiness stayed with him. Some boxers have it that way, like they're on their toes when they're not. Cats have it.

Technical Sergeant James Hugh LaCasse, twenty-seven. A Canadian from Brockville, Ontario. Short, compact, blond haired, sparkling blue eyes. "I had a lifelong desire to go to the United States," he said. "After completing schooling in Canada I felt I could get along better in the States and after living here for some time I felt it was my duty to my new-found country to do my bit in the service. After entering the service I found it was to my liking and I felt closer to the country as a whole and I decided I'd like to stay in. So it's more or less a personal outlook actually. The country did something for me and this was my small way of repaying it for letting me live over here."

Only it wasn't enough just to wear the uniform. Jumping seemed to carry it to where he felt it needed really to be. And so for Jim LaCasse, the extra of jumping became the extra he was able to give to his new country, and jumping to rescue made it exactly right. "I'd been exposed to the facts that there are more things in life than making a bundle of money and that saving a few people's lives now and then is more important than what your personal stake in life is. I found this type of work very satisfying. It reaps rewards in its own way—put it that way."

Jim got to Ladd in the latter part of April 1954, and the Howell story that Chapman spoke of occurred the following November. Second Lieutenant Nichola Howell, twenty-one, and his copilot, Second Lieutenant Richard Lill, twenty-two, were out on a routine training flight in their T-33 jet from Eielson Field, near Fairbanks, scheduled to fly to Nome via Galena. Over Koyuk Sound in the Bering Sea something happened to the plane and it went out of control and both men jettisoned the canopy over their heads and then released the explosive charge that blew them out of the plane. Howell didn't want to drift down too slowly in that subzero weather so he dropped free for almost five thousand feet, and when he finally saw water under him he popped his chute. He landed in the Bering Sea in water up to his chest. He looked around for Lill, from whom he had got separated while falling, but he didn't see him anywhere.

He waded through the icy water until he got on land and then he walked until he found an old abandoned trapper's shack. By that time his clothing was frozen stiff and he was not too far removed from that point himself. He went inside the cabin and tried to get the clothing off but his fingers wouldn't work. He managed somehow to gather some scraps together and start a small fire on the floor of the cabin and he thawed his hands and got his clothing and shoes off. When he got out of his flying suit, it stood up just the same as it did with him in it. He tried to thaw the suit but the fire wasn't nearly big enough and it only froze harder so that it was like a suit of armor. He huddled over the fire, naked, and waited. Outside, the temperature was just a shade above zero.

He kept the fire flickering for twenty-four hours, just enough heat to keep from freezing to death, and then he heard an airplane and he ran outside. Up in the plane La-

Casse and Chapman were looking down, searching. "We spotted him running down the beach," LaCasse said, "naked as a jay bird. We jumped and took care of him in nothing flat. No sweat."

LaCasse and Chapman stripped off some of their own clothing and put it on Howell and got him warmed up a little and then they asked about Lill. From what Howell could tell them, and from their own estimate of direction and drift, they figured that Lill was probably a few miles farther down the beach, perhaps on the other side of the Koyokuk River. They went to the village of Moses Point and there LaCasse engaged a native Eskimo pilot, Don Stickman, and flew with him in his bush plane to the village of Koyokuk.

"There I made arrangements for a thirty-foot native skin boat and three dog teams of seven dogs each and six natives. I agreed to pay ten dollars for each team and thirty dollars to the man who owned the team and fifteen dollars to each person who helped. We started out across the Koyokuk River with the boat on one sled. The lead team fell through the channel and in just a matter of minutes four dogs were dead.

"We rushed forward immediately. Roger Nassauk, the Eskimo driving the first team, fell in, too. We got him out, after fifteen minutes. Every time we tried to get him out the ice would break around the edges. Then we all returned to the village. We hassled it out. The language barrier was such that I had to make myself understood in a primitive way. The Eskimos have beliefs and disbeliefs. It was a bad omen to them that they had already lost four dogs and had nearly drowned a man. Besides, they have a natural fear of water in the winter.

"I was having trouble, and then I learned something from a white schoolteacher in the village, a man named Ed Rorke. He told me if I expressed myself in a manner to make the Eskimos believe they were part of a team, an American team, and were not being used as natives, they would have a different attitude. I gave them a little talk along those lines and he was right. It worked."

Then LaCasse got word through his radio from a search plane that a parachute had been sighted imbedded in the frozen Bering Sea. "We started out again. We took the last dogs they had in the village and that was very important to the Eskimos. The hunting season was coming up and they ran the risk of losing the dogs or overworking them so they wouldn't be of any value during the hunting season—and they get their food for the whole year then.

"We stayed on the coast ice. I didn't know the depth of the water and having witnessed one accident I was leery of riding in a sled. I learned how to ride, native style, one foot on the runner, half running and half pushing. At Norton Sound we followed the coast ice for about ten miles and then headed for the open sea. I decided it was better traveling in a boat than along the shore because of the pressure ridges built up along the shore.

"When we got to the edge of the ice, we tried to float the boat but it wouldn't float. So I asked for the aircraft overhead to drop me some exposure suits. The natives wouldn't put on the suits until I put one on first and waded out. We left the dogs with two natives and the rest of us pushed the boat to where it was deep enough to float. The water was about twenty-eight degrees. We waded up to our chests. It was exhausting trying to push the boat through the mud. We had to stop every ten or twenty feet. Finally we got it out into the Bering Sea and started the motor and headed southeast to where the parachute had been located. We were about two hundred and eighty miles from Russia at that point.

"We worked our way for about six hours but we couldn't make it to where the chute was. We headed in for shore again and we holed up for the night. At 8 P.M. we lit a big fire so the airplane above could spot us and the plane, flown by Captain Harry Cole, dropped us supplies. The natives were amazed how I could contact the plane and get it to respond. When I asked them if they wanted food they thought we would get out our guns and shoot some and then it came floating down out of the air.

"I requested Captain Cole to go back to where we had left the other natives and drop them some food, too, and tell them, if he could, to return to their village, that we were staying out all night. In the morning when we got up the boat was frozen in. We were stuck. I began to worry about the natives. We had already caused them all that hardship, losing their dogs, and now their boat was frozen in for the winter. All their equipment was lost to them—and they faced starvation for helping us.

"I radioed for immediate evacuation. Don Stickman came in again and landed on the beach. I paid the natives for their boat and equipment. That Christmas we made a drop over their village—toys for their kids and, what was more important, food, plenty of food. It was an experience, working with them. Their attitude was that they were a group team, being led by someone who knew what he was doing. But you couldn't push them too far. They had to know they were equals. Which they were, more than that."

When Chapman learned that LaCasse had been unable to get to the chute in the boat, he tried another tack. "He came down with Stickman in the light plane and landed five miles farther south on the beach and then he waded out to where the chute was, imbedded in ice. The parachutes are issued by name and it was important to make sure this one belonged to Lieutenant Lill. It was his, all right.

"The canopy was on the ice and the lines were under the water and the harness was on the bottom. He found a glove and a map and a hat—and that was all. He broke the ice and trampled around and tried to find the second man. No sign of him. Then he came back and went into the hills and looked for him. Chapman almost didn't get back himself. His part of it was worse than mine, believe me."

Lieutenant Howell was taken to the hospital and recovered very quickly. He achieved a kind of immortality—the only known man who lived through a day and a night of Alaskan winter as naked as the day he was born. The body of Lieutenant Lill was never found.

About two months after that an F-89 jet with a pilot and radar observer crashed alongside the Chena River, cutting a swathe through the trees, and Chapman and LaCasse went out in an SA-16 flown by Captain Cole. They ran into a little competition.

"The weather was real bad," LaCasse said. "Ice, fog, and snow. Visibility was about eight hundred feet. We spotted the survivors standing off the wing of their plane holding up night flares. That's how bad it was—night flares at high noon! We circled around trying to find a place to jump. We kept losing them. When we saw them for the third time we figured it was the last chance, that we'd better do it and get it over with, we might not find them again."

The SA-16 at that point was at minimum operational jump altitude of 800 feet. Chapman and LaCasse went out and cushioned in the trees. They uncoiled their ropes and started the tricky descent to the ground. However, it seems that while Cole was maneuvering the SA-16 to a jump position a helicopter, flown by Lieutenant Lewis F. Wells, also was poking around, and that a couple of other paramedics, Master Sergeant Ira Chichester and Staff Sergeant Willard Williams, were aboard—and eager to foul up Chapman and LaCasse.

You see, there is a nice rivalry between the SA-16 pilots and the chopper kids. They're always trying to prove to each other that their machine is the right one. Wells got his helicopter down low and Chichester and Williams dropped off the hoist. They got the survivors, got them in the sling, had them hoisted up into the chopper cabin, and then Wells went straight up, like an elevator. A real snatch case.

When Chapman and LaCasse got down from the trees and made their way to the scene they found Chichester waiting for them, calm and relaxed and looking like a man who had studied the face of a Cheshire cat for a long time and had it down real good. "What the hell are you doing here?" he asked pleasantly. "Hell, we got those boys out already."

LaCasse shook his head and grinned as he recalled that moment. "Professional jealousy. We each figure we can do the other's job. Actually we all need each other, but they tried to make us look like we were a day late and a dollar short. So we just chalked it up to a training jump."

Jim LaCasse has learned a lot in Alaska. He has learned that you can get people to work themselves to the bone and run the risk of starvation—if you make them know you think they stand as high and straight as you do. And he knows what comes on the face of a human being when it looked like the time was up and he handed over another chance. *"Saving a few lives now and then is more important than what your personal stake in life is. It reaps rewards in its own way."*

"Everybody Was Crying—Even the Indians . . ."

As Jim Stevenson started toward the airplane with the sack of bread slung over his shoulder his daughter, Sandra, ran up to him and threw her arms around his legs. "Be sure you get back in time for my brithday, Daddy."

Stevenson squinted down at the child. "You having a birthday?"

"You *know* it's going to be my birthday."

Stevenson put down the bread bag and swung the little golden-haired, blue-eyed child high in the air. "Of course, I'll be back, honey. I catch all your birthdays. By the way, how old are you going to be? Eight? Ten?"

Sandra giggled. "Three, Daddy. You know that."

Stevenson put down the child, kissed his wife, Gladys, waved Paul Andrick on toward the plane. A few minutes later Stevenson lifted the lightplane up from the strip at Fort Yukon on what was to have been a brief, routine flight across the Yukon River to Venetie Landing, just a little more than twenty miles away.

Two days later Rescue at Ladd was notified that the two

men were missing. Bush pilots had searched for them but hadn't been able to turn up a clue.

When I tried to look up Jim Stevenson in the little village of Nenana on the Yukon where he manages one of the Northern Commercial Company stores I was told he was away on a fishing trip. Nobody knew exactly where he was but somebody said an Eskimo was going to deliver some supplies and a case of beer to him by kayak. I scribbled a note on a piece of wrapping paper and put it in with the supplies and a few days later Stevenson got me by short-wave radio at Rescue headquarters at Elmendorf Field, Anchorage.

It was almost five years since it had happened and I asked him if he still remembered it well enough to tell me about it. There was no sound but the crackling of the radio for a moment or two and then he said, "Remember it? How could I forget it?"

A couple of days after that I was sitting in a little fishing cabin near Sunshine, not far from the Susitana River and Jim Stevenson was telling me what he could never forget.

Jim is a husky, blue-eyed man with the reddest head of hair in Alaska. He's in his late thirties now. During World War II he was a B-24 bombardier flying out of Italy and he achieved something unique—he was shot down three times and all over the same place—Vienna. Each time he managed to make it to Yugoslavia and the Partisans got him out.

After the war he went to Alaska to work for the Northern Commercial Company which has stores scattered through Alaska like those of the Hudson's Bay Company in Canada. There is a legend in Alaska, by the way, that the Russians could never conquer the territory because the N.C.C. wouldn't give them credit. Stevenson was made manager at Fort Yukon.

"There was a traveling mechanic in town for the Alaska Native Service, this Paul Andrick," Stevenson said. "He'd been in Alaska for only a couple of months. He came to Fort Yukon to go to Venetie Landing to work on some motors for an A.N.S. school there. Ed Toussaint, the bush pilot, was out of town and my own plane was in Fairbanks getting winterized. So I borrowed a brand-new Aeronca Champion that belonged to Ed to take Andrick to Venetie. I also was going to carry ten pounds of bread to the teacher there.

"In the course of going up, Andrick said he wanted to look at some caribou herds. They're pretty thick there at that time of the year and I guess he had never seen any before. We located a big herd and started following it up the Porcupine Range and we got up in the Coleen River and kept following the herd through the passes and the weather socked us in. It was plain damned foolishness. There was no excuse for it—to take that plane out for the first time. We iced up and were forced down on a glacier and broke a ski.

"In the length of time it took me to repair the ski it was necessary for me to preheat the engine again and soften the oil. The temperature was between forty-five and fifty—we never say 'below' here in the wintertime—and all we had was a small primus stove to heat with. I opened the cowling and put the primus right inside. With that temperature it took about three hours of heating and in consequence we had to bring gas for the primus out of the plane tank."

He managed to get the engine warm enough and he fired it up and got off. "And then we flew downriver for about twenty miles. I noticed my compass was about thirty degrees off course. By this time our gas supply was so low it would have been impossible to get back to Fort Yukon so I landed on the ice on the river."

Bernt Balchen said, "Vee go." And he named Gene Douglas, then major and flight commander at Ladd, to do the going. Gene moved fast. He sent four C-54's and two C-47's out on search from Ladd immediately and established a second, forward search base at Fort Yukon. He moved three LC-126's—shorter-ranged, single-engine Cessnas—to work out of Yukon. He set up another C-47 to shuttle back and forth over the 150 miles between Ladd and Yukon every morning with supplies, gasoline, and oil for the forward base.

Douglas, a full colonel in command of Rescue at Hickam Field, Hawaii, when I caught up with him, a big, light-haired, energetic man, told me "that flight got to be known as the eight o'clock milk run. People said they could set their watches by it." Douglas set up his own shop at the advanced post at Yukon. "The first thing I did was talk to all the people there. I tried to get all the clues I could, tried to find out the psychology of Stevenson, to learn what he might do in an emergency. He'd been over the route several times, he was a former bombardier, he was expected to be ingenious and adept at survival. We figured out the extreme range of his airplane and broke the area into blocks about thirty miles square and we started searching, beating the bushes with our eyeballs, trying to find out what happened to this aircraft."

Stevenson surveyed his situation and tallied his assets. For food there was bread, ten pounds of it. Nothing else. For protection against the fifty-below cold at night they had, for the two of them, one inner lining to a sleeping bag that he had found in the plane. Not the bag itself, but the mummy lining. For a weapon he had a .22-caliber automatic pistol. That was the sum of what they owned. "We camped by the plane for two days, living on bread and water. We melted snow for water. We couldn't dig through the ice—it was four or five feet thick. I had on woolen underwear, woolen pants, a woolen shirt, flying clothes, and a parka. Andrick was dressed about the same as I was. We had no radio in the plane, just the bare primary group of instruments. After two days I figured that it was just a case of walking. So we started out.

"That was about as tough a walk as I've ever had—and that includes the times in Yugoslavia during the war. We were on a fast-running glacier river and in places the ice was only a couple of inches thick. The snow keeps the ice warm and the current underneath cuts through. You'd walk along and you'd find yourself up to your waist in water. If you'd stay away from the cut banks you'd be all right, but we had to cross it now and then. When we got wet we'd just keep walking. Andrick wore glasses and they would steam up and he couldn't see. I'd have to break trail and he'd follow. We could walk only about three hours a day—that was all the light there was. The pistol was useless. We saw a caribou once but I couldn't think of trying to get him.

"The wolves would come up to within ten feet of us. We saw wolves so big we thought they were caribou. They'll come right up to your camp. All night long we heard them howling. We'd limit ourselves to one thick slice of bread in the morning and a thick slice at night. That's hungry country up there—no rabbits or anything I might have got with the pistol. There was a kind of deep orange berry we ate once in a while but it didn't do anything.

"Andrick had never slept outside a night in his life. It was his first time in Alaska. But that turned out to be a good thing. At a time like that one man has to be boss or there's trouble. He let me make the rules. We followed the Coleen, which runs into the Porcupine River, which in turn leads into the Yukon. There's an Indian superstition about the Coleen. The Indians won't trap that country. There's only one camp on the river, run by an old white man. Normally on a river up here we'd run into cabins, but not the Coleen nor the Chanjac. I knew that from where we were we had to cover about two hundred and sixty miles and we'd have to walk it all if we were going to get in. I'd just about given up hope of being picked up. I figured it was walk or curtains."

Douglas: "Each night we came home discouraged. The people in the village would pep us up and plead with us not to call off the search. Stevenson's wife would look at us each night when we came in and we couldn't look back at her, and when the little girl, Sandra, asked where her daddy was, we couldn't answer her.

"There was no hotel there. We used a house and fixed up a room upstairs with mattresses for the crews and Gladys Stevenson and Ed Toussaint's wife fixed breakfast for us. We rotated nightly from one place to another for dinner with the bulk falling on the hospital of the Fort Yukon Episcopal Mission. We'd come in for gas at noontime and the nurses would come down to the strip with hot coffee while we were reservicing the aircraft. Bush pilots came in with their own aircraft—five or six of them—and I put my navigators in their planes with them and the bush pilots placed themselves under my navigational control. I assigned them areas to search.

"One day at noon, while we were servicing the aircraft, I saw a man with a dog team coming down the trail. He and his wife owned a lodge on the other side of Fort Yukon. I saw him put a package in the aircraft. I didn't know what it was and I forgot about it. We had to service the airplanes out of fifty-gallon drums. Daylight was at a premium and we worked as fast as we could to get airborne again—we had only from 9 A.M. to 2 P.M. to fly. And that was not all good daylight but half twilight. We never stopped for lunch. After we were out flying a couple of hours that day we were cold and hungry and thought it would be a good time to eat. We wished we could, but we felt obligated to take advantage of the daylight, what there was of it. Then by chance we saw this package in the plane and opened it and it was a Mason jar with coffee and surrounding it were ham and egg sandwiches."

Where Gene was telling me this the palm trees were rustling in a light breeze and from a radio somewhere there was Hawaiian music. But Gene was thousands of miles away, back in Alaska, the place he says he loves more than any other.

"Each night we held a radio-telephone conference with the people at Ladd, back in Fairbanks. Mrs. Toussaint ran the radio station at Fort Yukon in conjunction with her duties as postmistress. She was a large, motherly woman—full of cheer and energy. She would call up on the ham radio on the schedule the bush pilots use and a ham would plug me in with my Center at Ladd and my Operations officer Captain Robert Marcum would get on the horn.

"I'd give him my clues and ask him the result of his interrogation of the crews that were flying the search out of

Ladd. We established identical plotting boards and assigned each square marked off by numbers so each of us could tell what had been searched. We'd lay on the search for the next day and Marcum would send up gas for the next day's operations. We gave the leftover gas to the bush pilots. Everybody at Fort Yukon pitched in. It was something to be part of. Each day we had to get fire pots under the planes before we could take off. We had to build a hood over the engines and light stoves under it to melt the engine oil. The batteries had to be taken out of the planes when we came in and brought to a place that was kept heated all night and then hauled out to the planes again in the morning.

"Remember we were operating out of a makeshift strip—we weren't on an air base where we had regular facilities for maintenance. But everybody pitched in. Everybody wanted those two men found—alive. There was one old sourdough Egil Salveson, a friend of Jim Stevenson, who worked day and night, gassing planes, everything. I don't know when he slept.

"Well, the search went on day after day with no luck. After a full week with no bath or cleanup or anything we came in from a long day, it was cold, and the head nurse of the mission met us as we came in and told us that she had arranged hot baths for all of us. The water was heated at the mission and then we were invited to have dinner at the mission afterward. I'll never forget the bath and the dinner, but it was a rough evening. We'd been looking for seven days and hadn't seen anything. But what was bad was the report I got that night by radio that the weather was getting ready to sock in. If we were lucky we'd have maybe a day, maybe two at most, before everything might have to be grounded. And once the weather closed in it might be weeks before it lifted again.

"Mrs. Stevenson had given up hope. She had already started to pack, planning to go back to the States. And what hurt the most was that the day after the next day was the little girl's birthday. It looked like it was going to be one hell of a birthday."

Stevenson: "We were walking down the river. It was about 2:30 P.M. and it was getting dark. And then I fell through the ice. I really fell in this time—up to my shoulders. We were carrying poles and it was the pole that kept me from going all the way. So we decided that day that we would knock off early and build a fire so I could dry out. Then I began to think how things were, and I figured we didn't have a ghost of a chance to make it. Our equipment was wearing out, especially our shoes. They were going to pieces. We had been lining the sleeping bag with the cardboard from the box that held the bread and that was what we had slept in each night—both of us crawling into this lining at the same time. We'd sleep for half an hour and then crawl out and move around and then get in again. It was some trick, but by now the bag was coming apart and all I could see was us with no shoes and nothing to cover us at night. And no food. Ten pounds of bread don't last forever no matter how you ration it.

"We were in the Yukon Flats as I figured it, between the Brooks Range and the Crazy Mountains. The weather pours in there—I'd often been held up for thirty days at a time flying from one place to another. The worst weather in the world, the Yukon Flats. There are no markers there. And it was no weather for anybody to be flying in. We'd been lucky so far with the kind of weather we had but I knew it couldn't last. I knew what had to come, how it was going to get, and all I could think of was that they hadn't been able to find us when it was relatively clear and what would happen when it closed in.

"We built a fire and I tried to dry off and Andrick was telling me that he had just taken out some life insurance before we started out when he saw some wolf tracks around our camp and he asked me should we tie ourselves into the trees so the wolves wouldn't get us and then this C-54 came over." Stevenson dragged on a cigarette and his blue eyes drifted and the five years were not so long, after all. "I never saw anything so glad in my life."

He was silent for a few moments, and then he gave a short laugh. "Andrick got so excited he threw his hatchet into the fire. God, we were lucky I fell in when I did and we had to make a fire!"

Douglas: "I was flying when Captain Smiley Whitmer radioed me that he had located them. He saw these two men, just outside the mountains by a stream, and he dropped a message to them asking them if they were Stevenson and Andrick to please wave their arms. They waved their arms so hard, Whitmer said, he thought they'd take off like birds. Then he dropped them supplies and a message: 'Stay put—we'll be in at daylight for rescue.' "

Stevenson: "They dropped us a full case of rations. It landed less than fifty yards from us. That night we dug into a beaver house to keep warm. Andrick sat up and ate all night. I sat up all night and smoked cigarettes."

Douglas: "We thought at first of getting a helicopter up from Ladd the next day, but that would have taken too long. The only thing that could get in where they were—about one hundred and twenty to one hundred and thirty miles away from Fort Yukon—was a lightplane. Our stuff was too big. What we could do was send out a C-47 to guide the lightplane in.

"That night Ed Toussaint and I flew down to Ladd and Ed got Stevenson's own Stinson that was in Fairbanks. He changed the prop on the Stinson because where they were was a close area and he put on a high-performance prop so he could get in and out in the shortest distance. I asked him to take along my copilot, a captain named Charles Neuvius—Neuvius was killed later making a glider pickup in a C-54. Then Ed asked a favor of me. He wanted to know whether his wife and Mrs. Stevenson and Jim's pal, Egil Salveson, could go along in the C-47. I knew it wasn't right, but how are you going to tell that to people who had worked their hearts out for us?

"In the mess hall that night at Ladd I just mentioned to the boys that we had found them. We got to talking about the little girl and how the next day was her birthday and when I got up the next morning with Whitmer and went out to the C-47 the boys brought me a wooden box and told me there was something in it for Sandra.

"We landed back at Fort Yukon, and I gave my space to the passengers who wanted to go and whom I felt obligated to let go. I asked Whitmer to radio me as soon as the Stinson was safely on the ground at the pickup point and when it was airborne and on its way back. Whitmer took off and Ed Toussaint was right behind him in the Stinson."

Whitmer got there first and he flew low over the two men. By then Stevenson had a ten-day growth on his face and his red hair and beard stood out against the snow as though his head was on fire. "Is that your husband?" Whitmer asked Gladys Stevenson.

"Yes, yes." She kept saying it. "Yes, yes, yes."

While the C-47 orbited the Stinson landed on his skis and picked up Stevenson and Andrick and then took off.

Douglas: "The C-47 got back to Fort Yukon first. So all the passengers were standing on the runway when the Stinson taxied in. The whole village turned out to welcome them. There were two hundred people there, most of them Indians. I think everybody was crying, even the Indians."

When Stevenson stepped out of the Stinson, Sandra broke away and ran up to him. He held her for a long time.

Stevenson: "I never knew there were so many people in Fort Yukon. It looked to me like half of Fairbanks was there. Everybody went into the store. As we entered, the first thing I saw on the counter was this cake. It was all covered with icing and there were three candles on it and it said on top: 'Happy Birthday, Sandra.' Gene Douglas's cooks down at Ladd had baked it. It was a surprise to me, of course, but not even Gladys or Sandra had known about it. I guess we all broke down for real then."

The candles were lit, Sandra made a wish as she blew them out, and the cake was cut into pieces, very little pieces, so that almost everybody had a bite. And then while Sandra curled up in his lap Jim Stevenson told of the eight days that had passed. When he had finished, Sandra was asleep.

Stevenson: "Then I told Gene Douglas what I had said to Andrick when we saw that C-54 come over us. I said, 'I'll never again complain about paying income taxes. Never again.' "

HAWAII

"I Had to Reply . . . in the Same Language"

On the morning of December 7, 1941, a Hawaiian boy lay flat on a rooftop in Honolulu and watched Japanese planes destroy Pearl Harbor. His name was Melvin Kealoha Ayau. He was sixteen years old. His own name, Kealoha, meant "happiness," and until that dark morning the name was one that belonged to him because he had grown up in his own land, among its beauties, its green forests, its waters. On that morning the name departed from him as he watched the death and destruction that were being brought to his home.

There is little of hate and little of anger in Hawaiian nature now. There has been violence on the land, much violence, but that was long ago, and it no longer lives in the hearts of the people. There is always time for song and for dancing and much time for love, but there is almost no time for hatred. But on that morning in the heart of the boy there was hatred for the first time.

It was now again a time of peace in Hawaii. People were gathered for a *luau*. There was on every face the serenity and joy that live so easily in the features of the people of the islands. There was music and there was the smell of food to be eaten and there were cups filled with drink. It was only with effort that Melvin Ayau was able to bring himself back over the years.

"I was with my sister, Lei, whose name means 'wreath.' We were having breakfast. We saw a drove of planes come over. We watched them strafe the hangars. Just about that time the radio broadcast came over that Pearl Harbor was being bombed and that all the people were to go up into the hills.

"Of course I didn't go up into the hills. I climbed up to the roof and saw them dive-bomb Pearl Harbor. I saw the oil tanks blow up there. I watched the whole thing for about an hour and a half. I wasn't scared or nervous. I saw the planes strafing the hangars. It sounded like marbles dropping on a tin plate. Then we got a call from my brother. They had hit a house in his block in the Pawaa Area on the other side of town. There is a big public school in front of his house. They were trying to hit all the big buildings. He thought his house was going to burn so I started up there.

"I drove my sister's car to my brother's place. I got out the hose and started shooting water on his home and on the surrounding homes on that block. The bombing was still going on. It was then that the shock of the whole thing hit me. There were wounded people lying on the grass in front of the school—they had been evacuated from Pearl and they were setting up the school to be a hospital. I helped them carry the people into the rooms. I was there until about ten o'clock that night." In those hours the boy ceased to be a boy.

"There was only one thing I wanted—to go into the Air Corps as soon as I was old enough. I wanted to go to flying school if I could make the grade. I had to reply to the Japanese in the same language."

Melvin Ayau is a young man of middle height with gentle features, large dark eyes, and a soft, musical voice. As he sipped his drink he told me how he went to the authorities in Honolulu on the day following the bombing and how they looked at him, and while they did not laugh—it was not a time of laughter, even over Hawaiian youths who wanted to become airplane pilots—they explained to him that he was too young and that even if he were old enough he would first have to go the mainland of the United States and that he would have to pay his own way.

He took on a job as a laborer. His family tried to dissuade him, of course. Who had ever heard of a native boy becoming a pilot in the American Army? It was not in the manner of Hawaiians. He spoke the English language but with an unmistakable accent. Here in Hawaii he was home. There, on the strange and remote mainland, he would be a dark-skinned native boy. A pilot, moreover, was an officer. The Americans were good, many of them, but they did not have many dark-skinned natives from Hawaii wearing the uniform of officers in their Air Corps.

It was as though Melvin knew the language of his parents no longer. Each week he put aside his money and he watched it slowly accumulate. He needed years and he needed money. He became one-minded, driven, hardened by a single passion. In August of 1943 he had enough money and enough years at last and he called his family together and told them he was going away.

Once again the entire family, together and member by member, protested. Perhaps the one who was hurt the most was his father, Edward Ayau. When the Japanese had attacked, Edward Ayau, a Chinese-Hawaiian, was foreman on a pineapple plantation on the island of Molokai. The horror of Pearl Harbor had shocked him, too—but it had produced a different result. Edward had no thought of vengeance. It was his belief that his people needed spiritual help. He had left his job on the plantation and had become a minister of the Hawaiian Protestant Church. It filled him with unutterable pain that his son was leaving him, and the pain was even deeper because his son was leaving to learn how to become a killer from the air.

When the family understood at last they could not stop Melvin they gave a great *luau,* the greatest in the family history, and they looked upon Melvin carefully and in sorrow, because to them he had already departed, and no one would expect to see him again.

Because of his age he had to bring his parents to the passport section before he could leave Hawaii. "They interviewed all of us—they thought I was still too young. And I had only enough money to pay my fare one way to the United States and there was not a soul on the mainland I knew or could call on for help if I needed it. If I flunked out, I would be stranded in the United States without a penny." Despite all that, Melvin somehow persuaded the authorities to permit him to go. Perhaps he communicated some of his fervor. He left his native land for the first time.

"I took my examination at Hamilton Field in California—and I passed. Believe me, I was the happiest guy in the world!"

On October 1, 1943, just twenty-three days after his eighteenth birthday, Melvin Ayau was sworn in as an aviation cadet. In April 1945, after studying and training in Texas, he was commissioned a second lieutenant in the Army Air Corps. He wrote to his family that one thing had been answered: a native boy from Hawaii with a curious accent could wear the uniform with the silver wings of a pilot and the gold bars of an officer.

From then on he awaited the orders that would send him back across the Pacific, back farther west than Hawaii, back to the little islands from which the airplanes had flown with bombs for the enemy. But it was not intended to be that way. Perhaps it was the *amagua* who was guiding the way. Perhaps it was Lono, who lived in the clouds, the clouds that Melvin knew now, too. First it was Brooks Field, at San Antonio, and more training, and then Lackland Army Air Base, where he learned to fly the twin-engined B-25 that was being used in New Guinea against the Japanese. He felt certain that he would get his chance then, but instead he was sent on to other air bases, always within the United States. And the war passed him by and the thing that was started in Pearl Harbor that Sunday morning was ended on the deck of a battleship. And by then Tokyo and Hiroshima and Nagasaki and Nagoya and the other places had paid the price for Pearl Harbor and the time when it sounded like marbles were dropping on a tin plate.

Lieutenant Ayau was at Lincoln Army Air Base, Nebraska, when the war ended and his chance for revenge was ended as well. But oddly he was not so disappointed as he thought he should be. For by then he had become interested in another kind of flying machine, the helicopter. He applied for helicopter training and began his transition in May 1946 and finished in July.

The helicopter is a gentler kind of bird. It is not made for death. It is clumsy, and no one would pretend it had any beauty. But it is not made for death. Perhaps that is why the boy whose middle name meant happiness and merriment took to it so well. Lieutenant Ayau became expert at flying the chopper, so much that he was used to fly them for demonstration purposes to acquaint the public with their unique capabilities. And then one day he was sent to the air base at West Palm Beach and he found himself assigned to something that was the precise opposite of what he had started out to do. He was put in Air Rescue, and now there seemed to be no question that the quiet *amakua* was mixing in his life.

He was sent up to the Rescue squadron at Selfridge Field, in Michigan, and his first rescue mission was the search for Major General Paul B. Wurtsmith, the brilliant Pacific war tactician who was reported missing with four other men in a B-25 in the Great Smokies, in September 1946. Ayau flew his helicopter all the way down from Selfridge. He had to make four stops for refueling before he reached Asheville, North Carolina, out of which the search was being conducted. Ayau and another helicopter pilot, Lieutenant David J. Andersen, were the only helicopter pilots working on the mission. Day in and out, in all kinds of weather, including snow and icing conditions, they wove their whirlybirds through the mysteries of the mountains seeking some sign of the missing plane. The mission ended tragically: General Wurtsmith and the four other men had been killed instantly when their plane crashed into Cold Mountain, North Carolina.

Ayau returned to Selfridge Field and in the months that followed he was checked out in other planes used in Rescue: the old PBY's, the familiar Catalinas of wartime; the B-17's which had served so well as bombers and which were being given a new lease on life as search planes; the L-5's, lightplanes on skis; the C-47's, the faithful gooney birds that were old when the war started and that seemed to get steadier and safer and more dependable the older they got.

Ayau relished the opportunity to enlarge upon his flying skills by learning how to handle different-type planes—but the more he flew conventional aircraft the more he loved his helicopter. The awkward chopper seemed almost to be a personal extension of himself and he came back to it always, fining himself down in its operation. In his hands it became a delicate instrument and he performed on it as a virtuoso.

From time to time, while he was stationed at Selfridge, Ayau applied for a transfer back to Hawaii. He had been long from home. There were places of beauty on the mainland and he had seen many of them. But for one who was born on the island there is no other place quite the same. In May of 1948 the miracle happened. He was assigned to Rescue at Hickam Field. After almost five years the native boy went home.

"It was wonderful. I never had thought it would come through. My family gave me a big *luau* to welcome me home. I was the first person in my family to become a United States officer. They were so proud of me." And perhaps the proudest of all was his father, the gentle Edward Ayau, who had found his own true vocation in travail. "You see—he had not wanted me to become a flier to carry bombs. But now I was doing the same as he was doing. I was *saving* people."

The pride went further than the Ayau family. It went out among the people and became a thing they all owned. Mel

Ayau was a *haole,* a native boy. And now he had become an American officer and boys from the mainland saluted him and he had responsibility and command, and they knew that when they saw one of the great planes flying marked "Rescue" that in it might be Ayau, their own.

There was perhaps only one thing that prevented Ayau's assignment at Hickam from being perfect—the Rescue unit there had not yet been assigned helicopters, which were just slowly filtering throughout Rescue. It was not until the spring of 1949 that the first chopper arrived and Ayau seized it and took it up, and it was a meeting of two old friends. It was reunion on the grand scale. And then, just two weeks after the helicopter arrived, it became something else.

On a warm day in April a United States Air Force captain named Edward H. Connor, who was stationed at Wheeler Field in the Wahiawa section of Oahu, took his wife to Haleiwa Beach on the western side of the island. Swimming is discouraged at Haleiwa. There is a powerful current there and a brutal rip tide and the water is studded with reefs as sharp as razors. And there are sharks.

Connor stretched out on the beach and Mrs. Connor wandered into the water. And then, a few yards out, she was gripped by an undertow and pulled out to sea. She cried out for help. Connor leaped to his feet and threw her an inflated inner tube. She missed it. He plunged into the water after her. He caught up with the tube and swam out to her. The two of them held on to the tube, which was only partly inflated and semi-buoyant. The current pulled both of them farther and farther from shore. About two hundred and fifty yards from land Connor managed to catch hold of a submerged reef. Mrs. Connor was almost spent. She clung to the tube and he held to the reef with one hand and on to her hair with the other, and he struggled to keep her head above water.

A man tried to reach them from the shore on a surfboard. He, too, was caught in the treacherous current and soon was fighting for his own life. A Coast Guard crash boat attempted to get to the three persons but was unable to do so because of the reefs. Other swimmers tried and were beaten back.

An appeal for help was made to Rescue at Hickam and Ayau went out in the chopper. He arrived twenty minutes after the call came in. His job might have been quite simple and quite routine except for one thing: the newly arrived helicopter was as yet unequipped with a hoist and a sling. Ayau looked below him. The man on the surfboard appeared to be holding his own for the moment. But Connor and his wife were obviously exhausted and in mortal danger. Beyond the captain and his wife, just a few yards, Ayau saw two sharks.

Ayau came down low and dropped a one-man rubber life raft, dropping it carefully so it would fall within Connor's reach. Connor caught hold of the raft and managed to get his wife into it. Then he started to climb in himself. He got halfway in and collapsed. He lay half in and half out, the weight of his body on the side of the small raft causing it to ship water. He had no strength to paddle. The raft began to drift out toward the open sea. Ayau saw that the captain and his wife were no better off than they had been. He watched them drift away from land and he saw the sharks again. He hovered over them, close enough almost to reach out and touch them and yet as far removed as though he had been a thousand miles away.

And then he had an idea. He swung the tiny chopper around until it was on the seaward side of the unconscious victims and he tilted it fifteen degrees and then, using the slip stream of the three rotors as a giant wind machine, he began to *blow* the raft toward shore. It was an exhibition of skill that riveted the spectators on the shore. Ayau shifted back and forth, ducked, rose, twisted as he dueled with the sea for possession of the two souls unconscious in the little yellow raft. Again and again a sudden shift in current, a swell, snatched the raft from his grasp and sent it drifting out to sea again. And each time Ayau swung around and got behind the raft and resumed his duel.

Slowly, foot by foot, he drove the raft toward shore, parrying the sudden thrusts of water, and presently he had it in shallow water and it was pulled in to safety. And then Ayau went back out and got behind the man on the surfboard and blew him in to land. And then he dipped his helicopter in farewell and returned to the base.

"They all lived," Ayau said. "Mrs. Connor had to spend three days in the Tripler Army Hospital but she recovered all right. They came down to the squadron to thank me. Since then I get Christmas cards from them every year." He grinned. "She was a panicky woman, they told me. All those sharks around them. . . ."

Ayau's spectacular improvisation caused something of a sensation in the Air Force. As far as anyone could determine a helicopter had never before been used as a fan. Ayau would not say he had invented the technique. He said only, "I never heard of it being done before and as far as I know I thought of it myself at that moment." In a citation labeled

"Outstanding Feat of Airmanship," Colonel Mills S. Savage, deputy chief of staff for Operations of the Pacific Air Command, said it for him: "The technique used in this rescue is unique and was conceived by Lieutenant Ayau while hovering over the swimmers and analyzing their predicament. This Command has no information of rotor blast being put to a practical use before. Since this rescue Lieutenant Ayau has practiced this technique and found he is able to control the drift of a life raft with remarkable accuracy. This procedure can also be used to blow a raft to survivors who might otherwise to be unable to reach it."

There followed an official commendation from the commander of the PAC, General Robert F. Travis, who said "the results of the aggressive action and superb display of ingenuity employed by you in utilization of the aircraft to the maximum extent in accomplishment of your mission reflect great credit upon your personal ability and to the United States Air Force." And so the gimmick that Mel Ayau thought up in an emergency was reported out to all Rescue units all over the world and other helicopter pilots studied it and learned how to do it and the chopper was given another capability to save lives. Mel was quite proud of that, of course, but in his secret heart the thing he was most proud of was that his people in Hawaii were told that one of their own *haoles* was a credit to the Air Force of the United States.

The Rescue unit at Hickam always keeps a small detachment on Johnston Island, and in the summer of 1949 Lieutenant Ayau was doing his week's tour of duty there. He happened to pick a good week. A USO show was brought to the island to entertain the troops. One afternoon some of the girls in the company went down to the beach to swim and Ayau's eyes fell on one of them and from then on he was more lost than any human being he had ever rescued.

Her name was Thelma Camacho. She was a stunning young lady, of Portuguese and Irish ancestry, black-eyed and black-haired, and Ayau was still reeling when he learned that she was leaving Johnston with the troupe the next day. She saved him from utter despair, however—her home, she told him, was in Honlulu.

"I asked her for a date when I got back there," Ayau said. His eyes wandered for a moment until he found her. He looked at her for a long time. Then he went on. "She said, yes. Well, we were married the next year." On June 1, 1951, their first child was born to them and they named him Melvin Ayau, Jr. Ayau and Thelma remained at Hickam until June of 1952, then he was transferred to the Rescue squadron at McChord Air Force Base in Tacoma, Washington.

He left behind a fine record. During the more than four years he had been stationed at Hickam he had participated in scores of missions, actual rescues, and endless intercepts—guiding in to safety airplanes that had run into trouble over the Pacific and were limping in on three, and, in one case, on two engines. That is one of the less dramatic functions of Rescue, shepherding in wounded aircraft. The plane gets in safely and nothing has happened. But the presence of the Rescue plane, within sight, is something the people in crippled aircraft never forget.

In May of 1953 a second child was born, a girl, and Mel and Thelma named her Lynette Moana Ayau. Moana means "ocean," the water that was linking her with Oahu, thousands of miles away. Their happiness was full brim—work that increased in satisfaction daily, a marriage of joy, two beautiful children. And then, in November of that year there was tragedy. Thelma and the firstborn, Melvin, Jr., were involved in an automobile accident. Thelma was injured and the little boy was killed. It was only the living presence of the girl, Moana, that preserved the sanity of her parents.

Ayau tried to lose himself in his work. He volunteered for mission after mission. He was named mission commander when a hunter and his wife, flying from Redmond, Oregon, to Grants Pass, had engine failure and crashed into the forest about ten miles north of Klamath Falls, Washington. "We located them," Ayau said. "There were many others. Some we could find. Some we couldn't." Somehow, in his lifesaving work for others, Ayau worked out a kind of personal peace. And then, in March, 1954, he received a magical set of orders: he was sent back to Hawaii again.

"It was good to get home." His greatest help now was his father who had for ten years devoted himself to giving spiritual sustenance to others and who now was close to his son who needed it so badly. "I became close to him," Mel said. "Very close."

Rescue had by now developed into a science. The techniques that Mel Ayau and the other pioneers had worked out so laboriously over the years had become refined into procedures—procedures that combined maximum efficiency and results with increasingly less left to chance. Among other things, Rescue and the Civil Air Patrol had learned to cooperate with each other in emergencies. Upon his return to Hawaii, Ayau, a captain now, was named a control officer, and he found a large part of his work was with the CAP.

"The majority of them are local—native Hawaiians," he said. "It is a good thing to work together this way—all wanting to do one thing, to help people in distress."

The choice was an ideal one. Captain Ayau soon was regarded as a kind of bridge between the Rescue unit and the local CAP fliers. He was a United States officer—and he was also a native boy. And by now, too, the value of Air Rescue was appreciated by other uniformed men who fly. At the beginning pilots had a kind of hesitancy in calling for help—some of them had the idea that somehow it was not manly or brave; this was one of the intangibles Rescue had to overcome—but that time had passed.

"We got a call that a Marine pilot had bailed out northeast of Kaneohe. He had been flying a jet plane, a boy named Lieutenant Paul Meyer, from the Kaneohe Marine Air Station. Major Richard Carpentier and I took off in a helicopter, an SH-19. One of the things that was nice about that mission was that our man in the cabin, the one who operates the hoist, was a staff sergeant named Mitsuri Kato—a full-blooded Hawaiian-born Japanese.

"An SA-16 got there thirty minutes before we did and they had dropped a life raft to Meyer. He was just floating. There were sharks and whales and manta rays in the vicinity. We could see them from the air. We set up a pattern to effect the pickup. We hovered over him and Kato dropped the sling and hoisted him aboard. It was one of the longest over-water helicopter pickups on record—ninety miles."

And there was the time when Rescue received a call from the Navy, asking whether a helicopter could be sent to an LST thirty miles south of Kahoolawe Island. There was a young crew member, a boy named Patrick L. Lord, who had been working in the tool shop and had injured his eye. The only thing that would save the eye was an immediate operation. The LST was about eighty-five miles from Oahu, a six-hour trip by boat.

A helicopter was indicated, but there was one thing: the chopper would have to land *on* the LST. And an LST is a very small vessel with very little space for even a chopper to crawl down on. Ayau was on helicopter alert and he volunteered to try. He had to admit he had never landed on an LST before but he said he'd like to make a stab at it. "I made two requests—to mark the center of the landing area and to have as many men as possible standing by so they could jump on the landing gear of the helicopter and hold it down when I got in."

When Ayau got over the LST he found another problem. His radio and the radio on the LST were on different frequencies and he could not talk to the Navy craft. Fortunately there was a Rescue SB-17 circling overhead with radio equipment for both frequencies. Ayau used the SB-17 as a relay. The radio operator on the SB-17 received his messages and passed them on to the ship, and then gave Ayau the answers.

"I sent a message through to have the LST lay still across the wind. The winds were about twelve knots. There was a pole in the front of the LST and superstructure in the rear and we had to come down in between." He had, in all, an area about seventy feet long and fifty feet wide, and an area that was not stationary. Plus the wind. The exact center of this area, as he had requested, was marked with a white cross. He made a broadside approach to the landing area and with exquisite precision slipped his chopper between the mast and the superstructure and gently set it down. When the wheels touched the helicopter was straddled exactly over the white cross.

"As soon as we touched down all hands jumped on the landing gear. We put the patient aboard and took off. We were on the deck all of about one minute. We took him to the island of Maui and transferred him to the SB-17 which was waiting there and he was flown back to Hickam. An ambulance was waiting on the field and rushed him to Tripler. They saved his eye."

At the time I listened to Mel Ayau he was a major and the senior control officer of the Rescue outfit at Hickam. That means he heads up the nerve center of the squadron—he determines how a search mission shall be put together, how much equipment will be committed, whether to call up reserve crews or other agencies to assist. It is he who evaluates the leads, sets up search plans, briefs the crews, and dispatches the aircraft.

The native boy who stretched out on his belly on a roof on the day of Pearl Harbor has made a long journey. There are many helicopter pilots who take out choppers and fly over the islands. From the ground, of course, it is impossible to know who is sitting at the controls. But there are Hawaiians who say they can tell, it is the native boy who now again uses his middle name, which means happiness.

"You must understand. The Hawaiians are a peaceful people," he said. "I cannot tell you how they feel—about the United States Air Force doing this kind of work. And don't ask me how they feel about the fact that I am allowed to be doing what I do." He looked up. "Hey, let's eat."

JAPAN, FORMOSA, OKINAWA

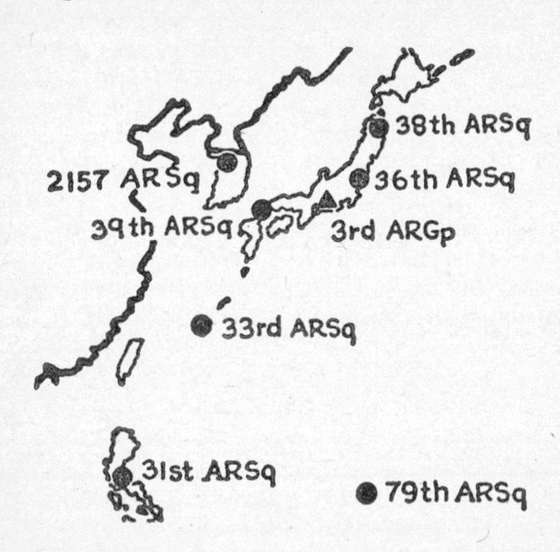

"Somebody Was Worrying About Me..."

Ito Haruo is a Japanese dead-end kid grown up. He's tamer now than when he roared hell up and down Honshu. He smiles once in a while. But the old anger is still there. It was in his hands that opened and closed convulsively and gripped the chair arms as he spoke. It was in the sudden hard, wild light that blazed in his eyes. It was in his mouth that closed on the end of a sentence like a steel trap. He is thirty-six now. He is short, plump, bald halfway back on his head. He wore a dark suit with the usual collection of fountain pens sticking out of his handkerchief pocket. With the sandpaper that lacerated his voice he was type cast for the Boss, a Japanese Little Caesar.

He talked a lot about himself. He talked defiantly about the old days. It was hot summer in the seaport town of Moji on Kyushu Island, southernmost of the four big Japanese islands, and the office of the Yamashita Steamship Company was noisy only as Japanese offices can be noisy. Haruo wouldn't raise his voice above the noises. His head was filled with bigger and older noises. His wife, Kazuko, died the year before, he said, and now there was no one but his three-year-old son, Yasugi. He was alone, but he had always been alone. That was his whole life. Even when people had tried to help him there was something in him that stayed alone so that he had only himself and his hates to depend on.

"I never had a family. I was brought up by my older brother. He tried to see that I had an education. I went to Shimonoseki High School but even before I was out of school I joined a gang. We were wild. We did many bad things." He turned to the translator and spoke rapidly, clenching his fists. The translator said: "He wants to say again how wild he was. He had evil friends and they did evil things."

"I signed on the crew of a fishing boat," Haruo said. "When I wasn't sailing I spent my time eating and drinking and gambling. And fighting. My brother could not control me and he was unhappy. Then when I was twenty-two I met a great man. He had wisdom. He told me I had to leave my bad friends and my bad ways. He said I could have an important future but that I must stop living as I was. I believed what he said and while I was still working on the ships I began to study. In 1941 I passed an examination and became an engineer and I was taken on a big fishing boat as an engineer. My brother was very proud of me. He had believed he had failed as my parent and now he was content. I traveled everywhere, and in 1943 I joined the Japanese Merchant Marine and served as an engineer on ships transporting troops and now my brother was very proud.

"On the second trip our transport was bringing troops to a small Chinese port. In the harbor we were attacked by American airplanes and then we were ambushed by Chinese soldiers on the coast. It was summertime and I was sick in my cabin with a fever and all I could hear were the American airplanes and I cursed them. I crawled off the bed and hid under it and listened to the airplanes.

"After that my ships were always attacked. It seemed to me that the American airplanes were looking especially for me. Five or six ships were blown up under me. Then in December 1944 an American submarine found us at Tsushima Island, between here and Korea, and chased us all the way to the China coast and then it fired two torpedoes and blew us up. The captain, bos'n, first mate, and I were the only ones who didn't drown. We hung on to pieces of the boat and got to a small island, it didn't even have a name, and we stayed there, starving, until a little Korean fishing boat picked us up. When we got back to Japan we found that the Government had sent word to the families of everybody on the boat that we had been killed. All the other families, I mean. I had no family except my two brothers, and I wanted my older brother, the one who had been as a father to me, to know that I was still alive.

"I found out that it was my older brother who was dead. He had been killed on Formosa by American planes during a raid. I hated Americans then, all Americans, and most of all Americans in airplanes. Now there was nobody in the world for me except my younger brother, Takano, and he was just a child. I went to him and we mourned our brother who was dead on Formosa." The anger exploded in him. He shifted in his chair as though he were chained there and was trying to break loose.

"I wanted to do anything to kill Americans, anything at all. The Japanese Government sent me to a shipbuilding yard in Tokyo but I asked for something else to do, to fight. I could not sleep. All I could think of was my brother dead. And then the atom bombs were dropped on Hiroshima and Nagasaki and I thought the next one would be dropped on Tokyo." The hooded eyes flamed. "That was not the way for a gentlemanly country like the United States to fight! Pearl Harbor was not gentlemanly either, but the purpose there was to attack soldiers. Your bombs killed innocent people!"

He lit a cigarette and took several fast drags. "In the first part of August in 1945 I got what I asked for. I was named captain of a suicide ship. They did not tell us what our mission was going to be but it did not matter. It was enough that I was going to kill Americans and that I was going to be able to die killing Americans. I went to see Takano, I thought it would be for the last time, and I went to a shrine and said prayers for my brother who was dead in Formosa, and then one night they called us in and said that the ship would sail on its mission the following night. Then when we came in to get our orders the next day they told us that Japan had surrendered."

After he received his discharge he was blind for a little while with his frustration, and then he returned to his home town of Beppu and established a small bakery shop and ran it with his younger brother, Takano, who was then thirteen. For two years he tried to make a go of it, but it did not work out. The times were bad and he knew very little about standing in front of a baker's oven and there was too much of the salt air and too much hate still in him.

"I went to Yokohama and became an engineer in the Merchant Marine again. We learned about unions from the Americans and we formed a seamen's union and I became a leader. The ship owner tried to reduce force by five men and I led a strike. We lost the strike and I made an agreement with the owner to resign if he would not fire the others.

"I went from one ship to another. It was hard finding work. They said I was a maker of trouble. It was about then that I met a girl and we were married and we took a little house here in Moji. We had a son, and for the first time in my life I had a real family. I still had a hard time finding anybody to hire me. I was away looking for work in October 1953 when I received a telegram saying my wife was sick and I hurried back to Moji just in time to see her die. I was alone again with just my son. I took a small room here in Moji with my son and I wondered how I would be able to bring him up."

Nobody would hire him and as the months passed his money ran out, and then one night, when he was alone and living his hatred, he received an offer to sail as engineer on a small cargo vessel, the *Koyo Maru,* of the Yamashita line. The only reason he got the offer was because the chief of the seamen's union in Aburatsu had written a strong letter of recommendation for him, emphasizing his skill and experience.

"The offer was delivered to my room at ten-thirty on the night of October 2, 1954. I had to wake up my son and leave him with a friend. I felt pity for the child but it was a chance to work. I caught a train at five twenty-five the next morning for Aburatsu. I got off the train at Miyazuki and went to Aburatsu by bus and there I met Minato Riichi, the captain of the ship and also the man who was agent for the line. On October 4, at six o'clock in the evening, we sailed from Aburatsu with a cargo of anchors and floaters bound for Nase in Oshima Island near Okinawa, with eleven crew members aboard.

"The next morning at six o'clock we developed engine trouble and we put in to Kuchierabu Island in Kagoshima Prefecture and they made repairs there. They tested the engines for a week and we left the island on the eleventh at eight o'clock in the morning. Three hours later the engines were still in good condition but the water was getting rough and the ship began to leak. The ship was an old one and with the rough water and the hard wind it began taking on water. We used hand pumps to get the water out but the water was coming in too fast and the main engine quit. The other engines would work for a little while and then stop and then start working again.

"About five o'clock on the morning of the twelfth all the men in the engine room were ordered out and the captain,

Riichi, ordered the ship abandoned. Before he did this he spoke to me, because I had had so much experience during the war on sinking ships, and then he ordered me to take charge of the abandoning of the ship. I told the crew to prepare food and water. They made a life raft. We had one lifeboat on the ship but it would hold only five persons. We made the life raft out of lumber used to bulwark the cargo. I tied four empty oil cans to the life raft to make it float better and then I used a long rope and tied the life raft to the bridge for the time being. By then it was blowing hard. I worked with the men and made a second life raft and tied it to the bridge, and then I had the bridge cut off from the deck so if the ship sank the bridge would float and not pull the rafts down with it. Then I ordered the crew to stand by and await the order to abandon. I still hoped that we might not have to go."

During the night the storm worsened. The winds built up and the seas became walls, and early in the morning Haruo saw it was hopeless. "At three-fifteen in the morning I gave the order to abandon. The first mate got into the lifeboat and the rest of us divided ourselves on the two life rafts. Captain Riichi took command of the port raft and I was in charge of the starboard raft. Some of the crew wanted to take personal belongings with them but I told them they would have to leave everything behind.

"By the time we got on the rafts the ship began to sink. It went straight down for a little while and then the stern went in and the nose stuck up and then the nose disappeared. The life rafts were thrown around when they hit the water and three of the men on my raft were washed off. They were rescued by Captain Riichi and taken to his raft. After a while they returned to my raft. By this time the ship had disappeared entirely. At six o'clock in the morning there was nothing but the life rafts and the lifeboat, all tied together to the wooden bridge. The reason I had tied them to the bridge was to keep us all together. I learned that by experience. We had some rice and some water and nothing else.

"The next morning five of the men wanted to row off in the lifeboat to find help. I tried to stop them. The wind had died down a little but the water was very rough. There were sharks all around us. I told them we were off the well-traveled lanes and they might float around for weeks before a ship found them. They would not listen to me. The five men got into the lifeboat. I gave each man two days' rations of rice—two handfuls—and a beer bottle of water. They rowed away. It turned out they were rescued two days later by a Japanese boat. They had come across a small island and had tried to land but the water was too rough. As they were being battered about they were picked up."

The men remaining on the two life rafts were Haruo, Captain Riichi, Tabato Juo, twenty-one, second engineer; Satomi Shiro, thirty-one, deck hand; Sato Tadatoshi, twenty-one, deck hand; and Takaki Takeoki, thirty-one, an oiler. "We had seven kilograms of rice and six liters of water. The rafts were about eight feet by four. We had just two blankets and the clothing on our backs. We spread out, three men on each raft, and we floated and waited. The only thing I had for a signal was a small mirror. It once had been in a compact owned by my wife and I had always carried it for good luck.

"The first thing we found out was that our water was bad. Oily ocean water had gotten into the containers. Then on the fourteenth the wooden bridge sank and we cut it off before it could pull the rafts down, and after that we tied the two rafts together. The wind died out but the water was still very rough and at night we could see a beautiful moon. It was very cold. The four drums holding up my life raft began to sink and the life raft was about a foot under water. We just lay there, covered by water, and saw the sharks around us. I will never forget the sharks.

"I tried to drink some of the bad water but I vomited it up. The rest saw how bad it was and nobody touched it. We floated for three days without water. We tried to catch small fish to eat but we never could. One day I saw big American planes flying overhead. They were B-29's and all I could think of was what they had done during the war. Still I flashed the little mirror at them, but they didn't see it.

"I started to talk to the men. One of them was twisted up with pain in his belly and another had a crushed foot, and we all thought that we would starve or die of thirst or drown. And the sharks were there all the time, waiting. I kept talking to them, and I told them about all the things that had happened to me during the war and how I had lived through them. They kept saying how it would be when a ship found us. I think I did not believe we would be found. Who would be looking for us? We did not come from a big ship that would be missed. It was a small, old freighter and who would miss us? I think that I had done things alone for too long and I did not think people helped each other.

"When I ran out of stories I began all over again. And then one morning one of the life rafts started to sink under the men and they got off it and climbed on the life raft I was on and we cut the other one off. It floated away. And my life raft sank farther down with the new weight, so far we could hardly see it or feel it beneath us, but we could see the sharks, more of them than ever before."

The Japanese vessel that picked up the other five men reported on the six still missing to the Japanese Coast Guard which in turn notified the Air Rescue squadron at Ashiya. But at the time the squadron was having its own troubles. The same typhoon that had sunk the *Koyo Maru* had struck Ashiya without warning. It broke the rudders of three of the SA-16's parked on the field. All were out of commission. There was only one Albatross in the squadron that could fly.

Orders to scramble were issued on the morning of the fifteenth at eleven o'clock. The SA-16 was refueled for a long search and Lieutenant Ted Lemcke took off with Lieutenant Jimmy Copps flying as copilot. Lemcke flew the plane south for forty miles to Yakujima, an island south of Kyushu, and then he started a slow search pattern over the wild waters.

"It did not seem that the life raft could hold us much longer and I was running out of stories. I told them a third time, and the men were past the point of listening. They were looking at the sharks and there were even more of them than before.

"Then I looked up and I saw the airplane and I saw it was an American airplane. The men began to wave at the airplane, even the man with the pains in his belly. The plane seemed to be scouting the area. The plane made a second pass and then a third pass and then we saw the plane come down but it did not come down to look at us—it had found the other life raft, the one that had started to sink, the one we had cut loose. Without the weight of the men on it it was still half floating and that was what the plane had seen. The only thought that was in my mind was that the pilot would think that that was the only raft and that everybody on it had drowned and that he would go away." Haruo paused. Then he said slowly: "I started to pray. I called all the Japanese gods. I called them by their names. I asked them to guide the plane to us."

Over a breakfast of bacon and eggs on a Sunday morning in Ashiya, Jimmy Copps, a pleasant-faced lad, related to me how the Rescue men had spotted the abandoned raft. It was about three-fifteen in the afternoon, he said. "We didn't see anybody on it and we decided to take some pictures of it. In maneuvering to take pictures of the wreckage we saw the raft with the survivors. Ted evaluated the situation. The swells were ten and twelve feet. The wind was ten knots, from ninety degrees. The swell pattern was from eighty degrees. There were oil drums we could see floating around. We didn't know how many others there might be."

The book for water landings says that the amphibian should be brought in along the length of the swells at right angles to the direction in which they are moving. But landing is also suppposed to be made into the wind, which is SOP for any kind of landing. In this case to land along the length of the swells would mean a cross-wind landing, and in water that was about twice as high as an SA-16 is supposed to challenge. And there were the drums. Colliding with one of them at the speed of a water landing could stave in the hull of the plane, could change it instantly from a rescue vehicle into a wreck.

The Rescue men knew one thing more, although nothing was said about it: even if the water landing was made successfully, if the plane was not dumped by the cross wind into a trough, if it avoided all the drums that might be floating around, with the additional weight of six men aboard, in that kind of water, it was pretty certain it would be unable to take off again. And the nearest land was miles away and the sea was building up again. There was a second SA-16 in the area by then, broken rudder repaired and sent out to join the search. Ted Lemcke got on his radio. He said: "I'm going in."

"We saw the airplane make four or five circles around the abandoned life raft and by now the men were waving and yelling as though the pilot could hear us. The waves were so high we could see the airplane only part of the time and we wondered how they could see us at all. I saw floats on the plane and I knew it could land on water but not that kind of water.

"I thought that even if they did see us all they would do would be to radio the Japanese Coast Guard so they could send a rescue boat. I did not see why an American airplane would take the danger to try to save some Japanese. But then they saw us and they came closer to us and I saw they were going to try to land. They tried it, but the waves were too high and they could not make it and they went up and I thought they would surely go away now but they turned around and tried again and still could not do it. But they tried a third time and landed on the water and do not ask me how I felt. I cannot explain to you how I felt."

"We made a cross-wind landing," Copps said. "We landed

about fifty yards from the raft and made our runout. A funny thing happened. When we landed, a box of sea-marker dye broke and spread through the inside of the plane. I could see Lemcke's teeth and tongue turning green.

"One of the boys on the raft got so excited he wanted to jump off and swim to us. We waved him back because of the sharks. We had to maneuver around the Japanese raft until we could run out our own six-man rubber life raft. The Japanese raft was breaking up and we were afraid it would damage our aircraft. We spent ten minutes circling the raft to get our own raft close enough. Then the Japanese survivors got on our raft and we pulled them in."

The survivors were startled to find themselves facing Americans with green faces and green lips and teeth and tongues, with a green pallor on all their flying clothing. They were given first aid by the medic on the Rescue plane and Lemcke and Copps turned their attention to their own sweat. They had one hope for a take off, the JATO bottles—Jet Assisted Take Off—which would give them a few precious seconds of increased speed, which might just lift them from the water that gripped them.

"We tried one take off but had to abort it," Copps said. "Even with JATO we couldn't get up enough speed. Ted elected to taxi the airplane to Yakujima—forty-three miles to the nearest land face. The seas were so rough we couldn't even recover our life raft. We called up to the SA-16 orbiting overhead and told them what we were going to do and they gave us our direction. We asked them to give our heading and coordinates to the Japanese Coast Guard so they could send us an escort. Then we started off."

The SA-16 is built to land and take off from water and its hull is shaped like a boat. But it is not a boat. It can take a beating, up to a point, but it is fragile, as are all things that fly. The seas tossed it around like a cork. "We were under water half the time," Copps said. "We couldn't open the windows to get fresh air. Due to the cross wind we had to run on one engine."

One after another, the green-faced Americans and the exhausted survivors began to feel the effects. The medic, working over his patients, became violently sick. Others sickened and vomited. The plane bucked the water on its one engine and fought the wind that tried to turn it around and dump it. It was a little after four in the afternoon when they started out. It was eleven o'clock, seven hours later, when they finally saw the south side of Yakujima and were picked up by two vessels of the Japanese Coast Guard.

"We were going into Ambo, a little village on the east

side of the island," Copps said. "We started to taxi, looking for a suitable port. We passed Ambo without even seeing it. The seas were too rough to go in close to the shore. We continued circling around the island and got up to the northwest side where the sea was calmer. We spotted a small Japanese village just before midnight and attempted to beach the boat. I opened the hatch over the pilot's compartment and held up an Aldis lamp to see the shore and I almost got swamped.

"The water got in the circuit box and burned out the radio fuse boxes. Then we attempted to beach. As we were going in I opened the hatch again and shot up flares to guide Ted in. We approached about fifty yards from the shore and then in the light from the flares we saw rocks." The water was strewn with them. Lemcke knew he could go no farther.

"The only thing he could do was to tie up the aircraft to one of the Japanese boats that had followed us around the island. The Japanese lowered a boat and attempted to get a line to us but it didn't work," Copps said. "We taxied up to the boat and threw them a line and then attempted to back off but the props wouldn't go into reverse because the circuit box had gone out from the water and we hit the Japanese boat and smashed in the radar dome on our nose. It was little damage actually but the water started to pour in the front.

"The Japanese Coast Guard men took off all the survivors. We went on board the Japanese boat after them and notified our Radio Control Center through the Japanese radio that we were tied up and where we were. The Japanese prepared a meal for us—our first since noon that day and this was after midnight. They gave us sliced ham and hardtack and an apple each. They really treated us fine. They showed us where we could get some sleep and I guess we all just went out cold. It wasn't until the next morning that we found out that the Japanese officers had given us their own beds.

"The next morning they woke us up at seven o'clock and told us an airplane was circling overhead. We made contact with them on the URC-4, the walkie-talkie, and they told us to try to get back to Ambo. The Coast Guard said they would tow us there. After an hour of towing we started to hit a swell system and the Japanese skipper suggested that we go into a harbor on the northwest side of the island. We notified the escort plane that we were turning around to make for the harbor. We reached an inlet at eleven o'clock.

"The Japanese lowered a small boat and towed us to within a hundred yards of the beach. We fired a Lyle gun and the Japanese Fire Department and half of the island grabbed hold of it and pulled us in. After we beached we decided to run up the engines to see if they were okay—no sweat. We cranked them up. We used our unfeathering switch and managed to back out and then we beached the airplane properly and tied up with the help of the local firemen."

The word that American fliers had saved six Japanese sailors spread through the island and soon the entire population swarmed down to the beach and many of the people came with food and drink. "They brought us soft-boiled eggs, all the way to the beach, and canned sliced beef and fruit and sugar cakes and muffins," Copps said.

The plane overhead notified the Rescue men that supplies would be dropped to them at three o'clock that afternoon.

"We sat on the beach," Copps said. "Thousands of little kids came around us. The people were all trying to talk. I guess they were trying to say thanks. The mayor came down. He could read and write English but he couldn't speak it. Other officials came down and some of them could say a few words in English. The fire department put guards around the airplane and we looked at the damage. The spark plugs were fouled due to the taxiing, the reverse mechanism relays were burned out, and there was the hole in the radar dome. We knew we couldn't take off with that because the water would come through.

"At three o'clock a C-47 from the squadron came over and dropped water, blanket rolls, food, and extra clothing. When the drops were made close, the people yelled and applauded. When they missed, they kept quiet, out of politeness. The C-47 notified us that they would send a replacement crew with mechanics and parts the next day by Navy boat from the base at Sesebo. The Japanese took us to a hotel. It was real nice—a two-story building with four rooms upstairs. They let us take a bath—first Japanese bath I ever had. We took it all together. The bath was right next to the kitchen and while we were bathing, trying to get the dye off us, we could smell the cooking.

"We shaved and got back into our uniforms and by that time all the dignitaries started to arrive. They served us a Japanese meal on little individual tables—spiced fish and squid and curry rice and sake and beer and fruit. About ten of the local big shots dined with us. One Japanese boy was going to the University of Oklahoma and he brought his American textbooks. We sat around trying to talk to each other until eleven o'clock and then we had to hit it, we were so tired. We went to sleep on Japanese beds and they continued the party.

"The next morning at six-thirty a Navy boat, the *Waxwing,* came in, and we dressed and had breakfast in the hotel—

half-cooked eggs, toast, coleslaw, and tea—and then we went to meet the relief crew and went aboard the *Waxwing*. We left Yakujima at nine o'clock for Sesebo and got in at eight o'clock that night. We spent the night on the boat and then returned by train to Ashiya, 150 miles away. We were still covered with sea-marker dye, our faces and clothes."

There was one thing Jimmy Copps remembered more than anything else, more than the hairy landing, more than the nightmare of the long surface trip on the water: "The Japanese hospitality amazed me. They went out of their way to be friendly."

Haruo lit another cigarette and he looked at its glowing end for a few moments. "We were exhausted when they brought us aboard the airplane," he said. "Our lips were broken open from the wind and the salt and the man with the crushed leg was suffering and the man with cramps was in agony. I do not remember anything after we were taken aboard the plane, not the trip on the water nor when they took us on the Coast Guard vessel. We were all almost unconscious that whole time. Later they took us off the Coast Guard vessel and we were brought somewhere on the island and we never saw the men who had saved us again." That was the end of Ito Haruo's story.

Haruo and I went out into the street. It was a clear, warm day. The sun was shining brightly. There were many ships and small boats in the harbor. Haruo walked slowly. His face was wrinkled with thought. "It is hard to tell how I feel. For ten years I hated Americans. Now I am embarrassed."

He looked out across the harbor toward the hills beyond. "You know, I never talked about this before. Now, when I told you about it, it was just as though I was seeing it for the first time. And I have just thought that when I was out there I was not alone then, was I?" He turned his face to me. "Somebody was worrying about me."

"Our Hearts Are Filled with Gratitude . . ."

Okinawa to many people is where there was a lot of fighting and now everybody goes to the Teahouse of the August Moon and watches the girls and drinks sake.

That is not a wholly erroneous impression as far as it goes. There was fighting on the island, some of the worst, and now the teahouse is filled every night. It has got expensive and commercial—it has now expanded to include a "Western" part for those who are tired of Oriental kicks—and it isn't much fun any more. But it's there if you're stuck in Naha and you want to see what inspires Broadway shows.

The impression does not go quite far enough, however. For there is a native people on Okinawa, the Ryukyuans. It is customary for native peoples everywhere to look leanly on foreigners who rule their lives, no matter to what degree. The United States has done a great deal for and in Okinawa. Hospitals, roads, schools. The Ryukyuans never had it that way before and parts of Naha look magnificent these days. But the United States has also taken over large pieces of geography and has turned them into air bases and military and naval installations.

A look at the map and a contemplation of the world as it exists today make that understandable and necessary, from our point of view. Trouble is that world conditions are less important to most Ryukyuans than what happened on the farm that season or how the fish catch was. And it is rough when a farm isn't a farm any more but a concrete runway, and it doesn't do much good to move the farmers somewhere else or give them money. They like what's been in their family for years, same as anybody else.

An American official who is in the middle of all this and who deals daily with the Ryukyuans is Paul H. Skuse, director of the Public Safety Department of USCAR—United States Civil Administration of the Ryukyu Islands. Skuse came to Okinawa originally during the war as a lieutenant commander with the United States Military Government. His original job was to get the natives out of the way of the shooting and to keep them from interfering with military operations. He came to know and like and respect these people whose land was being fought over in a war in which they had little interest, and when peace came he stayed on in USCAR. He has been there ever since, and his alert, keen face with its mustache and its mouth clamped around a pipe is one of the most familiar American faces in Okinawa. When I was in Naha visiting the Air Rescue squadron there I telephoned Paul Skuse and said I would appreciate listening to anything he had to tell me about Rescue. He invited me over to his office in the huge USCAR building.

I went there on a hot, drizzling morning over the new highway system that looks more like Westchester County than a Pacific island. Mr. Skuse had on hand some very impressive-looking Ryukyuan officials. He started out by telling me of some of the problems USCAR has to face in dealing with a people who are still bewildered by what is happening all around them. "These people were told by the Japs that when we caught them we would cut off the hands of the men and rape the women. They were afraid of us. They hid in the mountains and in caves and we were many months collecting these people and getting them to come out of the hills. But the United States Naval Military Government set up hospitals, dispensaries, and treated their wounds and supplied them with food and clothing and shelter and in time the Ryukyuan people realized they had been fed with a lot of war propaganda by the Japanese. They became deeply grateful to Americans for their kindness."

And then it became necessary to take their land. "That has affected nearly every Ryukyuan. Certain Leftist groups, Communists, and some people imbued with nationalist feeling have attempted to take certain incidents and use them as anti-American propaganda and also to promote a reversion movement to Japan—our taking over this land, for instance.

"We have lots of very effective programs to promote Ryukyuan-American friendship and to counteract the activities of these people, but I think that the work of the Air Rescue unit has been one of the most effective of these programs. The United States spends millions abroad for aid and everything, but it's the little things that count, and when Air Rescue goes out and saves some Ryukyuan fisherman or assists in the rescue of a disabled ship like the *Nanshu Maru*—that really hits home to them more than some of these big aid programs that Americans are good people and want to help them.

"Air Rescue has done a great deal to promote Ryukyuan-American friendship. They are always ready to respond. I call on them day and night when some Ryukyuan fishing boat or canoe is overdue—the relatives of these people notify the native police department who in turn request me to obtain the assistance of the Air Rescue unit. The local people now call them by name. They have called so many times they know just what they want. The Air Rescue people here in Okinawa have participated in countless rescue missions in the past few years and the Ryukyuan people are deeply appreciative."

Skuse pulled hard on his pipe and smiled. "You should see the old ladies with children and babies. They come here and they tell me they can't get on the air base. They tell me to thank the Rescue people for saving their father or their husband or their son. You should see them. You would understand what I mean." As Skuse was speaking the native officials nodded eagerly from time to time as they caught a word or phrase in English they understood. Mr. Skuse introduced me to Kenshin Nakamura, director of the police department of the Government of the Ryukyuan Islands, the native government.

"This is one of the finest gentlemen I ever met," Skuse said. "He speaks out frankly and openly as pro-American. Generally Ryukyuans are afraid to express themselves in favor of the Americans in case the Japanese ever come back." Nakamura has been a policeman for more than thirty years and he looks it. He is a compact, forceful man who wears rimless glasses over eyes that bore holes in you. He was chief of police before the war and during the war the Japanese picked him out of the police department and made him chief administrator of the Northern District of Okinawa—one of the very few native Okinawans to whom they entrusted a position of responsibility.

"Not only myself but every Okinawan felt he was going to be slaughtered and the women were going to be raped when the Americans came in," Nakamura said through Skuse's interpreter. "That was the way the Japanese military gave propaganda, in such a way that everybody believed it."

In the early part of July 1945 Nakamura had his first encounter with the dreaded Americans. "I was up in the mountains and just by accident I and two others met a platoon of American soldiers and they asked us questions and we all thought we were going to be shot. But instead of shooting us they just questioned us and let us go. We went back to our hiding place and we talked about it, and we thought the Americans were strange people because they didn't shoot us. For the first time we thought Americans might be different from what the Japanese propaganda said they were."

So effective had the Japanese propaganda been, however, that it took another full month of starvation before Nakamura and his friends could bring themselves to come out of hiding. "On the Fourth of July in 1945 a group of us came down from the mountains in northern Okinawa. At first we thought we were the only natives alive on the island. We discovered many other Okinawans and we were all starving. My group had been hiding out for three months and it was the same with all the others. Most of them were dying of malnutrition."

When Nakamura was restored to health he resumed his career as a police official. In 1951 he was selected as a national leader to tour the United States to study the operations of American police departments. "I was embarrassed to think about what the Japanese said during the war. Every chance I get I tell people how the Americans are and what I saw in the United States and what I think about them. I saw many things and I learned many things. The Americans are well disciplined and have a very high moral standard. The Americans were very nice to me. I did not take it that they treated me that way because I came from a foreign country or from a long way. It just comes natural to them, the same as they would do to anybody else.

"I want Americans to be made to feel the same way here. I want to do more than I do but I cannot because I cannot speak your language. So many times I want to express my personal views and appreciation but I cannot. There are no words to express our appreciation for the Air Rescue unit. They have been very cooperative and in many cases have risked their own lives and gone out to distressed vessels and conducted rescue operations. In many cases the persons who were rescued came to me and asked me to express their thanks to the Rescue people and in many cases I have asked the chief executive of my government to express appreciation to the Rescue men. But at this moment I want personally to express my own thanks to the individuals in the Air Rescue Squadron who participate in these rescues.

"There was the time when the ships were lost during the terrible storms and winds just last February—and there was that other time when two native fishermen went skin diving in the northern part of the island. They were trapped just offshore and one of the Americans tied a rope around his waist and tried to swim out and save them and there were hundreds of people on shore trying to stop this man. They didn't want him to lose his life—not even for their own people. Find out about these things and you will understand why my people feel as they do about the Rescue men."

I made a note to check into the story of the skin divers and then Nakamura said that two of the three other native officials there had been passengers on the *Nanshu Maru,* a vessel of 316 tons, which had departed Miyako for Naha with 146 souls on board and a crew of twenty-three, and ran headlong into the tempest that exploded the waters off Okinawa between February nineteenth and twentieth of 1955. Scores of vessels were disabled during that period, big and little ships, and some of them vanished with all on board and never were heard of again. During the storm, while winds that reached sixty-five knots tore across runways and airfields, United States Air Force and Navy planes took off again and again, searching out the crippled vessels that had radioed for help.

It was impossible for the aircraft to land on waters that were tossing ships around like toys, but the planes were able to direct surface vessels to the distressed and in many instances dropped flares to light up a wounded ship so that another vessel could find it and come to its aid. During that storm there were twenty-nine vessels of major size and fourteen canoes and smaller boats that were located. Most of these, with their total of 701 men, women, and children, were shepherded to safety. Shuhei Higa, chief executive of the Government of the Ryukyu Islands, said at the time: "As each vessel returns safely to port our hearts are filled with gratitude."

In at least one instance, that of the *Nanshu Maru*, the presence of aircraft overhead prevented abandonment of the ship with the certain mass loss of life that would have ensued. Juto Oshiro, a building engineer inspector attached to the Ryukyuan police department, one of the men Nakamura brought with him to Skuse's office, was one of the passengers on the *Nanshu Maru*. "We were caught in the sudden storm and the vessel was unable to move under its own power because of the heavy seas and the wind. We didn't know what happened to the ship at the time except that we had generator trouble, but when we got back to Okinawa finally we found the rudder had been damaged.

"The *Nanshu Maru* left the island of Miyako to the south at five o'clock in the afternoon on the nineteenth and about nine o'clock in the evening there was the storm and the vessel started pitching and the passengers had to tie ropes around their waists and secure themselves to the ship. This went on for many hours, all through the night, and most of the next day. None of the people on board had any thoughts about going to live. Especially a group of young girls who were making the voyage by themselves.

"The girls all crowded around the men and all the passengers were waiting for the order from the captain to abandon the ship. Most of the people could not swim. Everybody was thinking they were going to die any moment, as soon as the captain said to jump off the ship, and then out of nowhere this airplane was heard and we thought as soon as we heard it that we were going to be saved. It is hard to describe feelings at a time like that. By then the waves were washing over the deck and the winds were strong and even the passengers who couldn't swim were getting ready to jump overboard."

Traveling with Oshiro on that voyage was Police Inspector Mozen Toyozaki. "I saw this airplane about three o'clock in the afternoon when we had been in the storm for more than eighteen hours. The plane was flying very low. The plane circled around every ten minutes or so and I could see it was very low. When it came dark they dropped flares around the vessel. At first I thought the plane had flown too low and had crashed into the sea, but then I realized the plane was putting down a marker that could be seen from a great distance."

At nine o'clock that evening, guided by flares, a Japanese vessel arrived and stood by the *Nanshu Maru*. The crew of the *Nanshu Maru* took heart and all thought of abandoning ship was put aside. The engineers went to work on the generator and presently they got the main engine to function after a fashion. The next day an American Army tug went out to tow the *Nanshu Maru* into port. "In my usual working days I do not have too much contact with the Americans," Toyozaki said. "But this vessel, the *Nanshu Maru,* that I was a passenger aboard, I knew I was going to drown and all of a sudden Americans came in a plane and conducted a rescue and for the first time I felt that Americans were good people to come out and help out the lives of the Ryukyuans.

"As police officer I am assigned as deputy chief of the Miyako police station and there are many vessels in that area in distress and I have to send messages to Okinawa asking the police here for Air Rescue planes to come to Miyako. When just dealing with paper work you do not feel directly the importance of the actual work of Air Rescue but in this trip in the *Nanshu Maru* I experienced the Air Rescue operation directly. Now I know."

The third Ryukyuan, Chokei Kochi, brought by Nakamura, is superintendent of Public Safety for the local police. He said: "When American Rescue planes are out looking for ships in distress, the people who have their relatives and friends on board feel safe that the Air Rescue unit is notified and is on the scene searching. They feel secure. They do not have the old worries. Not only the people in Okinawa but in Miyako and Yaeyama, islands to the south. They just do not have the old worries."

"Pilots Not So Alone Any More . . ."

Rescue operates on both sides of the street in Formosa. The United States Air Force maintains a small Rescue detachment on the island, crews who rotate out of a squadron that is based elsewhere. The Chinese Nationalist Air Force, run by General Wang Shu-ming—"Tiger" Wang—has a rescue squadron as well. The United States has supplied most of the equipment and the United States Rescue people are teaching the Chinese fliers the technique of using it in rescue work. The Chinese Rescue squadron is just learning its business, but it is already good and it is getting better.

The introduction of the *concept* of rescue to the Chinese was in itself a revolutionary thing. It is not a very closely guarded secret that in the Orient there is very little that is cheaper than human life. There are more people than anything. The idea that anybody should go to any trouble, life-risking trouble sometimes, to save anybody else, was a new idea, for a time a startling new idea.

And yet, very quickly, it has had a wondrous effect. It turned out, after all, that the Chinese pilots were quite human and it made them feel better to know that if anything happened to them in flight there was somebody who would come out and try to help them, and that feeling better made better pilots of them, just as it has made better pilots of men everywhere else in the world.

Formosa is the name by which the Western world knows the island that has become the final stronghold of the Republic of China. It is a Portuguese word, meaning beautiful, and it was the name given to the island by the Portuguese sailors who first set eyes on it. To the Chinese the island is Taiwan and to the people who still call Chiang Kai-shek their leader it is the place from which they will someday return to the mainland. The dream is symbolized by a towering statue of Chiang—facing the mainland.

Taipeh is a badly overcrowded city with the nervousness, excitement, and drive of a city in the midst of a war. Although there are other pressing problems, the Nationalists have found time to do many things there—build new roads, schools, hospitals, better sanitation. But despite these improvements much of the native population of the island is as discontented with the presence of the mainlanders as Chiang's refugees are discontented being there.

It is always difficult when outsiders impose themselves upon a people, even outsiders as historically tragic as the voluntary exiles from China. It is difficult when a slumbrous, apathetic place becomes transformed, unwillingly, into a desperate, last-stand holdout; where bombardment and death are always just tomorrow, next week, or the week after that. For the many years that the Japanese controlled Formosa the people of the island were forbidden to wear personal adornment of any kind—no rings, brooches, necklaces, earrings. In their defiance they filled their mouths with gold teeth, the only shining things they could display openly. Today the men and women of Formosa smile their golden smile at the people from the mainland and, along with them, dream of the day when they will go back where they came from.

The Rescue commander in the Chinese Air Force is a

young, smooth-faced lieutenant colonel named Chao Sung Yen. I spent several days with Colonel Chao, in Taipeh and in the little town where his unit is based. Now thirty-seven, Colonel Chao was trained with other Chinese cadets at Thunderbird Field in Arizona during World War II and he returned to Chungking as a fighter pilot in 1942. He served in the Chinese Air Force in the Chinese-American composite wing of the 14th Air Force under General Chennault. Thoughts about Rescue came to him early. "A fighter pilot is alone over the water," he said. "He has no one. It is very difficult. I had the feeling that he should not be alone."

One day, while making a fighter sweep against the Japanese, part of the electric system in his P-40 was shot out. For an hour and a half he jockeyed his plane and finally brought it in to a forced landing just outside his home base. During that hour and a half he had had plenty of time to wonder what would have happened if he had had to bail out. Who would have come to help him? "A fighter pilot is always alone," he said again.

When the war ended Chao stayed on in the Chinese Air Force. "The first time I saw a helicopter was at harbor, Tsantao, north of Shanghai. Lots of American Navy boats. They told me it was for rescue purposes. From that day I know there is another job in Air Force, very important, air rescue."

Chao went on to fight the Chinese Communists, but the idea of saving lives, the lives of his own pilots, burned in his head, and then one day "Tiger" Wang ordered him to organize a Rescue service in the Chinese Air Force. "He picked me because I was known to feel that pilots should not be alone," he said.

When the Nationalists had to abandon the mainland Chao flew to Formosa in a fighter plane. "After I came to Taiwan I want to send two pilots to the United States to learn helicopter. Our Government bought four helicopters from the United States and I take examination and I am very lucky, I pass. After we have training in the United States in 1950 we start fly helicopters. From that time the Air Force—our Air Force—was the very beginning of Air Rescue. We had two H-5's and two H-13's. Last year our organization enlarged, built up, the United States Military Assistance Advisory Group—MAAG—gave us eleven PBY's, one more to come, and six H-19 helicopters. We start training from the first aircraft that got here.

"The first crew fly to Taiwan brought the PBY directly here. Stay here for one month to teach us how to fly. American Navy pilots. Seaplane is very different from land plane, take offs, landings, very different. Even we have flown airplanes for over ten years but we have never flown seaplanes. I think the seaplane is more difficult. The runway never moves but the sea moves all the time. So even when the Navy instructors been here thirty days we can just take off or land PBY on runway or smooth water, ideal conditions. But in open sea, or rough water, we just don't have experience."

When the United States Air Force established its Rescue unit on Formosa the Chinese and American fliers automatically turned to each other for help. The Americans coached the Chinese in the science of making open-sea landings. The Chinese, in their turn, passed along what they knew of their own geography and weather and terrain. "In everything we work with the Americans," Chao said. "The Chinese Air Rescue outfit is still in its beginning. We do not have experience. The American Air Rescue, they have passed so many years in work. When we work together, we feel very good, so many years fight together against the Japs and now together again. Almost all officers, Rescue officers at Clark and Tokyo and Okinawa, we almost all know each other. All Rescue people have same idea, help the others."

Examples of the smoothness of the traffic on the two-way street occurred within a few weeks of each other, he said. "In January 1955 four American jet planes came into Taiwan for landing. Very bad visibility. In peeling off for landing one got lost. He climbed to 6,000 feet and then radioed in and then bailed out. The Chinese operator at the control tower understand English a little bit, not too much. But he knows somebody bail out. He call me quickly.

"I sent out two PBY's and one helicopter. The Americans sent out an SA-16. Major Yang Chung Tien, flying PBY, found the American pilot in a rice paddy half an hour after he went out. He saw many Chinese farmers around. He radioed to helicopter, flown by Major Lee Shien Cheng, and guided him to where pilot was lying in rice paddy. Major Lee landed with helicopter and brought pilot out and took him to hospital. His life saved. We received letter of thanks from United States Far East Air Force in Taiwan for this."

Colonel Chao gestured to a Chinese officer he had brought with him that day, Major Cheng Kuang Hua. "Then he have his accident," Chao said.

Major Cheng, thirty-one, a native of the Province of Peiping, who also learned to fly at Thunderbird, has had a career of fighting Communists in B-25's on the mainland. He was shot down by the Chinese Reds in North China in 1947 and was interned in a prison camp in Hopei Province. "I was there six months," Cheng said. "Treated very badly, very little food, bad living conditions. They tried hard to propagandize and make me go over to their side. I escaped and walked twenty miles to the Nationalist lines. I went back to bombing again until I had the chance to come into Rescue."

On February 16, 1955, Chao sent Cheng out to practice water take offs and landings in the Pescadores. "The water in that area is pretty rough," Chao said. "About ten-thirty that morning I had radio call from landing strip on island off Pescadores: 'Your PBY, something happened. One pilot hurt.' During that day all of my PBY's are sent out, some in training, some in alert different parts of Taiwan. I don't have any more PBY's in commission. Helicopters are out of commission. So I got no aircraft, no way to get to Major Cheng very quick. So I go to the Americans."

Colonel Chao's manner in approaching the American Rescue people that day is a small story in itself. It was told to me by an American Rescue navigator, a captain with the wonderful name of Angelo Fortuna, which, in Italian, spells out messenger of good fortune, and which, I submit, is almost too ideal a name for a Rescue flier.

Fortuna told me that he, his pilot, Captain Bob E. Cooper, and their copilot, Lieutenant Edward B. Richter, were sitting around in their alert room—a tarp thrown over bamboo poles—when Chao pulled up that day in his jeep. "He began to chat with us," Fortuna said. "We had many pleasant interchanges before and there was no reason for us to believe that this was a distress situation. Then he very casually asked us if the helicopter pilot was there. We told him that Captain Roy L. Jackson was in his tent around the hangar. Colonel Chao thanked us and chatted for a few more moments, then he drove off. A few minutes later Jackson came running in with the story that Chao had requested the use of a helicopter to pick up a pilot injured in Boko Retto in the Pescadores!"

The distance was too great for a chopper and Cooper and his SA-16 crew scrambled. Cooper asked Chao if he wanted to come along. Chao accepted the invitation eagerly, taking with him a Chinese Air Force doctor, Captain Ma Cho Te. Chao had taken about fifteen minutes to make his polite conversation with the men. Exactly eight minutes after he finally got around to the point of his visit the SA-16 was airborne. "We avoided the artillery range on Formosa and went on radar for cloud coverage," Fortuna said. "No sweat getting there and we quickly located the downed aircraft. We also noticed a Chinese Nationalist gunboat patroling the area."

As Cooper and Richter began their sea evaluation Colonel

Chao glanced down and commented: "That is fine water, just a little chop." The situation was not too bad. The only thing was that the wind was coming from the same direction as the swells and since water landings have to be made parallel to the swells Cooper knew he had to make the landing cross wind.

"We made our approach and that startled Colonel Chao because he was used to the PBY, which lands into the wind, no matter what," Fortuna said. "There are no reverse props on the PBY and they have to do it that way. As we were coming down the Chinese gunboat—for some unknown reason—started veering toward our course. Just before we landed the boat came toward us and drove us into a trough. Chao thought we were crazy for landing that way, but he had the other example before him, his own damaged plane."

The engineer on the SA-16, Staff Sergeant William B. Adams, launched a rubber life raft and Chao and the medic aboard the SA-16, Airman First Class Reuben Garza, climbed into it. Cooper started to taxi toward the PBY. Cooper was upstream and making his approach to the damaged plane when the gunboat again did the unpredictable and suddenly cut in between the SA-16 and the PBY. Fortuna hastily pulled the raft back to the Rescue plane and Garza and Chao climbed back into it. Cooper put on power to avoid a collision with the gunboat. The paddles on the raft fell into the water and floated away.

"We circled, dragging our raft, trying to figure out what was the matter with whoever was giving orders on the gunboat, and then we came closer to the PBY again," Fortuna said. "It was a little tricky then because the PBY was drifting toward a nearby reef. We got between the PBY and the reef and told them over the radio about their danger. Just then a Chinese powered sampan chugged up and secured the PBY at the bow and pulled it away from the reef."

Because of the sampan the SA-16 could not now make a close approach to the bow of the Chinese plane and Cooper had to make a wide circle and approach from the stern. The taxiing was difficult because of an eighteen-knot wind and by now swells were breaking over the bow of the Rescue plane. When Cooper swung the plane around as close as he dared, Chao and Garza again climbed into the raft and Fortuna began to pay out the line.

"The swells were about six to eight feet high and made managing the raft difficult, especially without paddles," Fortuna said. "Then we received real assistance. A small, hand-operated Chinese junk pulled up and one of the men in it said he wanted to help. I gave him one of the lines to the raft.

They had better locomotion than the raft and they hauled it to the plane. I held another line from the raft so it was taut."

Chao and Garza climbed aboard the PBY and Chao got his first look at Cheng and the damaged plane. The plexiglass windscreen was shattered. The cockpit was half filled with water. Cheng was a mass of cuts and gashes—his face, neck, arms, and legs covered with blood. He told Chao that he had been shooting his water landings and on the seventh take off, into the swells and into the wind, a swell broke over the bow and tore off the prop on the port engine. The prop hurtled through the side of the aircraft and splattered Cheng with plexiglass and metal fragments.

It had taken exactly one hour and twenty minutes from the time the accident occurred to the time Cooper landed on the water. During that time Cheng had waited helplessly in the PBY, at the mercy of eight-foot swells that tossed the powerless airplane around like a piece of debris. Cheng was transferred from the PBY to the raft and Fortuna hauled the raft back to the SA-16. The men in the junk held their line so that the raft did not drift too close to the revolving propellers of the Rescue plane. Fortuna lifted Cheng into the SA-16 and Garza began to clean and dress his wounds. Captain Ma assisted in putting on the dressing and comforted the injured man.

And then there was almost an accident of another kind. "It takes time to deflate a six-man raft to get it back aboard," Fortuna said. "Most of the stuff in it had been lost anyway so Cooper said to scuttle it. I asked Adams for his knife to scuttle it—not that we didn't want the fishermen to have it but it's yellow, and if it were seen floating anywhere it would cause another mission.

"Adams gave me his knife and climbed aboard the raft to pull the plug to scuttle. Just then Cooper, thinking I had cut it adrift, started to move under full power with Adams still in the raft. I was holding on to the rope so Adams wouldn't drift out and I was almost pulled out of the plane. It was difficult for a moment until I could brace myself. I held on. Just enough line had gone out so that Adams had gone behind the tail of the aircraft. He went up on the swells and the tail came down and he had to duck fast.

"I roared above the engines to stop the aircraft until I could haul Adams back. Cooper stopped, and we got Adams in again. He wears glasses and they were covered with spray. When he climbed back on board he had a startled expression. After he was back on the plane we slashed the raft with the knife. But then, as we taxied away, I saw one of the fishing boats making for the raft and they salvaged it. I hope they painted it so we won't see it again.

"Garza did a terrific job with the injured Chinese officer. He cleaned all his wounds and made him comfortable. Major Cheng was very stoic and after Garza finished with him and covered him I gave him a cigarette. He turned on a sweet smile."

Because of the turbulence of the water and the wind, which was increasing, Cooper taxied for two miles to the lee side of a protective cliff west of the rescue scene for take off. The radio operator on the plane, Airman Second Class Donald W. Drumm, sent word on ahead, and when the SA-16 landed in Formosa a Chinese ambulance was waiting. Colonel Chao remained behind with the PBY and the rest of its crew. The damaged plane was hauled to a harbor in the Pescadores and parts were flown in and the damages repaired. Ten days after the accident the PBY was flown back to Formosa.

"It happened very quickly," Cheng said to me. "I was very happy that in such a short time they sent an aircraft down to rescue me. It makes good friends between the Chinese and the Americans. We are ready at any time to help an American pilot if he is in trouble." Cheng leaned across the lunch table at the Friends of China Club and showed me a small scar on his neck. It was the only thing he had left to bear witness to his experience.

THE PHILIPPINES, HONG KONG

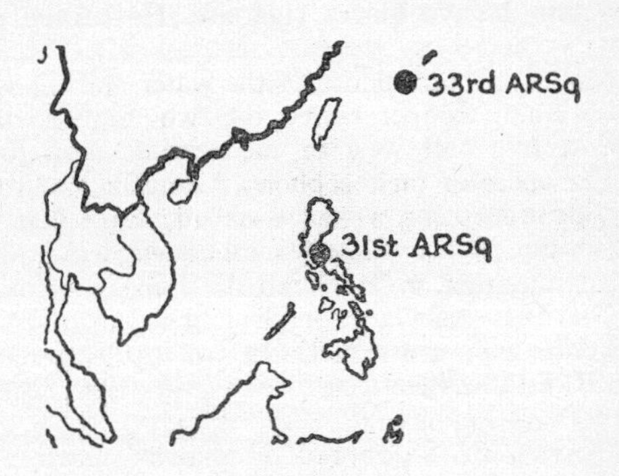

"I Have Been Shot. My Stomach Hurts . . ."

The Philippines belong to nobody but themselves now, but memories are still there, and some of the memories are warm and close and others are not. There are Filipinos who wish Uncle Sam was still around, the way he was before; there are other Filipinos who have stated publicly that they would rather see their country starve to death as a free nation than live fat and comfortable as a territory of the United States. There are Filipinos who want their fledgling democracy to learn what it can from the United States; there are men who have built careers on hatred for the country that ruled them and then turned them free.

The United States still has a lot of military in the Philippines and this, too, makes Filipinos stand up and shout at each other. Some see in the presence of American uniforms and airplanes and equipment a protection against anything that might come over from the other side of the China seas. Others see these uniforms and matériel as targets, elements of provocation, and wish they would get out.

It poses quite a problem for the Americans stationed in the Philippines and they have to walk a thin and straight and careful line. Every American there is more than a man in uniform: he is a reminder. In trying to make their new country stick, the Filipinos are as touchy and sensitive as any other proud people would be, and they are chary about who is looking over their shoulders. Having been more than friends to the Philippines it is difficult now for the United States to be just friends. And yet that is how it should be and must be.

Captain Alberto Geyls-Ramirez. He is a smallish man, dark-haired and dark-skinned with a gentle face and a soft voice. He comes from Arecibo, which is not far from Ramey Field in Puerto Rico where another Rescue squadron is based. He went to high school in Arecibo and then to the Polytechnical Institute in San German. After that he went to the University of Tennessee School of Medicine, in Memphis, and was graduated in 1949. He went back to Arecibo and interned at the district hospital there, was resident at the hospital for a year after that. He was in the Reserves all this time and in 1952, while he was engaged in private practice in Ciales, he was called into active duty.

He was sent to the School of Aviation Medicine at Randolph Field and then sent out to the 2nd Air Rescue Group at Clark Field, as flight surgeon. For quite a long time he also was flight surgeon of the 3rd Air Rescue Group in Japan, which meant that his area of responsibility covered a section of the world almost as large as that of the continental United States—all the way from Hokkaido, in Japan, to Guam, a distance of some twenty-five hundred miles. It was quite a position for the skinny little kid whose father ran a small drygoods store in Arecibo and quite a startling answer to those people who have strong opinions about the general capabilities of Puerto Ricans and other peoples whose skin is not so light as theirs.

Palanan is a tiny village of nipa huts on a little river emptying into Palanan Bay in the northeastern part of Luzon, one of the most isolated and primitive areas in the entire Philippines. The village lies back just a little way from a narrow strip of coastal land that is almost cut off from the rest of the island and the rest of the world. To the east lies the Philippine Sea and to the west the Sierra Madre with peaks that vault 5,000 feet. Nothing much has changed in Palanan for a long time.

Palanan has a police force that consists of one man, Romulo B. Mendez, which makes him chief. Mendez is a slender little man, not much over five feet tall and weighing just one hundred and fifteen pounds. On a March day he paid a visit to his superior to collect his monthly pay. "I went to him and asked for my money and I was told there was no money for me," he said. "We started arguing and he brought a gun out of his desk and shot me."

Mayor Bernardo of Palanan was a friend of Mendez. Mayor Bernardo knew little about medicine but he did know that a man does not live long with his belly ripped open by a .45-caliber slug. Clearly, if help did not come quickly he would lose a true friend and his chief of police. But there was no help. There was nobody remotely resembling a doctor in Palanan and Mendez needed more than a doctor. He needed a hospital and an operating room and the magic medicines. There were not even communications out of Palanan, no telephone, radio, or wireless. The nearest community of any size was Ilagan, which was only forty miles away, but those forty miles were largely a narrow footpath through a pass in the Sierra Madre.

There was no way to bring Mendez to Ilagan. And if, by some miracle, he could be brought there alive there were no hospital facilities in Ilagan either. For a little while it seemed to Mayor Bernardo that he was just going to have to stand by and watch his best friend die with the blood pouring out of his middle. Then in the back of Mayor Bernardo's mind a thought darted elusively, and he sat down and pressed his hands to his eyes and said words to the Holy Virgin to make the thought stop flitting around and come clear. It took minutes, and then he knew he had it straight; he remembered that somewhere he had heard that the Americans had airplanes they used for occasions such as this. And to an airplane a mountain was nothing.

But Mayor Bernardo had no idea how one obtained the service of one of these airplanes. He supposed it required much red tape and the influence of important people. There were official channels he should go through, he knew. But there was no time for channels. He sat down in the nipa hut that served as his home and his office and took a deep breath, then he addressed himself on a piece of paper to "United States Air Force, Clark Field." It was a presumptuous thing to do. It might cost him his office. But his friend was dying.

When he finished with his writing he selected a fast runner and told him to get the note to Ilagan as quickly as his legs would carry him and then get it on the wireless. Then he laid out Mendez in his own bed and stuffed some old clothing in the hole in his belly.

The runner started out, up the twisting trail through the Sierra Madre, through the little village of Melmel, then down the other side to Nassapan and to Amoboco and Tal-log, and finally to Mariano where the footpath broadened to a dirt road and he was able to get a lift on a carabao cart to the main road between Naguilian and Ilagan. And there he bummed a ride on a truck. It took him three days to make those forty miles from Palanan.

At ten o'clock on the morning of March 8, 1955, the director of Operations of the 13th Air Force at Clark Field was handed the following message:

> REQUEST IMMEDIATE HELP TAKE POLICEMAN MENDEZ SERIOUSLY WOUNDED IN PALANAN, ISABELA STOP CONDITION BETWEEN LIFE AND DEATH. MAYOR BERNARDO, PALANAN.

At 1015 hours an SA-16, piloted by Captain Williston L. Warren, with Captain Geyls aboard, was airborne and on its way over the 180 miles to Palanan.

Captain Warren arrived over Palanan but he was not exactly sure it was Palanan. From the air—and from the ground, too, for that matter—one native barrio looks very much like any other. He circled the place a couple of times but the people down below did nothing to indicate anybody needed help there. He dropped a message streamer—a weighted canvas sack—asking that if this was the place where the wounded policeman was would five people please lie down on their faces in the street.

The message was picked up and carried off, and a few minutes later five people lay down prone in the street. One of those five people was Mayor Bernardo, who knew that his long shot had paid off. Then Warren began to look around for a place to set down. Palanan was a short way up the river so he examined the river first. It was filled with floating debris of all kinds as well as with a dozen or more carabao luxuriously bathing. That eliminated the river.

He dropped another message, asking that the wounded man be brought down the stream to the bay. The wind was rising now so he put a can of evaporated milk in the canvas envelope to give it more weight. Then he radioed back to Rescue at Clark asking for a cover aircraft. At 1334 Captain Jack T. Woodyard was airborne in another Grumman Albatross. At 1435 Woodyard was over Palanan Bay. Woodyard evaluated the water and confirmed Warren's estimate of the sea conditions.

During all this time the wounded Mendez was being moved down the small river to the bay. "It took about an hour and a half to bring the policeman to the open sea from the village in a banca," Geyls said. "The banca was very narrow, just enough space for one person to sit up in it. When we saw the banca was reaching the sea we made a water landing about a mile offshore. We couldn't come in any closer because of the coral reef."

Geyls and two airmen, Staff Sergeant Leslie C. Gimmer, the engineer, and Airman Second Class Duane Moran, the medical technician, climbed into a six-man life raft. "We went to the shore to meet the wounded man," Geyls said. "The sea was pretty rough—eight to ten feet ground swells. It took us about an hour to make that mile into shore. Sometimes we were going in circles. Woodyard was covering for us and directing us to the shore. We couldn't see the shore because of the swells.

"As soon as we reached land I went to where the patient was. The canoe was pulled up on the beach. The wounded man was dirty all over—blue shirt and cotton pants—in filthy condition with lots of flies buzzing around old blood. But he was conscious and lucid. He said to me: 'I have been shot. My stomach hurts.' He also told me he had been unable to urinate and was in great pain—because of overextended bladder. Some old rags were stuck into the wound. The bullet had entered the right upper quadrant of the abdomen and had passed completely through him and out right under his shoulder blade.

"I got his history from him, that he had been shot three days prior, that he hadn't had anything to eat except a glass of milk given to him a few minutes after he was shot, and that from then on he didn't have any desire for food. He stated that nothing had been done for the wound but to cover it because they didn't have any medical officer or nurse except a sanitation officer who tried to give him first aid.

"I examined him. He appeared very dehydrated with a swollen abdomen, and he complained of severe pains when we tried to move him to check the wounds. I took his pulse. It was very thready and rapid and the blood pressure was obtained with a reading of sixty over twenty-four—a very low blood pressure, showing that the heart was failing."

By now the entire village of Palanan was gathered around the little banca in which Romulo Mendez was seated alone with his death already on him, the men in square-cut breech clouts and the women in shifts, all dark and small and silent as they watched another small, dark man busy himself with instruments they had never before seen to make the death leave the banca.

Geyls and Moran started an injection intravenously of 500 ccs. of dextran, a plasma expander—a substitute for plasma—and while the fluid was going into Mendez, Geyls gave him injections of 600,000 units of penicillin and a gram of streptomycin. "I gave him the streptomycin and the penicillin to check the peritonitis that had already developed," Geyls said. "Apparently he had a wound of the stomach with the contents of the stomach spread all over the viscera with stomach juice and undigested foods. He was still complaining about a desire to urinate, and I catheterized him to remove the excess amount of urine because the pain was also causing part of the shock. He remained stoic and did not complain.

"Then we proceeded to make arrangements to transfer him from the canoe to the raft and then to the plane. There were about fifty people around us and one of them was his little brother who was crying because he thought Mendez was dying. The people had stood in awe because of our landing in the water, and then when they saw I was finished they began praying and crying and thanking me all at once."

But the witnessing of miracles was not yet over for the people of the village of Palanan. While the dextran was being administered Geyls instructed Sergeant Gimmer to have a URC-4 radio dropped from Woodyard's plane, which was orbiting overhead, and then to send word back to the base hospital at Clark Field that Mendez's condition was critical. The reason for that was that normally Mendez would be taken to a civilian hospital in Manila but Manila was farther away than Clark. Gimmer stepped away from the crowd and began to make strange motions with his arms, almost as a jungle medicine man might do to exorcise evil spirits, and then, as the people watched with open mouths, the door of the plane opened and a package came tumbling out. Then a small parachute opened and the package floated down slowly to Gimmer's feet. There was a great, concerted sigh as Gimmer opened the package and took out a strange instrument of metal and began to talk into it. Some of the people backed away slowly.

Gimmer sent Geyls's message up to the plane and the message was relayed to Clark. The answer came back that if the added flight to Manila would lessen Mendez's chance for life to bring him to the military hospital at Clark. Then Gimmer used the radio for another purpose. First he questioned a native fisherman who could speak a little English about the underwater shoals and reefs, and he found out how the airplane, floating more than a mile offshore, could come in closer. With some of the fishermen standing at his side giving directions, he radioed the information to the plane.

Lieutenant Warren E. Lovegrove, the navigator, served as spotter in the bow of the plane, watching the depth of the water and the hidden dangers, and Captain Warren taxied the Albatross toward shore. When the fishermen thought the plane was not going exactly right they shouted to Gimmer who talked into the radio, and the natives witnessed how their instructions changed the course of the plane instantly. By that time it was very hot and muggy. The skies darkened and there was a feeling of rain. As the airplane approached, people fell on their knees and began to chant, waving their hands at the lowering skies.

Mayor Bernardo stepped forward and attempted to give a formal thanks in the name of the people of Palanan, as befitted the highest dignitary in the village, but he was too filled with emotion to say more than two or three words. Instead, he took Geyls's hand and held it. Then he stepped back and lowered his head. Mendez's brother moved next to the mayor and Bernardo put his arm around the little boy. At that moment one of the natives came up to Geyls and handed him the two canvas message streamers. One of the sacks still contained the can of evaporated milk, a valuable thing in that village. Geyls slipped the can out and gave it to the man.

"Then I tried to get the people to lift Mendez with the canoe and put it into the sea so I would have to move him as little as possible," Geyls said. "I knew that any movement would jeopardize his chances of living. But they said the canoe was safe only in the river and not in the sea. By that time the 500 ccs. I had given him were showing some improvement. I decided to give him another 500 ccs. but to wait until we got into the plane. Since we could not transfer him in the canoe, we had to pick him up and carry him out to the raft. We were about one hundred yards from the raft. We did this very gently. Everybody helped. We did it just as though he were in a litter. After we placed him in the raft we started back for the plane."

The swells were even higher now than they were when they had first paddled into shore. The last sight that Geyls had of the beach was of the people again on their knees waving their hands in front of them. He could see the moving lips but the surf drowned out the voices. Then the beach vanished behind the high water. "As we were going over the water one big swell hit the raft and one of the boys fell out of the raft into the water," Geyls said. "That was me. And I can't swim. I climbed back into the raft. In spite of all that we reached the plane in about twenty-five minutes. Captain Warren had gotten that close. It was getting pretty dark by that time—it was well after five. We still wanted to move Mendez as little as possible. From the raft we put him in a litter on the plane, and tied him up good because the swells were a little higher than before. After everything was set, the pilot requested my opinion on taking off with him and I said it was all right."

A JATO bottle had been installed on the starboard door while the airplane was waiting for the patient, and as soon as Mendez and Geyls and the others were aboard the port bottle was installed. At 1720 Warren started his take off. After a run of ten seconds he was forced to abort because the plane was lined up unsatisfactorily with the swells and had started to porpoise. The bilges, hatches, and JATO bottles were rechecked and Warren tried again. He got up despite the failure of one of the JATO bottles to fire.

And then in the confines of the noisy airplane Geyls began his battle against the minutes to keep Mendez alive. "When we were airborne I started him on oxygen," Geyls said. "His blood pressure was falling. We had a connection from the radio operator's seat to the patient and we gave Mendez the oxygen directly from the airplane. I gave him 100 per cent oxygen because of his condition, and then I started the second bottle of dextran on him."

As Mendez was being fed oxygen and dextran, Geyls and Moran stripped him of his foul clothing and washed his body with alcohol. Then they covered him with blankets. "He was a little uncomfortable because of the pain in his abdomen but otherwise he wasn't feeling too bad and I was trying to avoid morphine or narcotics because of his extremely critical condition. I didn't want to depress his central nervous system. He responded very satisfactorily to this treatment and the blood pressure climbed to one hundred and ten over sixty. About five minutes before getting to Clark the oxygen was exhausted. We landed at Clark about 1830, where an ambulance was waiting with an interne from the hospital. I went with Mendez in the ambulance and delivered him to the surgeon in the hospital."

Captain Allen H. Macht, the surgeon, saw that an immediate operation was necessary. "He was on the operating table for three hours," Geyls said. "He was given whole blood during the operation. Dr. Macht sewed up his stomach. One kidney was punctured in one of the poles. Fortunately he had had no internal hemorrhage in the lung so Dr. Macht didn't have to go into his chest. The main point on his condition was there had not been too big an internal hemorrhage so he didn't exsanguinate. The main problem was a severe infection of all the viscera in the abdomen and closing the wounds in the stomach and in the kidney. When he was sent back to the ward after the operation, he was still in a very critical condition. He had a very stormy night, but in the morning he was out of shock, with intravenous fluids feeding him and replacing the fluids lost in the operation. He was again very lucid."

That morning Geyls went to see him, and he asked Mendez, "Do you remember me?"

Mendez said, "You are the one who treated me in the canoe." The policeman held out his hand. When Geyls took it, Mendez squeezed it weakly.

"Are they treating you all right?" Geyls asked.

Mendez nodded. "I am very, very happy."

A lady from the Red Cross visited Mendez that day and he asked her to communicate with his people and tell them that he was very happy to be alive. She got the message through to Palanan. It worked in the same way in which the original call for help had gotten out—to Ilagan and then by runner.

During the next few hours Geyls and the others waited anxiously, but they discovered very shortly that men who can qualify for policemen in Philippine villages are pretty tough, even if they are skinny and undersized and look as though they ought still be in high school. "When we got him there everybody thought he was going to die, even myself," Geyls said. "His chances were very slim. But about thirty hours after the operation he was walking with the assistance of a medical corpsman and seven or eight days later he was discharged from the hospital as recovered."

Within two weeks Mendez was back in Palanan with his small brother and his good friend Mayor Bernardo. What happened to the man who shot him is known only to the Philippine Government. I think it may be fair to assume that public officials in Palanan don't get shot in the guts any more when they ask for their pay. What had happened to Mendez became folklore overnight, however, in the isolated barrios of Isabela, and it spread to the tribes in the hills where the people there told of it around the fires at night, of how the flying machine landed on the water, of how, even more unbelievably, a box was dropped by another flying machine, and how men talked into it and listened and how it was better than drums. And the story finally came to the ears of Ramon Magsaysay at Malacañang, the place that once was known as a palace and is known by that word no longer. It was something the people in Isabela would never forget, and neither would the man who came from the people and became their chief.

"Joy, Joy, Son Is Still Alive!"

The squat, close-faced little man finished writing his letter. He put down his brush and reread it carefully:

> TO: Li Mo-shih
> FROM: Li Yueh-hsiang
> Mother, Joy, joy, son is still alive. On Triton Island, April 7th, our boat was destroyed by a typhoon. I was among the seven survivors without food for nine days on the island. Later an American aircraft rescued us. At present we are in the Philippines. Until we meet again, there is nothing more to be said. SON

He slipped the letter into an envelope and brushed in the address: "Li Mo-shih, Hsia Tien Village, Chiung Tung District, Hainan Island." He handed the letter to an American officer and then lowered his eyes and muttered in harsh Hainan dialect: "It is a trick. It never will be delivered to my mother."

The officer took the letter without replying, then he collected similar letters from other Chinese in the ward of the Clark Field Base Hospital. It was a couple of months later that the officer, Captain Bryant M. Sharp, deputy Intelligence officer for the 13th Air Force, handed Li Yueh-hsiang a piece of paper and said to him in his own language: "Here is the answer to your letter to your mother."

Slowly Li Yueh-hsiang unfolded the paper and read:

> FROM: Mother
> TO: Son (Li Yueh-hsiang)
> This day was a blessing to hear from you. You are well and safe—JOY. I know about the big wind from the big people. You are lucky to be alive—big wind blew hard. We don't know when you will be returned home. You were born here on Hainan and hope you will come to your birthplace. We are well and happy. Don't worry. MOTHER.

Li Yueh-hsiang looked at the paper for a long time. His face was without expression. Then he suddenly ran up to Sharp and shouted, "Yes, when will we be returned home?"

Sharp said, "They're working on it."

It was one of the most offbeat rescues ever made in the Pacific. It started routinely enough. A series of violent storms had pummeled the China seas and a report reached Rescue at Clark—at 1620 hours, May 15, 1954—that two Japanese trawlers, the *Nippon Maru* and the *Houkoku Maru,* were missing. At 0638 hours the next morning Captain Dale R. Baker took off in an SA-16 on search. Captain Baker, a husky, blue-eyed officer, veteran of thirty-five B-17 missions over Europe in World War II, told me at Clark that on that morning he took a heading for the last known position of the vessel he was assigned to look for.

"About two hours before we got to the position we decided to let down to 2,000 feet. The weather was clear, the sea calm, and we thought we would just look on the way in. We were passing a small island on course, Triton Island, a barren place, and we didn't think too much about it. Bill Warren, my copilot, looked out as we were going past nothing but sand. A couple of minutes later he said to me: "I think I saw something moving there.' I said: 'Okay, let's go back and check.'

"We went back and flew over the island, and at that time we counted seven people on the island. We let down and made a low pass. They were all lined up without clothes and were waving their clothes. Then they kneeled down, as though in prayer. They were bowing the way Japs do, which led me to believe they were Japs. I circled, looking for a safe landing place. To the south of the island there were several schools of sharks, which led us not to land there. North of the island coral reefs ran out about half a mile from the island. We spotted a place and I landed about a mile north of the island outside the reef and taxied back toward the reef until the water began to get shallow.

"Then we got the life rafts out, and the navigator, Captain Turner O. Veith, and the medic, Airman Second Class Reuben Garza, took some water, some emergency rations, and a carbine of ammunition. He had to take the carbine and ammunition out of a drop kit because the island was close to the coast of China and we didn't know who it was. They started rowing toward the island and the seven people started wading out on the reef toward the aircraft. About a quarter of a mile out the water got over their heads and they started swimming. The raft reached them about half a mile from the island. They were all too weak to get into the raft without help.

"The first things they asked for were water and food—using sign language. We still didn't know what they were. They had cuts on their legs and bodies from the coral reef and salt sores. The medic took care of them while they were still in the raft. We got them aboard the aircraft and gave them all in-flight rations and all the water they wanted. While they were eating we tried to find out who they were and where they were from. We still thought they were Japanese.

"I drew a picture of a ship and by sign language tried to determine whether they were off a ship like that, but they shook their heads. Then one of them took the paper and drew a picture of a junk. We got out the map and through naming names such as Singapore and Hong Kong we figured out that they had left Singapore for Hong Kong. They finally pointed to the island of Hainan, and as we knew that Hainan was Chinese we knew that they were not Japanese at all but from Communist China."

As Baker taxied out and took off the thought occurred to him that it might be better to fly in to the French airfield at nearby Tourane on the Indo-China coast and turn the Chinese fishermen loose there. "As soon as we were airborne they continued to draw pictures and with those and sign language indicated there had been seventeen aboard the junk and that they had been swamped in a storm and had gotten on this island. They thought the others might be on other islands close by. We searched three other islands in the area, all just barren sand islands, about the same size as Triton, but there was nothing on them."

Baker and Warren talked about landing at Tourane and then decided not to. "Because of the situation in Tourane—the war in Indo-China and the feelings the French had for the Red Chinese—we figured it would be better for them to bring them in to Clark. We then radioed Clark to have security police and an interpreter waiting, that we were bringing in some Chinese from Hainan.

"On the way back, through sign language, they told us they had had nothing to eat or drink for eight days except birds' eggs and a little rain water. We finally made them understand the word Manila, and they all nodded as though well satisfied. When they first came aboard they were frightened but grateful. They were all young, except one, and he seemed to be the boss. He was in bad shape, but they all turned to him before answering any questions. They got a big bang opening all the cans and flight lunches. They didn't know how to open them, and we had to show them; we couldn't get the cans open fast enough. Got one open and they'd be ready for the next one. They finished them all."

Captain Sharp, who learned how to speak Chinese at Yale University and at the Air Force Language School, was waiting on the strip at Clark when Baker landed. Baker and his crew were interrogated by Intelligence as well. "And all our clothing was taken from us," Baker said. "It was sterilized. One of those heat treatments. It melted all the heels on the shoes and part of the shoes themselves. They looked like shoes the Arabs wear. They bought my airmen new shoes. But not me."

Captain Sharp asked the survivors whether any of them spoke Mandarin Chinese, which was what he had learned. One of the fishermen told him he spoke a little Mandarin and he confirmed the fact that all of the Chinese were from Hainan. "We are all from the District of Chiung Tung on Hainan Island," he told Sharp. "We departed Hainan on a fishing trip. Our crew numbered twenty-two. A typhoon destroyed our ship. Nine of us made our way to Triton Island. Two were washed away from the island the first day. We do not know anything about the rest of the crew members. The name of our boat was the *Na Kung Lwo*. It was capsized by the wind and sank under us."

The survivors identified themselves as follows: Chen Hsien-yang, forty-five, of Tan Men village; Hsu Kai-ping, twenty, of Tsao Chang village; Wang Kai-kuo, forty, of Sung Shu village; Li Yueh-hsiang, twenty-two, of Hsia Tien village; Huang Chao-yung, forty, of Lion Hua Chang village; Ting Tse-yeh, twenty-five, of Me Chang village; Wang Te-hua, forty, of Me Chang village. It was Wang Te-hua who acted as spokesman, and before they were taken to the hospital to be treated for exposure and hunger he expressed the gratitude of all of them for having been saved from death on Triton Island.

As soon as it was established that the survivors were citizens of Communist China their responsibility passed out of the hands of the Air Force into the hands of the State Department. From the beginning there was no question as to what would be done with them: they would be repatriated as quickly as possible, and no strings attached, even though at that very time there were a number of American airmen and American civilians who were prisoners in Red China and the United States had been seeking their release for a long time.

The only question was *how* to get the men back to China. Since the United States does not recognize Red China and has no diplomatic representation in that country, it was a complicated process. Arrangements had to be worked out through the offices of the British chargé d'affaires in Peking and the American Red Cross at Clark Field offered its own good offices in assistance. The first thing, of course, was to restore the men to health. They were suffering from serious malnutrition, shock, and exposure. The doctors at the Clark Base Hospital undertook to solve that problem.

"From time to time I called on the fishermen to see how they were getting along, since I was the only one who could talk to them, to find out what gripes they had or what wants," Sharp said. "Their main gripe was that the food was American food and they were not used to it and they were not getting enough rice. This was called to the attention of the hospital authorities and the diet was adjusted.

"They were provided pajamas by the hospital and subsequently clothing from the hospital supply—parts of old uniforms and fatigues. As they got better they got tired of sitting around the hospital. I asked them if they had any objections to working in the area—doing odd jobs. They all expressed a willingness to do anything we wished. So from that time on to the end of their stay they were given light work—cutting grass, painting barracks—always under supervision.

"They were removed from the hospital finally to the area near the stockade where the guard dogs were kept. They helped around the kennels and had a little more freedom than when they were in the hospital. All this time negotiations were going on through the State Department for their return home."

A few weeks after the men were out of the hospital one of them, Wang Kai-kuo, the one Captain Baker said had appeared to be the leader and who had suffered the most from his experience on Triton Island, had a sudden mental relapse. He broke down completely and had to be taken back to the hospital. "He was seriously ill," Sharp said. "He was brought around by shock treatment. Upon his recovery he stated that he did not wish to return to Communist China, giving as the reason that he was old and they would kill him if he went back."

From time to time, as the fishermen were being cared for at Clark Field and were putting on weight with vitamins and more food than they had ever had before in their lives, they were visited by representatives from the embassy of the Republic of China in Manila who brought them presents, clothing, and special Chinese foods. The representatives asked the men if they would consider going to Formosa to join the Nationalists there. Six of the fishermen said they preferred to return to their families on Hainan. Wang Kai-kuo was still undecided. No attempt was made to separate him from the other men.

On June 10 Chow Shu-kai, the Chinese minister in Manila, sent a note to Raleigh A. Gibson, at the American embassy in Manila, in which he said, "We are deeply appreciative of the generous assistance extended by the Air Force and yourself." As the months passed, the strain of waiting began to tell on all the fishermen. Their original feelings of gratitude gradually altered. They began to fight among themselves, they grew short-tempered, antagonistic, insolent. They started small fires in their frustration and threatened to hang themselves. The pressures these men were living under, with all the efforts to make their incarceration as comfortable and busy as possible, were thoroughly understood by the men in whose charge they were, and the Chinese were not punished for their acts.

Captain Sharp went to great lengths to explain to them frequently why it was taking so long to send them home. It was a delicate task. "They were aware that the two countries were not friendly but they didn't know why," Sharp said. "And from the treatment they were getting they couldn't understand it. They told me the Americans were their friends. They were very impressed by the treatment we gave them and were well disposed to us." Then he added with deep compassion: "They were only irritated at the delay in getting them home—and that is understandable."

Sharp, who alone of all the Americans could communicate with these lonely and frightened human beings, spent many hours worrying what could be done to ease their minds during the long waiting period. One day he suggested to them that they write to their families. He told them he would make every effort to see that the letters reached their destinations. The men were dubious, but he persuaded them to try. He procured Chinese brushes and ink and paper and the men who could write did so, and then wrote letters for others who could not.

Wang Kai-kuo wrote to his son, Wang Chieung-huan: "I assumed you knew our destination was the Paracels. It was on Triton Island that our boat was blown away by a typhoon. The outcome of the boat we do not know. I was among the seven survivors without food or water on the island for nine days until an American aircraft rescued us back to the Philippines. Please write and let us know if boat returned home. Until we meet again, there is nothing more to be said."

The letters written by the others were along similar lines. The men waited and Sharp waited with them, counting the days. It was Huang Chao-yung who received the first reply, from his wife: "Received your letter and glad you are safe and well. Everything at home is as you left it. I fixed your nets. I am going to wait for you, don't worry. Write to me when you are ready to come home. I will say you are well to many friends."

Huang read the letter several times and then he passed it on to the others. Then a few days later Ting Tse-yeh and Wang Te-hua jointly received a letter from a "Friend Who Can Write a Little": "Received your letters. Makes everybody happy and joy. Had no notice from the big people that your ship was lost. They do not say. Glad you are well and eating. People who picked you up—they have our best thanks. Sorry, sorry, Ting Tse-yeh, your mother died soon after you left to fish, much sorry." The postmarks indicated the letters were mailed on Hainan, air mail, went through the Canton post office, then to Hong Kong, and on to Manila. The "big people" mentioned in the letters from Hainan referred to the Communist officials on the island.

In February 1955 Captain Sharp was able at last to bring the glad tidings to the seven men. He informed them that arrangements had been completed to return them to their homeland, and that the American Red Cross had undertaken to pay for their passage back. They would leave, he said, on March 1, on a Cathay Pacific air liner. All the time Wang Kai-kuo had been at Clark he had wavered back and forth about going home. Now that the time had come he said he did not want to go. Sharp nodded silently and departed.

On the morning of March 1 Sharp returned with Richard E. Tomlin, the Red Cross field director at Clark Field—a veteran Red Cross official who had been a member of the team at Panmunjom from July to October 1953 working on the exchange of United Nations prisoners out of Korea. Mr. Tomlin issued new clothing to the six men who were scheduled to go: white shirts, white belts, western-style trousers, and black leather shoes. In addition he gave to each man a bundle of extra clothing.

As the clothing was being distributed, Wang Kai-kuo, who was seated in a chair apart from the others, became greatly agitated. One of the fishermen said to him: "We are leaving now. What shall we tell the big people and what shall we tell your family?"

Wang leaped to his feet and ran across the room and joined the others. He cried out that he wanted to go with the others. "I did not understand anything that was said to me before," he said. "Not all the time I was here. Now I understand that they are going home and I want to go with them."

Mr. Tomlin picked up a telephone and reserved another seat on the plane for Wang Kai-kuo and issued him clothing.

The seven men were taken to the Cathay plane and the aircraft departed. At four-thirty that afternoon the air liner landed at Kai Tak Airport, Hong Kong, and Mr. Tomlin turned the fishermen over to Mr. H. K. Tyler, assistant superintendent of police in Hong Kong. Mr. Tyler asked each of the seven men if he wanted to return home. Each man in his turn said yes. Mr. Tyler escorted them to the nearby border immediately and they crossed over the frontier into Red China.

There is just one thing more that should be mentioned. It was in July of 1954—less than three months after these Chinese fishermen were picked up, and while they were being given the benefits of the finest available medical care and decent comforts, and while negotiations were already under way with their government in Peking to get them home, that Red Chinese warplanes shot down a civilian Cathay Pacific air liner in the South China Sea, not very far from Hainan. There were American lives lost among others in that wanton and still-unexplained attack. And by a coincidence of which only truth could be guilty, it was Captain Dale Baker, the same man who rescued the seven fishermen, who also was involved in the dangerous rescue of the survivors from the Cathay air liner.

"The Third Time Is the Lucky Time . . ."

It was the way it is in Hong Kong. It was hot and sunny and clear and there was a ship in the water between Kowloon and the mainland and the little junks were clustered around it like terriers around a bear. Water taxis skimmed in the harbor like bugs and the ferryboats were filled, and in the streets native policemen, built like statues, moving with the precision and disinterested remoteness of robots, their varnished boots blazing in the sun like armor plate, guided traffic dominated by double-decked top-heavy busses that looked as if they belonged more properly in Piccadilly Circus than on the China coast.

The Indian tailors were busy measuring tourists for the clothes they make to order in twenty-four hours, handing them drinks as fast as they could drink them to make them maybe order four suits instead of two—where else can you get English material like this at this price—and the Chinese storekeepers were pulling other tourists off the streets to sell them watches that had world-famous labels on their faces and heaven knows what kind of works inside, only the tourist would be back on the ship somewhere in the Pacific before he found it out. There were pearls to buy and diamonds and jade and silks and cameras and perfumes, and it wasn't as though Red China was just a few miles away, you could get on a train or in a taxi and be at the frontier in a few minutes.

And now it was in the past, and Peggy Thorburn could talk a little. Her ear is fixed up where the bullet tore it apart and the knots inside her head are untied and she can tell of it as though it were something she had read in a book or seen in a film, the kind of film they make about Hong Kong. It was just a year from that humid other day in July when fighter planes from Red China had come out of nowhere and had shot the Cathay Pacific air liner into the sea, an unarmed commercial airplane, a plane plainly marked with its name and a Union Jack three and a half feet high and five feet long, a plane on course, on scheduled, normal flight. There were ten human beings killed that day—British, Chinese, American—and eight saved. And now, a year later, there was still no reason given for it. "I can't understand why they shot at us," Mrs. Thorburn said. After all the months the bewilderment was still there. "We are at peace with them."

To piece together the story of that senseless attack Colonel Larry Horras and I spoke to both Peggy Thorburn and to Captain Philip Blown, the pilot on the Cathay plane that day. Mrs. Thorburn's viewpoint was that of a passenger; Blown talked as a war veteran and professional pilot. Peggy Thorburn, still in her twenties, born in Perth, Australia, is an exquisite, small woman. She has sparkling blue eyes, perfect white teeth, and flaming red hair. She was secretary to the manager of the Charter Bank of India in Singapore when she met John Thorburn, an accountant in that bank. After their marriage he was transferred to the Hong Kong branch of the bank. They have two children and live in a lovely house with a fine view on top of a hill in Hong Kong. For many years Mrs. Thorburn's father lived in Singapore, and in July 1954 he decided at last to return to his native Australia and Mrs. Thorburn journeyed down to Singapore to visit with him before he departed.

"The route back was via Bangkok," she said. "We had quite a little engine trouble at Bangkok. We thought it was minor at the time. They had two goes at the engines. Once we actually took off and circled for a while and then landed again. Then Blown said: 'The third time is the lucky time.' And we left. That was about three o'clock in the morning.

We were all tired. We all went to sleep. The first time I saw daylight it was about eight-thirty in the morning. We were very close to Hong Kong by then. Blown was assuring one of the passengers who was anxious about making a connection at Hong Kong for the Philippines where her mother was ill. It was their voices which woke me up. I went to the ladies' room and got tidied up a bit for arrival. I wasn't back in my seat five minutes when the attack started. . . ."

Philip Blown, a trim, terse man with a small mustache, almost type cast for the role of soldier of fortune, comes from an adventurous family and has led a bizarre life of his own. He was born to an Australian seafarer in Tientsin, North China, served in the Royal Australian Air Force during World War II, flew in India for Deccan Airways—a private line owned then by the Nyzam of Hyderabad—and when the Indian air lines were nationalized he went over to Cathay Pacific and now had flown for Cathay for more than six years, making scheduled runs to Bangkok, Singapore, Saigon, Rangoon, Manila, Calcutta, and Borneo.

His official report of the attack by the Red Chinese planes stated:

> The departure at Bangkok for Hong Kong was the commencement of a normal and routine flight via the International corridor and through point 18N 110E. After being airborne we set course 065° at 20.19 hrs. GMT and duly passed the lights of Korat, Mekong River, and the Indo-China coast on track, as ground marks were quite visible and in good moonlight. The sun rose shortly after crossing the coast and Cape Bastion, the southern and most easterly point of Hainan Island, was visible from a range of 50 miles. Course was now 063° with a SW wind of about 15 knots blowing. 18N 110E was crossed exactly on Dead Reckoning Flight Plan time with reference also to Cape Bastion at exactly 23.29 hrs. All previous check points were passed also on time to plus or minus ½ minute, which showed the Met forecasted winds from Bangkok were accurate.
>
> Cedric Carlton (the first officer) turned to me as he passed the FIR 18N 110E position report to Steve Wong, the Radio Op, and said: 'It's time to turn on our new course,' to which I replied that I thought it would be better to hold to our present heading of

070° for ten minutes to avoid coming anywhere near Hainan Island. I altered course for Hong Kong at 23.40 hrs. GMT.

As we all sat in the lounge of the Peninsula Hotel, Blown then told me what happened next. "We had been stooging along on this bearing at 9,000 feet for about three minutes when for no apparent reason Cedric glanced out of the starboard window and said we had an aircraft on our tail. I looked out my window and saw I had one on my side as well, and my reaction was to anticipate that they thought we were too near their island. And so I disengaged the automatic pilot and started a slow rate-one turn toward the east just to make them happy. I thought they might be warning us.

"As soon as the aircraft started to turn they opened fire and for the number-one engine and the number-four engine straight off. And the reason I think there was also a third aircraft was because the rudder controls were shot away at the same time."

Peggy Thorburn: "First I thought it was something the matter with the engine again. It sounded like the conking of an engine—some peculiar noise—and I didn't know what it was. But then I realized the sound came from the rear and when I looked in that direction I saw a hole, obviously a bullet hole or a cannon hole, through the compartment of the ladies' room. I looked out the window, which was my natural reaction, and I saw the planes, red-nosed, coming at me from my side.

"I ducked right under the seat straightaway. And then I crawled up and told the woman who had been worrying about making the connection to the Philippines to get down, and I think by then the whole plane was alert. I crossed to the other side of the plane where the air hostess was, Esther Law, a Chinese girl, and I tried to pacify her.

"There was a lot of shooting going on, bullets flying everywhere. The plane was jolting. I think I was hit by then but I don't remember. I didn't know it at the time, but the wing was completely on fire. That was what Blown told me later. The whole tail of the plane was on fire, smoking very badly. We couldn't do much to defend ourselves. There were no messages from the pilot or anybody in the front of the plane to let us know what was going on. Then the engineer, a man named Cattenach, I think, came along and tried to get blankets out to pad the sides of the plane against the bullets. Then he got down some life belts, Mae Wests, and I remember undoing two life belts and throwing them to the front, and I barely got the third undone when we must have hit water."

Blown: "The aircraft caught fire and I knew it was not going to stay in the air long. The area on fire was from number-three engine right out to the wing tip. It was all burned away. As we zigzagged, they kept going all the time, strafing all the time, and using 20-millimeter cannon, incendiary bullets, and 303 ammo, the whole lot.

"They were piston-type engines, LA-9's, painted cream color with red cockades on the sides. I told the radioman to tell Hong Kong we were ditching and then they shot the radio out. We got one call in. It's a sort of helpless thing. You have to make the best of what's given to you. The aircraft was still holding together, so I flew into the water, that's all. I was waiting for it to fall apart. She had to be vigorously flown right to the water—no question of letting her go. If you let her go she'd have gone right on her back!

"We had no arms at all. I wished we had some. By George, it would have been handy! We wouldn't have felt half so bad."

Peggy Thorburn: "There was no warning when we hit the water, so I didn't brace myself for any shock. I rolled right out of my seat, I remember that. There were a few seconds of complete blank and then I was out of the plane and into the water. Mrs. Law seemed to be with me at the time and for a moment I thought we were the only two survivors. The others must have gotten out ahead of us, they were about thirty yards away. An American woman, Mrs. Leonard Parish, from Texas, and her little daughter, Valerie, who was six, were nearest me. Mrs. Parish asked: 'Have you seen my husband and my two boys?' I told her no. Nobody ever saw them again."

Blown: "When the plane was smashed into the water she broke up into three bits and we had to swim out of the cockpit because it was submerged, and it was then that I saw Peter Thatcher, a young American civilian connected with the American Army. I had met him aboard. We were chatting away, floundering in the water for a number of minutes before we saw the dinghy. Nobody had a Mae West on because it had happened, boom! suddenly, and we were scattered in an area of a quarter of a square mile. It was shark season at the time. We had seen them before the crash."

Peggy Thorburn: "I swam to the nearest thing that could keep me afloat, which turned out to be the dinghy, all packed up in canvas. I didn't know what it was. I was holding on to it for a while, at least ten minutes. I don't know whether it was my intuition or what, but as Carlton, the copilot, came drifting along I asked him whether this was anything. It was too well packed to be nothing. He swam over and shouted out: 'You beaut!' That's an Australian expression and it means the same as your 'hurray!' He hailed everybody to come as close as they could before he started to unpack and inflate it. It was a very rough sea and current and wind and he didn't want to drift too long before we all were in."

Blown: "It took about ten to fifteen minutes for the people to congregate to this spot. I was about fifty yards away gathering Mae Wests. About twenty of them floated up from the mass of flotsam and jetsam. I went back to the main group. As I approached, the dinghy started to inflate. Then Carlton and I got on the raft and we lifted the people in. That was nine of us. The others were shot mostly. I saw many corpses in the water. They were all floating face downward, which meant they were not drowned as their lungs still had air in them, else they would have sunk out of sight. So they must have been shot. I elected to leave the corpses in the water.

"When we were first floating and the oil on the water was burning, the airplanes that shot us down made one low pass. I say there were two then. Carlton reckons there were three. And then they went back in the direction where they came from."

Peggy Thorburn: "We got Valerie in the dinghy first and then her mother and then Mrs. Law, and I followed. The others got aboard very quickly. We were all very exhausted, I think. There were no signs now of any planes. We made ourselves as comfortable as possible. We lay back for a while. I think we looked ourselves over to see whether we were hurt. And I noticed Thatcher sitting next to me with a bullet in his arm.

"I had my ear shot. It was bleeding profusely. But that was not what bothered me. My chest and arms were hurting a bit. Mrs. Parish thought she had broken her collarbone. I think the only one suffering badly was Rita Cheong, a Chinese girl who had boarded the plane at Bangkok. She had her leg broken, mangled, and she had a wound in her forehead.

"Then I think I asked little Valerie to sit next to me because Mrs. Parish couldn't use her arms to comfort the little girl. She was feeling pain in her shoulder. Valerie lay on my lap most of the time. I put her head on my knee. Her mother said: 'Don't put her head in the dinghy.' It was full of green dye and her head was getting all green. Funny how you think of silly little things that don't matter.

"I asked Blown whether he had got an SOS out and he said that he had. Sparks had been plugging away all the time at the wireless, he said. He said the message must have been picked up at Singapore or Saigon or Manila or Hong Kong. He calculated the time it would take to round up the aircraft at Hong Kong and make the search. He tried to reassure everybody that everything would be all right, that the planes would sight us soon. It was a question of sitting and waiting. Valerie was asking many questions, as any youngster would. Why were we in the water—where was her daddy—where were her brothers—she didn't like being in a boat. I tried to pacify her, and presently she went to sleep."

A part of the SOS had got through: the fact that the air liner was on fire. Nothing about the attack. The message was picked up in many places. One of them was the civilian-operated rescue control center at Manila. The center relayed the message to Rescue at Clark Field—stating only that the plane was in flames and giving its co-ordinates. There was still no knowledge anywhere that the airliner had been shot down.

Captain Jack Woodyard, lean, lanky, six feet four, is one of the rare birds, a natural pilot, a man who was born to fly an amphibian plane and land on water. Woodyard and his crew were airborne in an SA-16 a few minutes later. He was followed immediately by Captain Dale Baker in another Grumman Albatross.

The two Rescue pilots had a complicated problem on their hands. From the information they had received they believed the plane they were going to seek was still in flight. They had to equate the location of the air liner at the time it sent out its SOS, its probable direction and air speed, wind velocity, and come up with a rough idea of where it might be four hours hence when the Rescue planes covered the 700 miles between the Philippines and the South China Sea. Woodyard and Baker worked it out over the radio: Woodyard would head in the general direction of Hong Kong. Baker would go to the last reported position of the Cathay plane. Then Woodyard would work back south and Baker would work north. And somewhere between them, if they were lucky, they might find the air liner before it was too late.

Blown: "We were drifting downwind in a dinghy toward Red China. The wind velocity was 180/20. We had ditched at 2346. Everyone was quite calm. There was not much hope of survival. We thought, this is it. There was nothing in it to indicate any future. We were drifting toward Red China. We thought we would all end up in Canton or a salt mine even if someone came out and fished us out. I mentally assessed the possibility of landing on a small island and getting some water and then stooging off again into the water."

And then the numbed derelicts in the little raft heard the sound of airplanes. They looked up first in terror, thinking that the warplanes had returned to finish what they had left unfinished, to eliminate forever all evidence of their cold-blooded handiwork, and then the terror flamed into hope, the first hope.

Blown: "It was our Hong Kong Air-Sea Rescue, the RAF, in the form of two Hornets, reconnaissance aircraft, and they came along and pinpointed our position and dropped a smoke float and then shortly they were followed by a Sunderland, a four-engine flying boat."

But the hope was destroyed as rapidly as it had risen.

Blown: "He couldn't land because of the roughness of the sea and the smallness of Tinhosa Island Bay. Six or seven times he had a go at it, but he couldn't make it at all." Then the Sunderland flew away and the people in the raft slumped again into their lethargy, with their hopelessness now despair, for they had seen a flying boat that was made to land on water come out to them and then be unable to land, and they watched the blue sea between them and the coast of Red China shrink before their eyes. Intermittently they heard other planes.

Blown: "Each time we heard engines we thought it was the Reds coming back again. We got out this yellow waterproof cover and threw a canopy over the people to make out the raft was empty in case the Reds came back looking for us, and that was what, in effect, caused all the stories that there was one survivor and no survivors, and all those sort of funny stories they got originally, because from the air with the canopy over the raft it looks as though it's empty, which was the idea, because if these guys came back they would not have shot on an empty raft, they would have thought their fishermen could get it and use it."

At 1103 hours, Tokyo time, Captain Woodyard instructed his radio operator, Airman Third Class Lawrence E. Rodriguez, to send the following message to Hong Kong: "Request to know if aircraft VRHEU has landed yet inbound to Hong Kong with one engine on fire." Hong Kong replied: "Air Traffic Control advises nothing heard from VRHEU since 8 A.M."

Peggy Thorburn: "I kept dozing. Thatcher nudged me to keep me awake. This continued until the two Hornets passed by us at high altitude. They came so fast we thought they had missed us, that they could not have seen us. We were under the tarp then and Blown had let out the marker. Shortly after that the Sunderland came down. That flew over us for a long time and we knew we were sighted.

"We were elated. We thought the Sunderland could land on the water straightaway and off we would be for home. But then it went away. I got disinterested. The planes were coming along and nothing was happening. I didn't care what was happening at that stage. We realized we were moving quickly toward the mainland. The tarp was flapping and making a kind of sail of itself and it was bringing us close to land. We pinned it down.

"I do remember that there was no thought of possibly being picked up at all. We thought we had two choices: to drift into the China coast or try to get away. It was a question of being picked up by the Communists or starving to death in a lifeboat. We started to paddle as hard as we could. We preferred to starve. We knew that the Chinese Reds wanted no survivors. It was just that they slipped up a little with us."

Woodyard radioed Hong Kong again at 1150 hours and was informed there was still no word on the missing air liner but that ten different airplanes were out searching and that a number of surface vessels were on their way to the last known position of the Cathay plane but could not get to the area for at least another six hours. And then fifty minutes later Woodyard received this message from Hong Kong: "Dinghy and survivors have been sighted at 11:37 A.M., position 1836 degrees north, 11028 degrees east." He was also told that the Sunderland was there.

Woodyard assumed immediately that the British flying boat would pick up the survivors in the raft and that as far as he and Baker were concerned that part of the effort was over. He decided to continue on, however, with the idea of scouting over the area, hoping that he might be able to locate individual survivors who might still be floating in the water. Thus far nobody, except the victims, knew anything about the attack by the Communist planes. Everyone still thought the air liner had simply had an engine catch fire.

So unaware of any Red Chinese involvement in the affair were the Hong Kong authorities that they sent a radio message to White Cloud Airfield in Canton, reporting that the air liner had had an accident and that the survivors had been located. Hong Kong also gave the Canton authorities the details and markings of the search planes going out of Hong Kong. The Hong Kong authorities were startled by the reply they received instantly from White Cloud: The Sunderland flying boat could remain on the scene. Other "warplanes" would be *"fired upon without warning if they approached land."*

Although Great Britain recognizes Red China, Anthony Eden later angrily charged in the British Parliament that this brutal warning was counter to "all international custom and behavior." But even this unpleasant reaction from Canton gave the world no inkling that the Cathay plane had been shot down. The Hong Kong officials interpreted it simply as another typical example of Communist Chinese intractability and unfriendliness. They passed the message on to all aircraft involved in the search mission and cautioned these planes to keep well away from the Chinese mainland.

Shortly afterward the Communists in Canton went a step further and issued another and even grimmer warning. It was one o'clock in the afternoon and Woodyard was approximately one hour away from his destination when his radio operator Rodriguez received a call from Hong Kong. Rodriguez copied down the message and handed it to Woodyard: "Message received from Chinese Radio, 'No military aircraft to *approach scene of accident*. Remain well clear of Hainan and await further instructions.' "

Woodyard read the message and then showed it to his copilot Captain Tommy Arnold. Arnold started cursing. "What do they expect us to do?" he said furiously. "We got to get those people out." He said this, it should be remembered, at a time when both he and Woodyard still believed that the Sunderland had picked up the people in the dinghy, when he thought there was only a *chance* that there might still be other lives that might be saved.

Woodyard said to Rodriguez: "Radio Hong Kong. Tell them: 'Roger, received message.' " And he continued on. When Woodyard reached a point about seventy-five miles from the raft he established radio contact with a French plane, a Privateer, and was informed by the French pilot, who spoke English: "We have spotted the dinghy with the survivors. It looks like two of them from here."

Woodyard realized then that the Sunderland had either been unable to get down to the survivors for some reason or that this was a different dinghy with other survivors. He immediately homed in on the Privateer's radio and shortly after two o'clock he spotted the raft, tossing about in a violent sea, about four miles from Hainan and about two and a half miles south of another tiny, high-cliffed island, Tachou Tao.

And he could see, too, why the Sunderland had been unable to land in the water: twenty-foot swells that would have battered the British flying boat, which was not designed for open-sea landings in that kind of water, into smithereens.

Woodyard made a rapid evaluation of the sea and its pattern. His only chance was the water near Tachou Tao where the sea was calmer, sheltered by the cliffs. But landing there would take him farther away from the raft—and closer to the China coast. He made up his mind very quickly.

As he gave orders to his crew to prepare for an open-sea landing he received a new radio from Hong Kong: "Remain clear of all facilities. Do not approach scene of incident until further advised." At the moment Woodyard was too busy to reply. Three minutes later he sent back his reply: "We have spotted survivors and have landed in water to pick them up."

Blown: "I hoped he wouldn't try to land—not where we were. The water was rough as hell. He would have broken up. An amphibian plane is not made to land in water twenty feet high. Some of the people were being quietly sick in their laps. I kept saying, *don't do it, don't try it,* when we saw him land. My God! That was gallant, that was gallant! We started to live again. We thought, this is it, we have a chance now. It took him a good hour to taxi where we were, two and a half miles, the water was so rough between where he landed and where we were."

The SA-16 sets low in the water. On its way toward the raft its wing tips were under the waves half the time and the water washed over the prow so that Woodyard and Arnold could not see more than a couple of hundred feet ahead of them. The wind got stronger and kicked the water even higher, and then the French Privateer got overhead and served as Woodyard's eyes, telling him, a little more to the port, a little more to the starboard. When Woodyard was halfway over, Baker arrived in his SA-16 and took over from the Privateer and he guided Woodyard the rest of the way to the survivors.

The engineer in Woodyard's plane, Staff Sergeant Douglas F. Blair, opened the hatch in the bow and stood there with a line. Rodriguez and Airman Second Class Cecil R. Smith, the medical technician, stood at the opened door in the rear with another line. As soon as they got close enough to the raft the men cast the lines. Blown and others caught them and the raft was pulled up to the plane. Arnold, Rodriguez, and Smith braced themselves at the open rear door and Blown began to pass the survivors aboard. The first one handed up to Captain Arnold was the little girl, Valerie. "It was worth my whole career to pull that little girl in," Arnold said.

The Chinese girl, Rita Cheong, with a broken leg, and a deep gash on her forehead, was in the most serious condition.

She was carried gently into the plane and stretched out on the floor. Blown was the last to climb aboard. He went up to the cockpit immediately. "What kind of accident did you have?" Woodyard asked him.

"Accident, hell! We were shot down!" Blown said.

Blown: "I told him to get the hell out of there fast, that these boys were going to come back. He said he had some top cover, some Navy planes, and it wasn't anything to worry about. And I felt a great relief then. If they had come back, without top cover even Jack Woodyard and company would not have got back."

As soon as Woodyard discovered the true reason for the crash of the Cathay plane he radioed Captain Baker and passed along the word and asked him to relay it to the other aircraft. The information was sent on to Hong Kong, and this was the first knowledge the world had of the atrocity.

Woodyard taxied back to the quieter waters off Tachou Tao and with the help of a couple of JATO bottles he lifted the heavily-loaded Albatross into the air. As the navigator, Captain Albert F. Smith, set a course for Hong Kong, Rodriguez, Smith, and Blair attended to the four men, three women, and the child, and when Arnold was no longer needed in the right seat up front he joined to help.

Rodriguez wrapped Rita Cheong in a blanket. She clutched his hand. "Don't leave me," she said. "Don't leave me." Peggy Thorburn's ear was half shot off and was dangling. It was severed so badly that Smith, the medic, did not want to bandage it. He was afraid the blood would clot and when the bandage was removed later it would take the ear with it. Mrs. Parish had a broken collarbone. Valerie appeared to be uninjured, but she was cold and wet and crying. Rodriguez took off his own jacket and wrapped it around her and tried to comfort her. Esther Law was suffering from severe lacerations, bruises, and shock. Thatcher, Blown, Carlton, and the fourth man, Lue Fuenn Fong, from Bangkok, were all suffering from shock and bruises, and later, in Hong Kong, it was discovered that some of the bruises were bullet wounds.

Lost forever in the waters of the South China Sea were Mrs. Parish's husband and her two children, Lawrence, four, and Philip, two, as well as the following: Mrs. H. M. Finlay, wife of the British Consul at Medan, Sumatra; G. H. Cattenach, engineer on the Cathay air liner; Young Nam-ying, a Chinese student, from Hong Kong; Tie Tian Chuang, from Bangkok; Steve Wong, radio operator on the air liner; Rose Chen, the other stewardess, from Hong Kong.

Peggy Thorburn: "We were all given cold water. It was

quite a treat. Our lips were dry and our throats were parched. Tinned biscuits were issued to us. I suppose they were full of vitamins. I was holding on to Rita's hand and it wasn't long after that that I realized she went quite cold on me. I thought it was just imagination on my part. I looked down at her eyes and saw how the pupils were dilated—and I realized—she was just not with us any more. I called the medic to confirm it and he covered up her face. Then we arrived at Hong Kong and landed quite safely at Kai Tak. An ambulance was there to greet us and we were taken straight to the hospital."

Mrs. Thorburn looked around the hotel lounge for a moment, at the people sipping their drinks. The hum of voices, which had seemed to vanish all the time she and Blown were talking, suddenly welled. "When your aircraft showed up we couldn't believe our eyes," she said. "It was a miracle to see them land. We knew that the Reds would shoot them down if they could."

Blown nodded. "I'd like to say it was very gallant. They seemed to care very little for their own safety. I really do. I think they are most brave, really."

On July 26, three days after the attack and rescue, the governor of Hong Kong, Sir Alexander William George Herder Grantham, made the following statement: "I should like to take this opportunity of placing on record my appreciation of the gallant action of the captain and crew of the Grumman amphibian, belonging to the United States Air Force, when they rescued some of the crew and passengers of the Cathay Pacific Air Lines Skymaster, which was shot down on Friday morning. It was a splendid operation carried out in very difficult conditions, and is worthy of the highest praise."

And on that same day John Thorburn wrote this letter to the American Air Attaché in Hong Kong:

> My wife is among those who had the great fortune to survive the events which followed the attack of the CPA plane by the Red Chinese on Friday last. She would not, repeat, not be alive and safe today but for the truly magnificent work of the United States aircraft who carried out the rescue operations and provided aerial protection after the dinghy had been located.
>
> My wife has nothing but the highest praise and deep gratitude for the courage and skill of the crew of the Rescue plane who picked them up under seemingly impossible conditions and treated them with

> such kindness during the flight to Hong Kong. I would ask you to accept on behalf of your compatriots my heartful thanks and gratitude for all which they did to bring my wife back to me and her babies. If it is possible I would particularly appreciate it if you could convey to the captain of the Rescue plane the sentiments I feel. I'd like to meet him one day and shake his hand. Till then, God bless him and his crew.

I thanked Mrs. Thorburn and Captain Blown for the time they had given me. Mrs. Thorburn left the hotel and went back to her house on the hill. Blown checked in at the Cathay office in the hotel lobby and then he took off for Kai Tak to make a flight to Saigon. Larry Horras and I crossed the street to the water front. The sampans were beginning to leave the sides of the big freighter. The afternoon sun lay pink on the houses across the water. An airplane was coming up the long dog-leg approach to Kai Tak from the open sea. The air was dry and it was still very clear and getting cool.

Men and women hurried to the slip to catch the ferry. People were lined up in front of a money-changing booth. Three Chinese school-girls passed, giggling, in sweaters, skirts, saddle shoes, and bobby sox. A Chinese monk, deep in meditation, walked slowly by them without giving them a glance. A British officer, riding crop under his arm, hailed a taxi and rode away. A slender, beautiful Eurasian woman crossed the street and entered the hotel. It was more British than London and more Chinese than Peking. It was the way it is in Hong Kong.

SAUDI ARABIA AND "LITTRELL OF ARABIA"

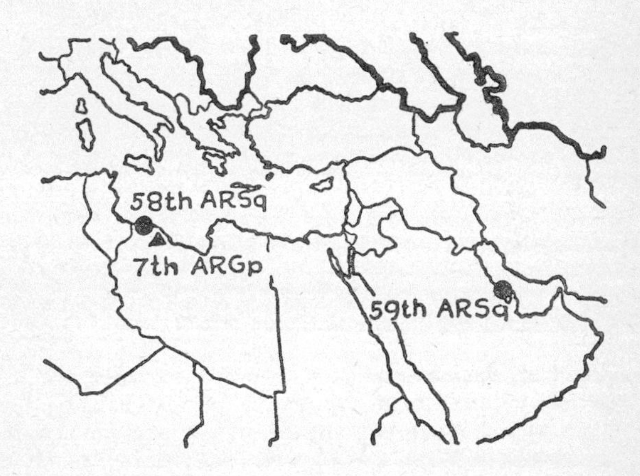

"Allah Ma'ak . . ."

Dhahran, on the east coast of Saudi Arabia, is a place very few American boys would choose to pass any time in, not five minutes of time, not even though it looks out on something with as exotic a name as the Persian Gulf. And yet with the world being what it is today quite a few American boys in the Air Force have to spend quite a little time there. And they discover in no time at all that Arabian days are murder and that whoever wrote *Arabian Nights* never tried Saudi for size.

Dhahran is labeled officially a "hardship station," which means a twelve-month tour without wives or families and the boys start counting the days the hour they arrive. The usual greeting to a newcomer when he steps off a plane and looks around for the first time is: "Brother, if I thought I had to spend three hundred and sixty-five days here I'd commit suicide." Everybody has a calendar and everybody marks off each miserable, hot, windy day as it passes, and during the empty, lonely nights men dream about their next station and pray that it may be a nice place this time, maybe like Devil's Island.

Uncle Sam has done his best to make the physical conditions of the airmen as comfortable as possible. Quarters are new and excellent and air-conditioned and the food is good and healthful, if monotonous. And whenever possible planeloads of airmen and officers are taken up to Cairo for a couple of days to see how it is in the world these days. And yet there is little doubt that in any popularity contest for overseas Air Force bases Dhahran would be a powerful contender for last place.

Among other Air Force units in Dhahran there is a Rescue squadron. It must be said that Rescue enjoys a unique standing throughout the Middle East. In that part of the world where countries are so pathologically jealous of their borders, Rescue planes alone may fly across these borders without special diplomatic permission. They have a kind of supra status that is tacitly recognized by all the governments.

The men in this squadron—a kind of American Foreign Legion—sweat out their twelve months of exile with other Americans with thousands of square miles of the emptiest desert on the face of the earth around them, where even the Saudi Arabians call it the Rub' al Khali—the Empty Quarter—and they wait for the occasional therapeutic flight to Cairo and each day make an X on the chart that reads out the passage of the years. And on the door of their Operations shack they have hung a little sign: "You call, we haul, you-all."

That indefinable thing called morale obviously cannot be too high. But it is not altogether bad. Because men learn from these things. For one thing, when a man gets sprung from Saudi he never beefs again, no matter where he is sent. But, more important, through all the irritation and sandpapering something else emerges in many of them. It is one thing to risk your life trying to save the lives of people you'd maybe like if you knew them. To do that for people like the guy who just spat at your feet as he passed you—that's something that perhaps is special.

Let us consider the experience of Ed Albers. Major Edgar H. Albers, Jr., thirty-three, World War II troop carrier pilot. A total of 193 missions during that war. Air Medal five times. Missions dropping paratroops in Normandy, southern France, Holland, Brussels, the Ardennes breakthrough. Twenty-one months of that in slow transports that were unarmed and unarmored clay pigeons for flak. A nice, sober, decent, quiet American, pleasant-faced, light-haired, low-voiced, a good grin.

In January of 1955 Ed Albers was put in Rescue and was

sent down to Dhahran. His reaction was normal and need not be enlarged upon. He was not exactly sure what Rescue was all about or even what it was. It was an assignment, and not a very good one. After a month in Dhahran Ed still knew very little about the concept of Rescue but he was beginning to feel he understood about the concept of hell. Then one day word came down from the Bahrein Flight Information Region—which is something like our CAA Air Traffic Control—that some men working for the Qatar Petroleum Company had turned up missing.

Qatar is a British company with an installation at Tarif on the Persian Gulf in the Trucial Oman Sheikhdoms, a British Protectorate. The Trucial sheikhs do not recognize the King of Saudi Arabia as their ruler and since King Saud has put forth claims to their land, especially since oil was discovered there, there is bad blood between the Trucial sheikhs and the Saudi Arabians and there is occasional shooting along the border. Because Britain, which has dominated the Persian Gulf for a century and a half, supports its Trucial sheikhs in their denial of the sovereignty over them of the King of Saudi Arabia, the Saudi Arabians take a very dim view of the English, and a corridor, about twenty miles deep, has been established along the southern border of Trucial Oman south of which King Saud says the British may not pass.

On this particular occasion five employees of the Qatar company—two of them English, the other three natives—had gone out the previous Wednesday, the twenty-third, in two jeeps equipped with two-way radios, and a truck, prospecting for oil. They had got themselves lost, which was not difficult since they were moving across a trackless desert with only shifting sand dunes to break the monotony. The jeeps had run out of gasoline and oil, and water was getting low. The three natives had taken off in the truck to look for help and had not returned. All this was told to the Qatar people over the radio by the Englishmen who had remained with the jeeps.

An SA-16 was sent out of Dhahran with Captain James A. Parker just after three o'clock on that Saturday afternoon carrying a para-rescue team that was prepared to jump out onto the desert. Soon after he was airborne Parker contacted Tarif 300 miles to the southeast by radio and was informed that Qatar's own lightplane had made a search and had found the truck—but that the truck apparently had been abandoned and there was no sign of the three natives. Parker was given the location of the truck, which was in the middle of dunes known as Uruq al Maraykhah, about forty miles south of Tarif, and he headed in that direction. At the same time Major Louis A. Griffing, the squadron commander at Dhahran, took off in a helicopter for the island of Bahrein to question the RAF people there and see if he could get any more information.

Parker located the truck but no men. He returned to Dhahran at eight o'clock that night and he and Griffing pooled their meager knowledge. Griffing had found out very little in Bahrein beyond the fact that Tarif was equipped to refuel airplanes if he wanted to use the strip there as a base of operations. Griffing, an earnest, careful, painstaking officer, laid on the mission for dawn the next morning: one SA-16 to fly direct to Tarif; one helicopter to stage down to the same place, landing at Um Said on the Qatar Peninsula, another British protectorate, for refueling en route; a second SA-16 to fly cover for the helicopter. He then named his new man, Ed Albers, who was working as Operations officer, as mission commander.

Albers left the next morning in the first SA-16, flown again by Parker. Griffing went down in the helicopter. Parker's plane landed at Tarif at nine o'clock. Albers was met on the strip by a man named Ken Maude, superintendent of the Qatar company's Tarif installation, and by a Captain Spence, the chief pilot for Qatar there. Spence told Albers he had been out searching again that day and that he had made radio contact again with the jeeps and that the Englishmen were not in any immediate danger.

Albers then directed Parker to get his plane refueled, fly out to where the jeeps were stalled, and speak to the stranded Englishmen by radio. If the Englishmen were in bad shape to jump the para-rescue team; if they were not, to inform them that a helicopter would bring gasoline, oil, and water that same afternoon. When this was accomplished, Albers went on, Parker was then to continue on and search for the three natives.

It developed then that the information that Tarif was gaited to gas airplanes was somewhat optimistic. "We had to use a hand pump and get the gas out of fifty-gallon drums," Albers told me in Dhahran. "It took almost two hours to replenish 200 gallons of gas." While the refueling was going on, Spence took off again in his lightplane and returned with information that a truck, sent out the previous night by the Qatar company, was within sight of the jeeps, and the Englishmen no longer needed help.

With this new intelligence, Albers altered his plan. He now directed Parker to fly to where the jeeps were and to ask them, as soon as they were refueled by the company truck, to drive over to where the abandoned truck was and report on what they found to Parker in the air. Parker got off just before eleven o'clock, homed in on the jeeps by radio, and made the request. He then flew back to Uruq al Maraykhah again, spotted the truck, and then, reasoning that the natives might have struck out on foot for some isolated settlements to the south, he started his search in that direction. He made a detailed search of this area of probability and found nothing.

At two o'clock that afternoon he returned to the abandoned truck. The jeeps were there by then and the Englishmen informed him that the natives had apparently spent at least one night there and that when they had left they had taken whatever food and water they had. From what traces were left of their footprints if seemed the natives had headed not south, as Parker had guessed, but north, toward another air strip the Qatar people maintained about twenty miles south of Tarif.

Parker radioed this information back to Albers at Tarif and Albers instructed him to conduct a creeping line search from the abandoned truck to the air strip and that if the results were negative to continue on to Tarif to gas up again. By this time the desert wind was blowing hard. There was a haze over the sand and a gauze of dust. Parker saw no one and returned to Tarif. By now Griffing had arrived in the helicopter and so had the second SA-16, which had flown cover.

The three thirsty Rescue aircraft posed a problem for the limited facilities at Tarif. First, and most important, it turned out that, contrary to the information Griffing had received in Bahrein, there was not very much high-octane gasoline on hand—just eight fifty-gallon drums. Moreover, there was insufficient food at the tiny establishment for the Rescue crews and no place for them to sleep. There also seemed to be among the Qatar officials a feeling that now that the two Englishmen were all right there was little need for any further search. Looking for the missing natives was useless, someone said. They were Bedouins and were familiar with the desert and were in all probability safe with some local tribe somewhere. It was a plain waste of time to look on the Arabian desert for Arabians.

As Major Albers told me all this he raised his eyes and looked at me gravely. "This was when I began for the first time to understand the meaning of Rescue and the meaning of the words in the Air Rescue code. Because Major Griffing—politely but firmly—wouldn't buy what they were selling."

Griffing, Albers said, would leave nothing to chance. He refused to call off the mission until he was certain of the missing natives.

Griffing realized, however, that his men and airplanes were too much for Tarif to handle. He sent Parker and Albers back to Dhahran in Parker's plane and directed the pilot of the SA-16 that had flown cover—and which still had plenty of gas—to return to Dhahran, too, but to swing around to the abandoned truck site first and look around there for fifteen miles on either side. After the SA-16's got back to Dhahran, Griffing continued, one was to remain there on normal alert. Albers was to gas up the other one to full capacity and return to Tarif the next day. As for himself, he would remain at Tarif with the helicopter and its crew—Maude agreed to take care of them.

"The next morning, Monday, I flew the SA-16 back to Tarif," Albers said. "As soon as we got there Major Griffing and I got together with the oil people and this is where I really learned about Air Rescue. The British said: 'Everybody is okay, quit.' And I figured: 'Okay, let's quit.' But Griffing said: 'We can't quit.' I said: 'Well, they don't want us to do any more and they're sure the natives are all right. And I'm sure they're all right.' And then Griffing looked at me for a minute and he asked me: 'Would you stake a man's life on that opinion?' And I said: 'No, I wouldn't.' And so we decided we were going to look some more."

Maude said he could not send any of his own people who could speak Arabic along with them because of the twenty-mile corridor and the interdiction against the British. Griffing located a native interpreter but the man had never flown before and he was afraid to begin then. After a long talk Griffing persuaded him to climb aboard the helicopter. Griffing got in the chopper himself and the pilot, Lieutenant William A. Lyell, took off. Albers climbed back into the SA-16 and took it up to fly cover for Griffing in the chopper. Below on the landing strip the oil people watched and shook their heads.

The native interpreter told Griffing in the chopper about a string of oases that were scattered along the desert below Uruq al Maraykhah, about sixty-five miles south of Tarif, the same oases Parker had had in mind, and Lyell turned his helicopter in that direction. The first oasis, as it appeared, was even smaller than Albers had imagined. A few palm trees. A house or two. He wondered how there could be any life there. But as the helicopter came down to land he saw life, a great deal of life. Women appeared from nowhere, holding their veils over their faces and fled behind the trees to hide. Men came out with long Arabian rifles and took up positions of defense.

"It must have been quite a sight to them," Albers said. "Most of them had never seen an airplane up close before and probably none of them had ever seen a helicopter. It must have looked like a magic carpet out of the skies." Lyell set down a good ways out of the village—out of rifle range—and the native interpreter walked toward the village shouting that he was coming in peace. When he reached the village, he explained that this was not an act of war, that no one was attempting to conquer the oasis, but that men, American military men, were searching for three native men who were lost and who might be dying.

As Griffing came up, the look of awe that was in the eyes of the people changed to something else. The flying carpet was miracle enough, as it was in the old legends, but the fact that white men were using it to try to find lost Arabs was a different kind of miracle—and perhaps a greater one. The elders of the tribe consulted with one another and then one of them, an old man with a fine white beard that rippled in the light wind, stepped forward and said that no one at the oasis had heard anything about the missing men. As Griffing thanked him and turned to walk back to the helicopter the old man laid down his rifle on the sand and said: "Allah ma'ak." The interpreter said: "He is saying, 'May God go with you.' "

With Albers circling overhead, the helicopter took off again, as the Arabs down below watched and the women came out slowly from hiding. The chopper went down to the next oasis and the same scene was repeated, and again there was no news of the missing natives. It went on like that, hedgehopping from one oasis to another. They were now in country of high dunes. Albers was flying at 1,000 feet indicated and sometimes he found himself less than 200 feet above the dunes and once or twice the dunes were higher than he was. The helicopter poked its way along, seeming, to Albers, most of the time to be almost on the earth.

It was at about the sixth or seventh oasis that Griffing finally was successful. When the interpreter told the people what they were about, heads began to nod. Two of the missing natives were there, being treated in a native house. Griffing was led to the house. The two men were stretched out on pallets. Their faces were seared from the wind and the sun and they were just beginning—after all those days—to be able to swallow a little water. It had taken them three days to walk across sixteen miles of desert, and these were

Bedouins who knew the desert. One of them, in a hoarse whisper, told the interpreter that the third man was worse off than they were, that they had separated and he had collapsed and had been found by the people of another oasis and taken there.

The two men were carried out of the house by the people of the village and were brought to the helicopter and placed inside. Then the people stood back and looked on silently as the rotors swirled lazily and then faster and the iron carpet went straight up and then away. Lyell went directly to the other oasis and the third man was picked up, this one half-dead, and placed aboard with the others, and the helicopter returned to Tarif. By the time it got there the SA-16 had already landed and Albers and his crew were waiting on the strip.

The three natives were lifted out of the helicopter and carried toward the infirmary. One of them, the last one to be found, raised his hand, and the men carrying him paused. He turned his head painfully to Griffing and said: "Shukran ya a'khii." The interpreter said: "He says, 'Thank you, brother.'"

Not long after that Griffing wound up his tour in Dhahran and was rotated out. Ed Albers was named squadron commander to succeed him. It was a good choice. Ed had found out about Rescue, the part that goes beyond the flying business, and he had found it out by himself. That made it a little easier to pass along to the others, the new boys, as they came in and looked around and wondered why under the sun they had ever joined the Air Force.

"Littrell of Arabia . . ."

The four local sheikhs entered the villa in the little village of Tagiura just outside Tripoli and greeted their host gravely. They seated themselves and for a little while they sipped tea and in courteous Arabic discussed casual things, and then at last they came to the reason for their visit: an act of violence was going to be committed against the next American who appeared in Tagiura.

The situation had developed in this manner: there were many Americans stationed at Wheelus Air Force Base. There was an American radio range station nearby. There were beaches. The soldiers traveled back and forth from these places at high speeds in military vehicles, thundering through the narrow, quiet streets of Tagiura, frightening the natives, their children, their animals, driving native carts against the walls in panic. There was more. There was a drinking establishment, created by the Italians of Mussolini, of cursed memory, when they ruled Libya, an establishment regarded with disgust and hatred by the nondrinking Moslems. American airmen now patronized this saloon. In it there were many fights, sometimes with knives.

For a long time this had been tolerated, the native leaders said, even though Libya now was a free and independent nation under its own king, but it could no longer be tolerated. While driving their own cars madly through the twisting alleys of Tagiura many American airmen drank beer and tossed the bottles and cans out of the window when they emptied them. Two days before one of the bottles, which had contained the forbidden alcoholic drink, had struck an elderly sheikh in the face. The airmen had roared with laughter.

This last insult had been taken by the people of Tagiura as a final outrage. They had resolved to assault the next American who passed through the little town. They believed if all the people in the town participated in the attack then no individual could be punished, even if the victim was killed.

One of the sheikhs put down his cup of tea. His mouth tightened as he looked at his host. "I was the one who was struck by the bottle that had contained the beer. But I do not want this act of violence to take place. Therefore, we have come to you to see whether something cannot be arranged to settle this matter in peace and to prevent similar affronts in the future."

The host listened to the lengthy account of abuse. When his guests were done, he meditated on what they had told him and then asked for more time to consider the problem, quoting the ancient Arabic proverb: "Speed comes from the devil." The sheikh who had been struck by the bottle nodded approvingly. "We have faith you will find a solution."

The four Arabs rose and bowed, murmuring, "Falyouafika Allah,"—May God give you health—and left the villa. The host sat down and pursed his lips and then he called out to his wife: "Hey, Ellen, what do we do about this?"

The host was not an Arab, not a wheel in the community, but an American; not a member of the diplomatic corps but a major in the Air Force, William Leon Littrell, who collects his salary from Uncle Sam not to settle difficulties of this nature but to fly airplanes. This visit, however, and others like it over many months, was testimony to the unique status Bill Littrell has achieved in the eyes of many Arab leaders, in Tripoli and other places as far away as Dhahran in Saudi

Arabia. These Arabs have come to know him, to trust him, and often to regard him as a bridge between their world and the world of the foreign military that has been imposed upon them.

Bill and Ellen, after talking the matter over between them, called upon Colonel Rollen H. Anthis, the base commander at Wheelus, one of the largest of American overseas air bases. They sat down with Anthis and his Arab liaison man, Wadie Deeby, who advises Anthis on local relations. Bill related what the sheikhs had told him and their warning of the riot that was impending.

"If I get the trucks off the road—keep them out of Tagiura—will that help?" Anthis asked.

"I believe it will, sir," Littrell replied.

"And the bar. Supposing I put it off limits to all American airmen and officers?"

"Yes, sir."

"Go back to your friends, Major Littrell. Thank them for their courtesy in warning us in advance and tell them that the matter will be corrected."

Littrell gave the word to the four Arab leaders. "Call off the planned demonstration," he said earnestly. "Your people will bear witness that this does not happen again." From that time on military vehicles by-passed Tagiura. The bar, deprived of its American trade, withered and died. There was no outbreak of violence in the streets of Tagiura.

That was a couple of years ago. Today the whole affair has been forgotten. Americans wander through the streets and back alleys of Tagiura unmolested, on the best of terms with the native dwellers and tradespeople there. Many Americans have rented houses in the town and their children play in the streets.

This may all sound like a very small matter, involving one obscure community. And yet in that smoldering part of the world, where the smallest spark may set off a brush fire, it quite probably averted a serious clash that at the very least would have resulted in the injury or death of one or more Americans, and which might have spread to other places in North Africa where, owing to the tone of the world today, Americans are required to live in uneasy proximity with native peoples whose history has made them hypersensitive to foreign uniforms. And it was averted because Arab leaders could call upon someone who spoke their language and in whom they could invest their trust. Arab thinking and pride made it quite impossible for these sheikhs to have presented themselves in the role of supplicants to the base commander in his office.

It had to be done somewhere in a house over the traditional three cups of tea, the first one bitter, astringent, and foamy; the second sweeter but still foamy; and the third sweet and not so strong as the others and flavored with roasted almonds—the first drunk in honor of the guest, the second in honor of the host, and the third, and most important, in honor of Allah. It was the kind of thing that has made many persons, both Western and Arabic, refer to this remarkable American officer as "Littrell of Arabia."

Bill Littrell is a tall, gangly, blond-haired man from North Dakota with a profound respect and admiration for the Arab people. In addition to his regular duties he has spent the last eight years of his life slowly penetrating the mysteries of the Moslem world, learning the customs, habits, history, religion, and even the maddeningly difficult language. He is a Rescue pilot and a very good one—some of his deeds in that field have become legends, as I shall presently relate—but on his own time he has gone far beyond the activities of an airplane jockey and has entered an infinitely more difficult area seeking for touchstones that can make the people of one race know and understand and perhaps even like the people of another race.

He could not have come from a more unlikely background for this. His father was a drug salesman in Minot, North Dakota, and Bill enlisted in the Army in 1938 and found himself assigned to the cavalry. He spent two years currying horses and cleaning stables in Fort Meade, South Dakota, and then was sent to the Signal Corps school at Fort Monmouth, New Jersey, where he studied radio operations and mechanics. In 1942 he was commissioned a second lieutenant in the cavalry and was assigned to Fort Riley, Kansas, as an instructor in radio theory at the school there.

"At the end of the year I found there were only two things that had priority over the ground-force schools; one was flying in the Air Corps and the other was jumping with the paratroops. I applied for both and was transferred into pilot training," he told me. In March 1944 he was sent overseas as a B-24 commander, assigned to the 10th Air Force in India, bombing through Burma, Siam, the Andaman Islands, Indo-China, flying back and forth over the "hump." In all he flew a total of sixty-two missions, with 522 combat hours.

In May of 1945 he returned to the United States as a captain and after seven changes of station applied for more overseas duty. He was an instructor at the base at Walla Walla, Washington, when the war ended, and he had just about given up hope of getting out of the country again when he was given the opportunity to accept a non-specified assignment that promised to get him overseas within thirty days. "I grabbed at that and received orders in two weeks to transfer to the 475th Air Base Group—search and rescue—with a permanent duty station at—Walla Walla."

Rescue was brand new then and Bill had no idea of what he was getting into. All he knew was that he was sore as a boil at getting assigned to the same place he was. He was made detachment commander of the Rescue unit but he continued to bombard his superiors with requests for overseas duty. In 1947 a call came through for volunteers to go to Saudi Arabia. This produced a minimum of excitement everywhere except in the heart of Captain Littrell. Not long afterward he was in Dhahran.

"I arrived in Saudi in March of 1948. It was desolate. This was the first Air Rescue Service equipment to be sent overseas as part of the organized Air Rescue Service. We had one B-17 and a five-man crew. I was the flight commander. Our missions were looking for trucks lost on the desert, barges that had torn loose from moorings and had blown out into the Persian Gulf.

"We had ten officers initially. We had no air-conditioning for the first two years—at a place where the temperature ranges up to 130 degrees. The average daytime summer temperature was 115 degrees. There was another temperature, the 'sun-soaking temperature.' That was how hot the equipment got. The plane on the ramp got as high as 180 to 190 degrees. It was impossible to work on it in the daytime. On most missions we flew only in our shorts."

In May of 1948 word was received that a B-29 flying down from Germany was lost. The last reported position was 100 miles north of Cairo, and Littrell flew up there, to learn on his arrival that the plane had exploded in mid-air and had crashed in the Saudi Arabian desert. He returned to Dhahran and was informed that Bedouins had picked up the radio operator from the wreckage and had cared for him for three days in a tent and then had brought him, with broken bones but alive, to Dhahran. "It was then," Littrell said, "that I first became interested in these natives."

Before Littrell had departed from the United States for Dhahran, Colonel Richard T. Kight, the then commander and father of the Air Rescue Service, asked him to make a study of methods of ground transportation on the desert. "Our first concept of Air Rescue in that area, due to lack of proper equipment at that time, was to drop a para-rescue team to the person in distress and then bring him out by ground transport. Colonel Kight asked me to study this. We learned that many Arab tribes in that area of responsibility were hostile, and so I was disinclined to drop para-rescue men at any which place."

To make Rescue more effective and to safeguard the lives of his men, Littrell took it upon himself to explore the desert and its peoples. "I made many, many trips on the ground, testing various kinds of vehicles, and at the same time began to study the natives seriously. I began to pick up the language."

It was obvious from the start that if Rescue was to function with any success in Saudi Arabia that the hostility of the natives had in some way to be neutralized. Littrell flew to Riyadh, the home of King Ibn Saud, and outlined his ideas to the old monarch and his son, the Crown Prince and present King of Saudi Arabia. In Riyadh and also in Jiddah he met many Saudi Arabians, and his interest in this people developed, and in some wondrous way he communicated this interest to these strange and aloof men.

Slowly, bit by bit, an atmosphere of trust developed, which paid off almost immediately when a coordinated survey mission of ground transportation was set up, consisting of persons from all branches of the United States forces and Saudi Arabian forces. Littrell participated in that survey and his mounting stature in the eyes of the Saudi Arabians proved invaluable.

It was at this time that Bill met Ellen Keller. Their lives have become so interdependent, their interests and desires so parallel, that I would like very briefly to give a little of Ellen's background here. Ellen Keller was born in 1924 in Niederweisel, Germany, of Swiss-American parentage. She went with her family to Youngstown, Ohio, in 1931. Her father was employed by the United States Steel Corporation as a design engineer.

"After graduating from high school and a business-machine course I went into the Civil Service at the Air Service Command at Dayton, Ohio, at Wright-Patterson Field," Ellen said. "As this was during the height of the war I wanted to get in on the big show, and as I couldn't get recruited for an overseas position at Dayton I packed my bags and with twenty dollars and a bus ticket went to Los Angeles. I worked for the Firestone Corporation and at other places but all the time I was trying to make contacts for an overseas job. However, due to my German birth—although I had entered the United States as a Swiss citizen—no one was interested in hiring me. I realized there was only one possibility left and I decided to try that: I joined the WAC in Los Angeles."

She finally got overseas as a German interpreter and after a year in Bremen she was discharged. Then she worked for a year and a half as interpreter for the Denazification Branch of Military Government in the Bremen Enclave. In 1947 she returned to California. She signed a two-year contract with Aramco—the Arabian-American Oil Company—and went to Dhahran in March 1948. Three months later she met Bill. "I was intrigued by him because when he was not working he went off by himself on a spit of sand in the Persian Gulf and fished and stayed out overnight," she said.

In his nights of fishing and staring at the waters of the ancient gulf Bill was doing a lot of thinking. He had known nothing of Rescue when he got his disappointing orders transferring him from Walla Walla to Walla Walla, but since that time he had learned a lot. He had been infected by Dick Kight with Kight's own concept of Rescue and he had participated in the lifesaving work himself.

But he saw Rescue in still another light: its chief handicap in Saudi Arabia was the animosity of the wild bands of nomads. And yet from his gradually increasing knowledge of the Arab way of life he knew that hospitality to a stranger was part of the religion of the Arab. Could not Air Rescue in some way serve as a span to these people in whom he was becoming so deeply interested? Would not Rescue, as an ideal, as Dick Kight saw it, strike a chord in those proud, untamed hearts?

And if this could be done, then would not Rescue itself benefit? Bill talked over his ideas with Ellen and he very quickly infused her with his own enthusiasm. I have come to know these two people well, and it is incredible how well they complement each other. Bill is quiet, thoughtful—a stoic, Dick Kight calls him. Ellen is forceful and determined, an outspoken, handsome woman who has learned to live for herself by living through Bill, whom she just plain adores.

Ellen knew that as tough as it was going to be for Bill to penetrate to any depth in the Arab world it was going to be a lot tougher for her—being a woman. The Arabs would stand away from Bill just because he was a Westerner and a Christian, thus an infidel. But she was a female, and she knew that Arabs agree that women have a definite function in life but that that function is not sitting around the counsel table.

Bill talked more and more about the things he was thinking, to his own men, to the Aramco people, to the Arabs he was getting to know, to anyone who would listen. And back in Riyadh his missionary work was beginning to have its effect as well—the old King, Ibn Saud, was coming to regard Rescue as an asset to his backward, underdeveloped land.

One day King Ibn Saud assigned two of the officers in his own air force to work with Littrell's Rescue outfit as interpreters and liaison men. And that day Littrell knew that he had taken a giant step. The two officers, Lieutenants Hakeem and Ruzi, members of noble families and distantly related to the royal family, were given the initial task of breaking through the archaic governmental system that prevailed in the country.

Traditionally, each province had its emir, each district had its emir, and each village had its emir, and in their own bailiwicks these men were laws unto themselves. Aliens who entered their places were promptly locked up until clearances came through from the King—and that might take a very long time, communication being what it is in Saudi Arabia.

As direct representatives of the King, Hakeem and Ruzi were authorized to speak for the monarch and break through these log jams. The two youths were taught English in Dhahran for two months—during which time Bill and Ellen tuned up their Arabic—and then they were shipped to Dick Kight in Washington to be trained in Air Force schools for jumping, survival, and rescue.

One of the amusing things that turned up was that when these boys were given desert training in the United States it was assumed that they could teach their teachers, coming from Saudi. It developed that neither one had ever been out of their native cities in their lives and that they knew nothing of survival on the desert. When they completed their training they were returned to Dhahran and Littrell.

Rescue as an operation was making itself heard in Saudi. Early in 1949 the unit at Dhahran received its first helicopter, an H-5, and shortly thereafter two Englishmen in a small motorboat crashed on the island of Halul in the middle of the Persian Gulf. The island is about one hundred yards in diameter, which explains how men can collide with an island, and the British were stranded there for two days. To make it pleasant for them during their sojourn there it so happened that a boat had crashed in the same place sometime before and the victims had never been rescued and their skeletons were still lying around. The two Englishmen contemplated the bones and wondered when the two skeletons would become four.

Word of the missing boat got to Dhahran, and Littrell

went out in the chopper with another pilot and found the men. The chopper set down and Littrell got out and calmed the derelicts. Then he put one in the helicopter and sent it off. He remained with the other one until the helicopter returned and picked them up. In the short time between trips Littrell himself got the idea how it was to sit and stare at bones—and he *knew* he was not going to get stuck there.

The different worlds of American and Arabic thinking were demonstrated to Littrell not very long after this incident when a young American second lieutenant flew to the island of Bahrein in the Persian Gulf on a training flight and on the way back ran into a dust storm and a high wind and was blown south. He was forced to land on the beach at the town of Oqair. Native soldiers escorted him to the local emir and the lieutenant was confident that he was going to be lined up in front of a wall and shot.

The emir, a gentleman of vast courtesy, wanted only to find out where the lieutenant came from so he could get word to his home base, and in traditional Arab fashion offered the American officer tea before he questioned him. The tea was spiced with cardamon seed and after one taste the lieutenant decided he was going to be poisoned instead of shot, or maybe drugged *before* he was shot. He refused to drink the tea, which was a mortal insult to the emir and almost did get him shot. The emir, controlling himself with great effort, had the lieutenant taken to a guestroom in his own house while he pondered his next step. The building, as is customary in that torrid land, was dark and had very thick walls. The lieutenant now was convinced that he had been put in a dungeon, preparatory to execution. He refused all food and water, believing these must be poisoned or drugged, and in a very short time he had worked himself into quite a panic.

The emir sent out a camel courier to Hofuf and from there got word through to Dhahran, and Littrell left immediately by truck for Oqair. When he reached there he found the emir in a state of high indignation at the lieutenant's refusal to accept his hospitality—and he also found the lieutenant half-dead from lack of food and water. Using what Arabic he knew and utilizing an interpreter when he came to a linguistic dead end, Littrell went to great pains to explain to the furious emir that it was only owing to ignorance on the lieutenant's part that he had acted as he had and that no insult had been intended. And as he spoke he himself realized how tragic it was that absence of understanding could produce a situation of this kind, how both the emir and the lieutenant had suffered so needlessly because neither had been properly informed of the other.

The emir, pacified at last, ordered the preparation of a feast, and the lieutenant, once he found out how wrong he had been, apologized with great sincerity.

"On the way back to Dhahran I realized that if we were going to do business with these people we had to have some more understanding of them," Littrell said. "I immediately started indoctrination courses in Arabian customs and ways." The most industrious student at these sessions, of course, was Littrell himself. The more he studied and learned about the inhabitants of the desert the more he felt a subtle and almost mystic kinship with them. And what he learned he communicated to Ellen so that they grew together in knowledge and understanding. And in their love for each other.

In January of 1949 Bill pulled off one of his great coups as a pilot, the kind of thing flying men yarn about when they get together. "You heard about the time when Bill Littrell. . ."

A man named Schuyler P. Henry, the assistant chief geologist for Aramco, was stricken with acute appendicitis while working in a camp at Wadi Dawasir in the middle of the Rub' al Khali—the Empty Quarter—the place that is desolate even by Saudi Arabian standards. Littrell volunteered to fly a doctor from Dhahran to the camp. There was no air strip at the wadi, but while Bill was on his way over in a B-17 the people at the camp cleared away rocks and then ran an automobile back and forth and in that way fixed up a fairly smooth place for Bill to land on.

When Bill was over the wadi he radioed down a request that the car be driven near the strip to raise dust so he could see what kind of wind he had. Then he made a perfect landing in the big four-engine plane. The doctor examined Henry and said that he had to be gotten to the hospital right away as his appendix had ruptured. That didn't seem to pose too much of a problem until Littrell tried to crank up the B-17 and discovered that his number-four engine was frozen. And he didn't have the equipment on hand to fix it.

If he ordered another plane out of Dhahran, it would get to the wadi after dark and of course there were no lights for a plane to land in the camp at night. And if he waited for a plane to get down the next morning, the doctor pointed out, it probably would mean bringing a corpse back to Dhahran instead of a geologist with a pain in his middle.

There was one thing Bill could do: try to take off on three engines. He called his crew together and polled them —this was not the kind of thing he would order any man to be part of. They said if he was willing, they were willing.

Bill looked over the strip carefully, then he got into the car and drove three quarters of a mile beyond the limits of the strip and marked out a lengthened approach. More rocks were removed and more earth was flattened by tire wheels. A little more than a mile beyond the point to which he extended the strip, and in direct line of take off, were a few jebels—hills—about two or three hundred feet high. He would have to clear those. He left the automobile parked out beyond the end of the extended strip to give him a fixed object on which to line himself and then he told everybody to get into the plane. It was then that he noticed that he now had a nice cross wind, coming from the west, at about fifteen knots. The sane thing would have been to flatten out a new strip so he could take off into the wind, but it was beginning to get dark, and, besides, the desert wasn't right in that direction.

So he started moving, with only three engines to draw power from, into the cross wind. "The normal procedure would have been to use only the number-two and number-three engines—the two inside ones—at first with full power until enough speed was achieved to counteract the unequal pull that would be made when I cut in with the functioning number-one engine. But because of the terrain on which we had to take off, however, I could not bring in the number-one or number-two engines because I needed the power of the number-three engine to counteract the cross wind from the right.

"Attempts to apply power on the number-two engine resulted only in the airplane vaning into the wind. I worked with my engineer, Technical Sergeant John B. Trusolawski, and built up to eighty-five miles an hour on the number-three engine alone."

And then Littrell dropped half flaps and raised the airplane into the air *on one engine*—and when the plane was *clear of the ground* he applied full power, with split-second timing to the number-one and number-two engines. "We went on three engines for about two and a half miles before we got aloft," he said. "It was really no danger at all. We had the whole desert to go on." Including the jebels, which roiled with dust as they skimmed over them so low they could have reached out and scooped up a handful of sand.

He got Henry into Dhahran, landing on three engines, and the geologist was operated on within the hour. There was very little doubt that his life was saved by Bill Littrell's ice-blooded gambling and his incredible coordination. Bill got praised up and down the line on that one, all the way to his big boss, Laurence S. Kuter, then a major general in command of MATS. It was quite characteristic of Littrell that in his own report on the mission his praise was only for his crew who chose to chance it with him.

Bill also was told privately that he was something of a lunatic, that people didn't take off in B-17's on three engines. "I wonder what would have happened if they had known it was on *one* engine." Bill grinned. "I'd have been court-martialed."

By this time it was getting near the end of Bill's scheduled year of duty and, as has been mentioned elsewhere, the boys count the days and minutes in Dhahran even now—and at that time they didn't have the posh air cooling and lush quarters they have today. Bill astounded Dick Kight by putting in for a year's extension, probably the first time any such request had ever come from Dhahran. Kight thought that the heat must have affected his boy and he checked back to make sure.

"They would give me only six months," Bill said. "They thought I must have holes in my head." The only thing that seemed to offer an explanation was that Bill had a girl in Dhahran and that she herself was bound there by her contract with Aramco. That was partly right, of course, but only partly. Bill was discovering that he had found something in life and that that something was with the Arab people. And he knew he still had work to do there—work that he felt he could do best himself.

For by then Rescue was getting a little fatter. They had gotten their second B-17 and their para-rescue teams and they had Ruzi and Hakeem to go out on missions to smooth the way with local tribes. But there was still one very big problem, as yet untackled: immediate entry into foreign countries.

"Our area of responsibility included all of the Middle East through India, a part of East Africa, and north to the Russian border. At that time it usually took from three to seven days to get a clearance, which would have been prohibitive in an emergency mission." And so Littrell plunged into a campaign to carry the message of Rescue beyond the borders of Saudi Arabia. It was a struggle against time—the six more months that had been allotted him—and a struggle against age-old suspicions and fears and almost pathological nationalistic prides. He went to Iran, Iraq, Syria, Aden, Oman, Trucial Oman, Pakistan, Eritrea, and Egypt to bring the word that Rescue was available to all who needed it. And after that to try to coordinate emergency Rescue clearances.

He journeyed with Air attachés and State Department

men and everywhere, at first, he collided with the same stone wall of distrust: why should a nation, even the fabulously wealthy United States, want to risk its men and equipment to save the lives of foreigners? Was it not truer that Rescue was just some secret, nefarious imperialistic plot the United States had dreamed up somehow to extend its control over other countries?

And when he managed to persuade doubtful government officials that this was not the case, that Rescue was nothing more than it said it was, he encountered specialized dreads. Iran, for instance, while admitting finally the value and humanitarianism of Rescue, was frightened about Russian reaction to permitting American military planes to have free access over her territory. Supposing Russia demanded the same privilege?

To all these objections Littrell could respond in only one way, with his honesty, his enthusiasm, and his genuine love for the people in that part of the world. And with this simple, unorthodox and—from a professional diplomat's viewpoint—wholly naïve approach, Littrell scored 100 per cent success. He obtained for Air Rescue carte blanche to fly anywhere on missions of mercy, with total disregard for national frontiers. This freedom of the air for Rescue planes obtains to this day—and it is *only* Rescue planes that possess this privilege.

When Littrell's six months' extension almost was expired he applied for a second extension, and this time everybody was sure he was losing his marbles for good. "I had to have Air Force approval and then have a session with the medics to prove I was not psychologically unfit," he said. The doctors, after lengthy tests, were forced to admit that Captain Littrell was exceedingly fit, physically as well as psychologically, and that Dhahran, a kind of tropic Siberia in the Air Force, was for him the best of all possible stations. He was integrated, within himself and with his work. Wisely, he was permitted to stay there.

From July through December of that year he worked with the Saudi Arabians and the Aramco people on desert problems. The biggest headache of all still was driving on the desert. The terrain, with its stones, sand, dunes, soft spots, the heat, the distances, all made surface transportation a nightmare. Tires lasted a pitifully short time and then came apart into little pieces, and even while they were still intact they had trouble keeping vehicles moving.

"I had a sudden idea—to put C-47 airplane tires on weapons carriers and ambulances," Littrell said. "It worked marvelously over the lava flows with their needle points. We were able to go anywhere with those ten-ply tires. I worked with Richard C. Kerr, the transportation boss for Aramco. Now Aramco has similar tires, in six-ply, for all its vehicles."

Among the lesser problems that Littrell had to cope with at the moment was the lovesickness of Lieutenant Ruzi, his Saudi Arabian liaison officer. It appeared that while Ruzi was in the United States he had married an American girl and he was having some difficulty in getting her to Saudi. He appealed to Littrell for help.

Bill was more than a little dubious. Although the girl was of Syrian descent, from what he could gather from Ruzi she was thoroughly Americanized. Looking about him, Bill could see how Moslem women were required by custom and tradition to live in Saudi, the most primitive of all the Arab countries, and it was difficult for him to see how an American girl, whatever her ancestral background, could adapt herself to the restraints that would arbitrarily be imposed on her. However, Ruzi continued his importunings, and in 1950 Littrell succeeded in getting the girl to Dhahran.

"It was amazing," Littrell said. "She became very Moslem —veil and all. No sweat."

"Except that every once in a while she visited me and took off her veil and relaxed," Ellen added.

When Littrell's second extension expired Colonel Richard J. O'Keefe, the base commander at Dhahran, allowed Bill to linger a few months more to wind up the myriad tasks—many of them self-imposed—that he had been working on. It was in March that Ellen's contract with Aramco expired as well, and soon after that Bill and Ellen were married.

They spent their honeymoon in Tehran and followed that with a trip through India, Thailand, and Singapore. Upon their return Bill was rotated to the States. They arrived in Washington in July 1950, and Littrell was assigned to Air Rescue headquarters there, given the assignment of writing a treatise on desert rescue in the Middle East, including tribal relations, transport, climate, geography—a field in which he was an unquestioned expert. His finished work was sent immediately to the Arctic-desert-tropic Information Center at Maxwell Field, Alabama, to be used there as a bible of its kind.

"After that I worked in the plans section of Headquarters and all the time I was campaigning to get back to the Middle East. Ellen and I went to Georgetown University in the evenings and studied Arabic and other subjects dealing with the Middle East—geography, economics, religion, politics, history." Littrell wrote his term paper on the Empty Quarter, a small masterpiece in its way. In February 1951 he was promoted to major.

In July 1952 Bill and Ellen got their wish: Major Littrell was assigned to the 7th Group Headquarters in Tripoli, supposedly to be sent from there back to the squadron at Dhahran. Since Dhahran was a hardship station and wives were not permitted there, it was planned that Ellen should live in Baghdad and Bill would get up there to see her when he could. It did not work out that way. When Bill arrived at group headquarters they decided to keep him there. There was a housing shortage in Tripoli at the time, and for five months Ellen remained in Washington, occupying herself during that time by working in publicity at the Eisenhower campaign headquarters. She got to Tripoli in December, and the Littrells moved into a new hotel—so new it was not even completed.

"The first night she was there we went to the Officers Club and we heard of a fabulous Arab villa that many officers had looked at but wouldn't tackle due to its primitiveness," Littrell said. "The next morning we drove out to see it. We took one look and said: 'This is it!' It had eighteen rooms, ten in the front for storage, servants' quarters, and so on, and then a large patio with the remainder of the rooms leading directly from it. There were four large pillars, a marble stairway to the roof, and it was fancily decorated—the hand of Fatima, the Arab good-luck omen, weird colored walls, and so on.

"It had stood empty since the day it was built five years before. The rich Arab for whom it had been constructed had died just as the house was completed and it is a bad-luck omen among the Arabs to be the first to move into a dead man's house."

There were several obvious reasons why other officers' wives had looked at the house and had said no. There was no electricity, no plumbing, and the only water came from a native well in the kitchen, a bucket-and-rope affair. There were no outside windows, all windows opening into the patio. However, for the Littrells the house had one virtue that made everything else unimportant: it was a true Arab dwelling. And they were both so deep in Arab feelings by then that they knew they could be happy in no other kind of home.

They entered into an agreement with the owner, Sheikh Hadj el Hadi Treesh, to rent the establishment provided improvements would be made. Only Bill and Ellen Littrell could have wangled them from the sheikh. It was necessary to erect seventeen poles to bring electricity and a telephone into the house. A water tank was installed on the roof. The Arab toilet was replaced with modern Western bathroom facilities, and the house was repainted.

"All this work took three months," Littrell said. "However, we moved in immediately. It was like camping out. We started a small garden in the back. We had a native well in the rear and we got a camel to draw water—the way it has been done since Biblical days."

At the outset their Arab neighbors were more than a little suspicious and unfriendly, but something occurred one morning a week after the Littrells moved in that seemed determined by destiny. Bill had gone to work as usual. Ellen was still in bed. Very little progress was being made in the promised alterations. It was pouring outside. In all, a dismal discouraging moment when even the most dedicated lover of the Arab way of life might have some self-doubts.

Ellen was indulging herself in a small case of the blues when Na'ami, the son of the owner of the house, burst into her bedroom shouting: "Madam, Madam, come quick!" It appeared that his father, a highly respected man in the community and one who had made his pilgrimage to Mecca, was involved in a bus accident somewhere between Tagiura and Tripoli.

Ellen threw a raincoat over her nightgown and got into her car with Na'ami. She knew nothing of the neighborhood then, nothing of the roads. She drove to Tripoli, leaning out of the window from time to time to ask people, in Arabic, about the accident. When she got to Tripoli she drove to the bus terminal and learned that the bus in which the aged sheikh had been riding had collided with railroad tracks and that the passengers had been shaken up but were not seriously injured.

She drove back to the house with the boy, and when they got there they found a large crowd in front of the dwelling. Na'ami told the people that the beloved sheikh, his father, was all right, and how Ellen had gone out in the storm to try to find him. When he was finished the people closed in on Ellen and took her hands and kissed them. "From then on, we were in," Bill said.

After that work speeded up amazingly. On the day the last thing in the house was finished Bill took Ellen's hand and they walked around their home. It was exactly as they had dreamed it might be. It was new—but it also was ancient, as Arab houses had been for centuries. They walked to the rear and watched their camel draw water. They stood silent. "We were home," Bill said.

From the start the Littrell house became a meeting place where Arabs and Americans could come and talk and listen and learn to know each other. It was an oasis, where racial animosities and old ignorances could be set right. When they had Arab guests, out of courtesy to Moslem religion and custom, Arabic ways were strictly followed: no alcoholic beverages, just tea and Arabic foods.

"One of the things that always used to amaze the base personnel at our place was the Marabuts," Littrell said. "This is a tribe that stick knives into themselves. The base surgeons used to stand there and watch the knife go in, the skin come to a point on their backs and then break through. But when the knife was pulled out there was no sign of a wound—although the knife went completely through the body. The docs said they stuck themselves clear through their livers but they don't know how it's done.

"The performers listen to the drums beating and they sway back and forth and the incense is burning—right in our patio. They use American knives. They put them right in their eyes, clear to the hilt. The surgeons were confounded—but the Arabs and Americans get together and it all makes for good relations." The Marabuts also ate cactus and glass and tried to persuade Littrell to swallow some. "They said it would not hurt me, but I never tried it."

The Arabs they entertained were quick to return hospitality. The Littrells found themselves being invited to native parties, weddings, and when they could they brought with them other American officers and their wives to spread the warmth of this mutual friendship as widely as possible.

As soon as they were settled in their house, Ellen took on a job in civilian personnel at the base and began to screen the natives who applied for employment there. Her two houseboys, Mohammed and Ali, worked with her, and word got around very quickly that only honest natives would be taken on, natives who would have to pass a blistering interrogation by Mohammed and Ali.

There was the thing with the vehicles and the beer bottles and the bar, and there were other things, street brawls, for instance. Hardly a week passed in the beginning when Littrell was not awakened in the middle of the night to act as peacemaker in some fight between American airmen and natives. It seemed to be the thing he was born to do. With his status as a field grade officer and his knowledge of the Arabs and their language, he was able, quickly and effectively, to cool off hot tempers and quell disturbances that might have vaulted into larger and uglier things.

Of the Arabs, Bill has many things to say, based on his studies of their religion, history, geography, climate, and—possibly most important—economics. This is something that only he should tell in length for only he can tell it the way it should be told. I may, perhaps, quote one thing he told me. "Realizing the conditions that exist it becomes apparent that there is a real problem which has a difficult solution. To relieve the desperate situation of the Arab it is first necessary to take his mind off his immediate problem—that of enough food and clothing for today.

"Then it will be necessary to begin a long campaign of education. As the education is assimilated the Arab will learn ways of improving his own position. After this has occurred, he will be in a situation more comparable to our own—and we will be better able to understand each other." So long, it might be added, as people like Bill Littrell keep working at it.

PANAMA, CENTRAL AMERICA

"The Big Ditch . . ."

To most Americans the Panama Canal is as much an American waterway as the Mississippi River. What is sometimes forgotten is that this big ditch cuts right through the middle of an independent Central American country, the Republic of Panama. And that crowding hard on both sides of the Republic of Panama are other Central American countries, many of which have a predilection for dictators, Communism, and anti-Americanism.

The Canal is only slightly more than fifty miles long and the Zone is only ten miles wide—five miles on either side of the Canal—and there are places on both Atlantic and Pacific ends where one side of the street is Canal Zone and the other side Panama. The difference between these two sides of the same street is sometimes startling, the difference between primitive, squalid, tropical slums and something that looks like a residential section in Palm Beach right opposite each other. It is there for all to see and for the dwellers on the native side to brood silently on and to envy and in the end to hate.

Jammed together in the Canal Zone are perhaps more United States military installations—Army, Navy, and Air Force—than in any comparable area anywhere else in the world. And the Panamanian cities are filled with big American cars and American uniforms and American wives spending a lot of American money.

It makes a field day for anyone who wants to take a belt out of Uncle Sam, and in that part of the world that has never been an unpopular thing to do. Remember this is where the American is a "gringo" and the United States is the "Colossus of the North."

The attacks can come from large nationalistic causes or they can spring out of the smallest things. For instance, the topography of the Zone is such that airplanes must come in low over towns to land and take off, and they make a lot of noise. Flying begins early in the morning when people are sleeping and continues during the day when children are in schools and adults are working. When a teacher has to stop what she is saying or a businessman has to interrupt a phone conversation while a big multiengined job is roaring over the roof it is an irritation. After weeks and months and years it can get to be more than that. It can get to be something that demagogues make campaigns out of and newspapers print editorials about.

It so happens that the SA-16, which is used by Air Rescue, is without question one of the noisiest piston-driven airplanes in the air. It is so noisy that a little container of absorbent cotton is regular equipment, so that the people inside can stuff their ears. Anyone who has ever heard one of these jobs take off or anyone who has ever ridden in one would never mistake it for anything else.

It was interesting then, to the air people in Panama, to read the following editorial published by the *Star & Herald* in Panama City recently. This newspaper, which reflects local opinion, printed the editorial after an accident in which three Rescue fliers were killed while searching for a missing airplane. The newspaper told of the tragic crash—which I will relate a little later on—and then said:

> We who live close to Albrook Air Force Base have become so accustomed to these mercy missions we are apt to take them for granted. We forget that nearly every one is fraught with danger, especially when involving landings in small airports tucked among dangerous mountain peaks unknown to pilots. . . .
>
> Yet there are those who complain about the racket planes make taking off from the field in the early morning hours or late at night. They resent also the low flying near the Administration building in Balboa. Even non-air-minded persons must know that planes cannot just drop onto an air strip. If their

> path lies over schools and dwellings they still must take it.
>
> With the exemplary record of these fliers it would seem more grateful on the part of us civilians of the Pacific side to doff our hats to the pilots and wish them happy landings. May God bless them all on their missions. . . .

The top United States military man in that area is Lieutenant General William K. Harrison, Jr., commander-in-chief, Caribbean Command, whose headquarters is in Quarry Heights overlooking Panama City. General Harrison's job goes far beyond the purely military, of course. A thoughtful, intensely courteous gentleman, he moves on the highest diplomatic levels in a region where most presidents are also generals and wear uniforms far fancier than his.

With the knowledge produced by long experience in an exceedingly delicate post, General Harrison made the following statement early this year: "I don't know of any activity in our Armed Forces that contributes more to the furtherance of United States policy in this part of the world than the Air Rescue Service. The courage and skill and the diligence of these crews who go out at all hours of the day and night when people need help—help that is not confined to our own airmen who go down or to other military people, but to anyone who needs it—have made an ineradicable impression. It is certainly an example of the willingness of our American people to give real help where it is needed."

And if it means anything General Harrison is United States Army—not Air Force.

"No Importa, No Importa . . ."

"The only thing that bothered me was there was no one around I could say good-by to in English." Doc Berry grinned. He lit a cigarette. It took a little doing. The air-conditioning in the Albrook dispensary had broken down and the Panama heat and humidity lay over everything like a wet rag. Matches were hard to get going, and when they were lit the limp cigarettes were hard to draw.

Captain Charles A. Berry and his side-kick, Captain Charles H. Barnes, are flight surgeons at Albrook. They both answer to the name of "Chuck." Together with their flight nurse, Captain Antoinette Kelso, they are medicine for Rescue in Panama. Berry is a big genial, round-faced young man. Barnes is a runt, cocky as a bantam, a cigar bigger than he is always jammed into his face. Tony Kelso is a redheaded doll.

It's a rare mission that goes out of Albrook that doesn't find one or more of this trio aboard—and not one of them actually is in Rescue. They are all three attached to the base dispensary and they have full-time jobs caring for the needs of officers and airmen and all the dependents stationed there. The Rescue business is on their own time, often after an eight-hour day or a long night. But the magic of this Rescue thing, which I have endeavored to bring out on these pages as best I can, has entered into them, and they'd fight being left out any time, no matter how rough it looked.

I shall deal in more detail a little later on with Tony Kelso and Chuck Barnes. Right now I'd like to tell a little about Chuck Berry. It's odd how easily you may be fooled. Berry, as I have said, is a pleasant man, and you know instantly that he must have what is called a good bedside manner. He doesn't look soft but you'd never label him a muscle man. The kind maybe who gets out and plays golf once a week, nothing more. You can see him back in his home town in Indio, California, in a nice office with Western-style furniture and a practice that includes a lot of old ladies and after office hours getting picked up by his good-looking wife, Adella, and going out to the country club in the red Ford ranch wagon. . . .

Just before midnight on April 28, 1954, a call came in to the Radio Control Center at Albrook reporting that an American seaman, James Mitchen, twenty-eight, had fallen into the bilge in the engine room of a tuna boat, the *Sun Dial,* during a storm at sea. The message had it that Mitchen had a severe pain in the head and a severe pain in the lower part of his back and that two lumps were developing in the lower back. The *Sun Dial* was more than forty-eight hours out of Panama.

Forty-five minutes later another message was received from the *Sun Dial.* Mitchen was in extreme pain and there were no medicines aboard the *Sun Dial* to give him relief. Because of his pain it had not been possible to move him from the bilge for an hour and a half after he fell in. When they finally got him out he was laid on his stomach and from then on they couldn't touch him, he hurt so bad. And there he was, in his bunk in a little fishing boat, screaming every time the boat pitched, and a dozen men standing around and staring at him and nobody able to do a thing. Then all radio contact with the *Sun Dial* was cut off because of weather conditions.

Communication was not re-established until seven o'clock the next morning. By then the report was that Mitchen's condition had worsened and so had the weather. With those seas in that weather a water landing was out. Word was sent to the *Sun Dial* that a plane would be sent out to drop some medicine to relieve Mitchen's pain. Then a plan was set up to evacuate him. The nearest port was Esmeraldas in Ecuador, 105 nautical miles away. At its cruising speed of nine knots the *Sun Dial* could make that in about nine hours. The tuna boat was directed to go there. A plane would be waiting to pick up Mitchen.

Captain Ralph A. Bass took off in an SA-16, intercepted the *Sun Dial* on its way to Esmeraldas, and made a successful drop of the medicine. From this point on the story is told by Chuck Berry. "We worked it out with the Radio Control Center that the time it would take to go to Esmeraldas and pick up the man we would have to make a night landing down there and a night take off in a very short field, so it was elected we would use a C-47 which can do things like that. We left, with Major William J. Alsleben at the controls, and flew toward Esmeraldas, searching for the *Sun Dial* as we went. We located the boat in the Caribbean and tried to contact them by radio but we were unable to do so. So we signaled them with Aldis lamp signals in Morse code and told them we would meet them in Esmeraldas. They told us they could get in there at nine o'clock that night.

"We went on to Esmeraldas. It's a seaport town. A big river empties there. The town is on one side of the river and there is a big island in the estuary and the landing strip is on the mainland on the other side. We got there just after dusk. The landing strip was filled with cattle. We had to buzz it a couple of times to make the cattle get off before we could set down. There was no lighting on the field at all. After we touched down an Ecuadorean who runs a little radio there came out and sort of guided us.

"We talked to the fellow and to some other natives who came along and found out just about where the tuna boat would have to come in. It was almost dark but we could see a couple of banana freighters out in the harbor and we figured that was where the *Sun Dial* would have to go—there was a channel or something there for boats of that size. The question was how was I going to get from the strip out to the boat when it got there.

"They told me there was a native who had a cayuco, a hollowed-out log, with an outboard motor rigged onto the end of it. I made a deal with him, for seven dollars, to take me out to where the *Sun Dial* was going to come in. Major Alsleben stayed with the plane. The copilot, Captain Coleman Adams, and one of the enlisted men, Airman First Class Michael Wynne, climbed into the cayuco and the native owner and his assistant climbed in after us and we started out.

"By that time it was dark. You know how it gets dark in the jungle. Just blackness. We had to go back upriver, against the current, to get around this island that was in the middle. We couldn't go the other way because the waves were breaking too high on that side. One native sat in the back and operated the motor. The other native was in the front with a long pole, shoving things away. All kinds of things were floating down current against us. We could see the stuff going by all the time. We didn't know whether they were crocodiles or logs. But the natives were skillful navigators. They managed to avoid getting smacked too hard.

"We went around the island and then downstream. Then we came to one of the freighters that was anchored out there. It was a British boat, pretty fair-sized. We got there just before nine. That was the time the *Sun Dial* was due in but there was no sign of her. We couldn't see her anywhere. We boarded the British freighter and talked to the captain to see whether he could make contact with the *Sun Dial* by radio. I remember the captain thought it was a little peculiar to see American officers coming up out of a native vessel to take care of an injured seaman on a tuna boat that wasn't even around.

"While we were talking we saw some lights to the northwest. The British captain said, 'If that's your boat, they're going to go aground!' He gave some sharp orders and a signal light was brought out. They talked back and forth. It was the *Sun Dial,* all right. The British captain told them they were in extremely shallow water. The *Sun Dial* replied that they would stay where they were until they could get a pilot to guide them into the channel. They also requested that the doctor come as quickly as possible because the man was very ill and in great pain. He was cut quite badly and they thought he had a fractured spine.

"We sent the cayuco back to town to pick up a pilot and a customs man. When they came back the British captain gave them gasoline."

Then the captain spoke to Berry. "It's very foolish for you to go out in that water. It's pitch dark and there's a storm coming up." Berry reminded him that there was a man gravely injured aboard the *Sun Dial.* "If you feel you have to go for your patient at least leave the two other Americans here," the captain said. "There is no need to risk their lives along with yours."

Coleman and Wynne spoke up in protest immediately, but Berry agreed they could be of no assistance in the treatment of the injured man. So they remained aboard the British freighter and Berry climbed back into the cayuco with the customs man and the pilot and the natives started moving the log out toward the *Sun Dial.*

"It started to pour. It was really dark. You know how waves break and you see the phosphorescence? That was all we could see. We got pretty well sprayed. The cayuco would ride up a swell and smash down. I was thoroughly soaked. I was in the middle, squatting down, holding on to my doctor's bag.

"Then I noticed that the phosphorescence was *inside* the boat, all around me. I put down my hand and saw that there was six inches of water in the boat. I told the navigator in bad Spanish about it and he just said, *'No importa, no importa.'*

"I tried to bail with my cap but I didn't have much luck. This went on for about half an hour and the water was getting deeper and deeper in the cayuco. I saw my bag floating away. I reached out and just managed to grab it. Then a large wave hit us and swamped the motor and it wouldn't work any more. We turned sideways and started to drift and then the boat was swamped. I could feel the sides of the boat under water. The boat was not sinking but it was below the surface of the water, all of it.

"It was lightning by then and in the flashes I could see the natives. I still held my bag between my knees. My shoes were off. I tried to bail again, and when the lightning flashed I could see the natives were scared to death and they were trying to bail, too.

"I thought we had bought the farm—that we were through."

Then Berry suddenly remembered he had a flashlight in the leg of his flying suit. "It was soaked, of course, but I got it out and it worked. So I tried to stand up when we were not being wallowed and I tried to signal an SOS aiming both to where the freighter was and also toward the *Sun Dial.* And also to the town. We were going up and down, and the swells were hiding us and it was difficult for them to pick up the SOS.

"Meanwhile the people on the freighter had become worried and were signaling to the *Sun Dial:* 'Had we arrived?' The tuna boat signaled back: 'No,' that we were not there yet and where were we? They were all trying to see into the water. Then someone on the *Sun Dial* saw my SOS. They put a boat over the side with two men from the tuna boat in it and headed for where they could catch my SOS.

"They finally reached us and hauled us out of the cayuco. I thought I had been snatched from the dead. All the time we were wallowing around, all I could think of was there was no one I could say good-by to in English." The small boat from the *Sun Dial* brought them all to the tuna boat and Berry climbed aboard.

"I went right in to see the patient. They had him in a bunk. I felt very likely he had a fractured spine. There was a lot of skin torn out from his side. From the amount of pain he was in shock. I felt, too, that he had a ruptured kidney, he had urinated blood. I gave him some demerol, intravenously, to relieve the pain. I had to give him a fairly large dose. They brought me some dry clothes and meanwhile, with the pilot on board, they had started around the channel.

"It took about an hour to bring the tuna boat to where the freighter was. We put the patient in a motorboat and covered him with blankets. I took a plastic pillowcase and put it over his head. Movement was extremely painful for him. We started back up the river. The idea now was to get back to the aircraft.

"It was still pouring. We ran aground one time. We spun around in circles and finally got free, and after a long, long while, got back to where I had started off in the cayuco. The landing strip was still quite a distance from the shore and we had to figure a way to get the patient to the airplane.

"We got some natives to get a truck to move the patient to the plane. They brought a dump truck and loaded him on it. It was still pouring rain. The truck started back up the road to the landing strip. We all tried to hold the litter off the floor of the truck. Every time we hit a bump the patient would scream with pain. We made it back to the strip at last. By now it was four o'clock in the morning and pouring like I've never seen it pour."

They got Mitchen into the SC-47 at last and then made preparations for take off. "There were no lights. We got out flares like you use on a highway when you get a flat tire and we ran them along the runway and put a lot at the end so that we would know where the strip ended. Then Alsleben revved up the old plane and he got her off. We got back to the base at seven-thirty and got Mitchen into the Gorgas Hospital. He had a fractured lumbar spine, a retroperitoneal hemorrhage, and a ruptured kidney. But he lived."

That was Jim Mitchen.

"He Could Only Mutter Something . . ."

Antoinette Kelso is probably the tiniest captain in the whole United States Air Force. She is exactly five feet and one-quarter inch tall, which, as it happens, is exactly one and three-quarter inches below regulations—the book says nurses have got to be at least five feet two and no argument. But as has been mentioned Tony has red hair, flaming red, and she also has green eyes, and she also has everything else that ought to go with that combination, inside and out, even though she weighs less than a hundred pounds. When she applied for a nurse's commission in the old Army Air Corps at Mitchel Field toward the end of World War II and she had to get on the scales to be weighed and measured she raised herself just a teeny weeny bit on her toes and somehow conned whoever was putting down the statistics into not looking down.

It may be said that the inch and three quarters have never been missed since.

From July 1944 to August 1945 Tony worked as a surgical nurse in a general hospital in England. Then she came back to the United States and put in six months at Fort McClelland in Alabama, then she separated from the service. She worked as a civilian nurse in a hospital in Memphis after that but her heart wasn't in it. Flying was in her bones. She took lessons and got a pilot's license, but even that wasn't good enough. She moved over to the Kennedy Veterans' Hospital in Memphis and that was a little better, because there were ex-flyboys there and she could talk about the good old days, but it still wasn't the real thing.

In 1951 she went back into uniform at Keesler Field in Biloxi. Two years later she went to air evacuation school and in August of 1954 she was sent down to the Canal Zone as flight nurse to team up with big Chuck Berry and little Chuck Barnes. Both doctors briefed her fully on her duties in the dispensary, pulses to be taken, needles to be stuck, pills to be given, charts to be filled out; and the air evac part of it as well, flying along with planeloads of patients being moved Stateside for special treatment.

But the docs also talked a lot between them about Rescue business, and Tony's eyes began to get big and pretty. Soon she asked, "Hey, how about me?" The two Chucks smiled and shook their heads and reminded her that, after all, she was a woman and an undersized one at that. Then the green eyes began to do something else than just get big. They began to snap. Somebody once said something about the power of a woman and not to underestimate it. It took just about two months for Tony to declare herself in.

On October 7 Rescue got a call that a seaman on a ship at Puentes Arenes off the coast of Costa Rica was bleeding internally from a perforated ulcer and Chuck Barnes went out in a Rescue plane to save him. Tony was aboard. Before Chuck Barnes could start arguing the plane was off.

They found what they thought was the ship but they couldn't make any contact with it by radio because they couldn't locate the ship's frequency. They dropped a message in a cylinder asking the ship to indicate in some way what frequency it received and broadcast on, but although the message was picked up nobody on the ship answered it. So they landed anyway.

"It was my first water landing," Tony told me. "I was so excited I forgot to mark it down in my diary. We put out a six-man life raft and I got in with Dr. Barnes. The water was pretty choppy. We were bounced up and down. We had this training in school but that was in a swimming pool. We couldn't come up close to the ship because of the swells so they lowered a lifeboat and met us a short distance from the ship.

"We boarded their lifeboat and went up the side of the ship by boat ladder. We got the patient and put him in a wire basket and lowered him into the lifeboat, transferred him to the life raft, rowed back to the plane, and took him aboard." There was no time or equipment to analyze the patient's blood so they gave him the anti ab group factor that permits the use of any type blood and then they gave him a transfusion as the plane headed back for Panama.

The man was delirious by then and fought like a wildcat all the way back to Albrook and Tony had a little time with all of her hundred pounds, but when the SA-16 landed Dr. Barnes gave out that maybe Tony had something in her pitch that a doctor needs a nurse no matter where it was, and from then on nobody said no when Tony said she was going along.

In a very short time Tony Kelso was like a fire horse—fire pony really—and when she heard a Rescue plane getting warmed up—and an SA-16 makes a noise like no other airplane in the world—and she was on her own, or could get another nurse to swap shifts with her if she was working, then she was off. It got so that if Barnes or Berry didn't see the runt tearing out and climbing aboard they'd think something was missing from the airplane, like a prop or a landing gear.

Less than a month after the Puentes Arenes business an Englishman named John Charles Mowbray Taylor, twenty-eight, a geologist employed by the Anglo-Ecuadorean Oil Company, stationed at Ancon, an oilfield about one hundred miles from Guayaquil, was laid low suddenly with polio. He was brought to the Hospital de Infecciosas in Guayaquil but he was no better off there—there was no iron lung in the hospital or anywhere else in the city. A British doctor and nurse team went to work giving him artificial respiration with their bare hands, and a radio appeal was made for help.

An iron lung was loaded on a C-47 at Albrook and the plane took off with Chuck Berry and Tony at 9:45 P.M., but fifteen minutes later an engine went out and the gooney bird had to return to Albrook. The mechanics worked like maniacs, and at 1:48 A.M. the plane went out again and landed at Guayaquil at six in the morning. A truck was waiting to take the lung to the hospital.

"When we came in with the lung, tears rolled down John Taylor's cheeks," Tony said. "He tried to speak but he could only mutter something. The British doctor and nurse had given him artificial respiration from eleven-thirty the night before. I'll never forget how swollen their hands were."

Taylor was put into the lung immediately and shifts were set up to watch over him. Everything went fine until that evening. "I was specialing him," Tony said. "It was about five o'clock and all of a sudden all the lights went out and the iron lung stopped functioning. I tried to call for the British nurse to see if she could call the hotel where the doctors were staying." She couldn't get the nurse, and she found out that the hotel didn't have a telephone anyway. So she was on her own, as though she were the only nurse in the world.

Her first thought was that Taylor had been kept alive all one night by artificial respiration, so she wheeled him out of the useless lung and went to work on him with her hands, only she had to do it alone. She isn't built for this kind of wrestling, remember, but she managed to keep Taylor breathing. All the time she kept yelling at the top of her voice for somebody to find out why the lights went out, and nobody could understand her. "I felt so helpless—my Spanish is so bad."

Her strength began to ebb, and after a while she knew she was getting too weak to give Taylor what he had to have so she rolled him back into the lung and began to operate the hand pump on the lung, which was another kind of back-breaking thing only it was different effort and she was able to do it.

She had to work the pump at the normal respiratory rate, twelve to fourteen times a minute, and once she got Taylor in the cycle she could not break it or it would impede his breathing. The more exhausted she got the more she had to watch her precision work to keep the rhythm. And all the time she was trying to get somebody to do something about the electricity.

It turned out to be a very minor thing. An attendant in the hospital poked around at last and found that a fuse had blown, a simple fuse. He put in a new one and the lights went on again and the lung started to work. Tony sat down gasping as if she had just run up a mountain. Fifteen minutes later the fuse blew again. It appeared that the wiring in the hospital simply was not gaited for the load the lung was imposing on it and for the rest of that night Taylor was kept alive by the electricity when it was there and by Tony Kelso when it was not.

In the morning they loaded Taylor into the C-47. The oil company supplied an auxiliary motor and the lung was set up inside the airplane. They had to punch a little hole in the fuselage for the exhaust pipe of the auxiliary engine but they kept the thing operating all the way back to Albrook.

A few days later the *Star & Herald* came out with an editorial headed "USAF's Mercy Missions." It commented first on the mass of equipment spread out in the Zone and how it was ready to act in case anybody started any shooting. And then the piece continued: "They have a self-assumed mission, however, and that is the type of operation with which we in Panama are most familiar. It is a mission of mercy. And scarcely a week goes by in which they are not called upon for some new emergency."

The editorial told in detail of the Taylor incident and how he had been brought to Gorgas Hospital and concluded: "Human effort had done all it could, at great cost of time and energy, not to speak of the abnegation we have learned to expect on the part of doctors and nurses. Geologist Taylor is in good hands. It is to be hoped that so much effort may not have been spent in vain.

"After all is said and done in this era of arming for defense against aggression it is good to know that the millions, billions, spent in warlike weapons of defense are mighty useful in such crises as those so frequently presenting themselves on this Isthmus. The Caribbean Command, especially its air component, is a great weapon of defense. But it also is a potent agent of mercy. As such it never fails when a call for aid comes from any of these Americas."

Exactly one week later, while Taylor was still touch and go at Gorgas, another oil specialist, this time an American named Philip Snare, was stricken with the same disease. There was one slight difference: Snare got his in Quito, Ecuador, which is located at an altitude of 9,000 feet in the South American cordillera. The iron lung was loaded in the C-47 again and Barnes and Tony got in with it. Major Clayton Wilson flew the old gooney bird at an altitude of 14,500 feet all the way and everybody had to stay on oxygen. It was just after seven in the evening when they arrived over the Ecuadorean capital.

Now nobody ever lands at Quito after sundown. The airport is not even lighted. And Quito is like the bottom of a deep cup, surrounded on all sides by mountains and peaks. With the responsibility of the crew and Barnes and Kelso and the airplane itself on his shoulders, Wilson got on the radio and asked the people at the airport to find out whether it would be all right for him to land at Guayaquil, which is a safe, sea-level field, and then fly up to Quito at dawn the next day.

The answer Wilson got was that the delay might cost Snare his life. The patient was breathing with extreme difficulty and at any moment the respiratory muscles might weaken and then fail. Everybody on the plane agreed there was only one thing to do—go on in.

Wilson radioed down for whatever lights he could have. People below drove four automobiles out to the strip and turned on the headlights. Wilson circled once with the silhouettes of the mountains so close he felt like a ball in a roulette wheel, and then with illumination from eight headlights he brought in his airplane on a strip he could barely see. It was one of those things where everybody wanted to go up to the cockpit and just look at the pilot, but there was no time for that.

"Snare had total paralysis," Chuck Barnes told me, "of all the respiratory muscles and was breathing with the use only of the left sternocleidomastoid muscle—the large 'strap' muscle on each side of the neck. He'd been on oxygen for several hours prior to our arrival and was not getting enough oxygen exchange in his lungs and was quite cyanotic—oxygen starvation.

"He was in an apartment in town. They had attempted two hours earlier to give him artificial respiration but had discontinued it because of the excruciating muscular pain that goes with acute polio. As long as he was keeping up with some oxygen they had felt it better to desist until they *had* to use artificial respiration.

"We put him in a local ambulance and gave him positive-pressure oxygen with a pneolator—a machine with which you can suction out people, give oxygen under positive pressure, or by just straight flow. We brought him out to the airfield."

They could not put Snare into the C-47 while it was parked there waiting for daylight to take off because it was too cold and also because the C-47, on the ground, sits at a steep slope. They found an old mission near the strip and outside the mission they found a generator. So Clayton and his boys moved the lung into the mission and Chuck Barnes and Tony prepared to sit up all night with their patient. The Rescue boys went in to town to get some sleep for the trip back.

And then it happened again, in the same ghastly way it had happened with Taylor. "At three o'clock in the morning the 100 foot cable between the lung and the generator burned out because of the load," Barnes said. Tony got on the hand pump again and Barnes went out into the night feeling his way along the length of cable trying to find the break. "I finally found it," he said. "I spliced it in the dark—by Braille, I think. Then I had to find the fuse box and then the bum fuse. When I had replaced that it started again. It took between an hour and an hour and a half, and all that time Tony was pumping by hand."

Snare was brought to Panama City and put into Gorgas and introduced to Taylor. The two men breathed in their little mechanical houses and got to know each other pretty well. Barnes and Berry and Tony visited both men from time to time and watched them get better, a little bit each day, and then Snare and Taylor got well enough to be moved away, Snare to the States and Taylor to England. The two men shook hands and said they had to keep in touch with each other because they had something in common, the same people and the same airplane and the same thing of glass and metal and wire that had all combined to keep them living.

Major General Reuben C. Hood, commanding general of the Caribbean Air Command, the top airman in that theater, told me that in his dealings with the proud little countries in that area Air Rescue and its boss, Colonel Edwin M. ("Mike") Ramage, were the most potent plus he had. They are the silent background to all his dealings with his opposite numbers from the Central American countries, because few of these countries, in one way or another, have not had a hand extended when it was needed.

It might have been a very little thing: a man will scratch his leg in some native village. Gangrene. A few years ago he was a dead man. He was only a short distance, in miles, from where he might be saved, but that short distance was through jungle or over mountains. He just gave up and his family mourned him while he was still alive. But now a missionary or a trader gets on the short wave and a little while later, maybe only minutes later, a helicopter comes along and the people clear a place in the jungle and the chopper comes down and takes the man away. Half an hour later—maybe it would have taken a week's trek on foot—the man is in a hospital and getting filled with the wonder drugs.

And he returns home at last, the man who perhaps had never ridden in anything more modern than an oxcart, and he never forgets the wonderful flying machine that came down in his back yard and took him away. And his family and the village never forget. And nothing anybody can say or write about Americanism and Good-Neighbor Policy can ever mean more than that, this little thing.

Or it may be a big thing, with hundreds of people involved, like the floods in Bolivia or Honduras, where the Rescue planes shuttled back and forth, bringing in everything that was needed—medicine, clothing, food, doctors, technicians, carrying out sick and injured. As Dr. Berry put it: "The natives around here have a great respect for us because we feel for people."

"The Hope and Salvation of the World Today . . ."

As has been indicated in these pages the young men of the Air Rescue Service have won for themselves a very special place in the deepest part of the hearts of many plain and silent people around the world. It is not very often that this feeling can come out beyond a brief prayer or a handclasp or a thank you. But on very rare occasions it can emerge crystal clear as something else, and at those times, wherever it happens, it is happening for all the other people in all the other places who never had a chance to show it but who would show it in their own way, the same way, if they could.

Early in January of 1955 an SA-16 was probing around

in the mountains of Colombia looking for Dr. and Mrs. G. O. Rockwell, of Houston, Texas, who were lost in their Bonanza lightplane somewhere between Cali and Medellin. The Rescue plane got itself boxed up in a blind canyon in the Cordillera Macarena and came to a dead end. The pilot was Captain Cullen D. Hardin. Lieutenant Colonel Joseph C. Smith, Operations officer for the Rescue group in Panama, was flying in the right seat. With them were Lieutenants Javan Bayer and James Watson; Staff Sergeant Edgar W. Callaway, the radio operator; and Airman First Class James R. Bartlow. The last message received from the plane came in at Albrook at 1125 hours on that January morning: "We're making a crash landing."

Captain Hardin and Sergeant Callaway were killed instantly. Airman Bartlow was thrown clear of the aircraft, which started to burn on impact, and by one of those miracles was scarcely scratched. He picked himself up, and although the plane might have exploded at any moment he went back into the flames and dragged out the other three men—three trips, three men.

He did not have the strength to carry them far enough away from the blaze in his arms and so, with a calmness and presence of mind that are beyond belief under those circumstances, he went back into the burning plane a *fourth* time and pulled out a couple of one-man life rafts. He inflated the rubber rafts and put the other three survivors in them and dragged them through the clawing brush and matted trees until some Colombian natives appeared and gave him a hand.

The natives put Bartlow on a burro and picked up the other three men and started out for a tiny community called Jardin. Jardin was less than four miles from where the SA-16 plowed in. It took six hours to get there through the jungle and up and down the hills. The natives had to hack their way with machetes, and it seemed that the stuff started to grow back before the last man got through.

Halfway to Jardin the little group was met by another party of Colombians from Jardin, led by a bearded patriarch who was white-faced and exhausted and gasping for breath from his own efforts to get through the jungle. This elderly man, Dr. Gabriel Pelaez, the doctor in charge of the Jardin Hospital, gave first aid to Smith, Bayer, and Watson, and then administered sedatives to ease their pain. Then the two groups continued on to Jardin.

Now this little village of Jardin in the Andes with its 1,500 souls has one small hospital. The hospital is the special pride of the people of Jardin. It is almost more of a show piece than a hospital to be used for real. It was filled with the latest medicines, but in minute quantities, and it was clean and it was new, and in possessing this hospital the men and women of Jardin knew that although they were lost in the Andes they were civilized. Much of the medicine had never before been used and possibly never was intended to be used. It was enough that it was there and that people in bare feet could stand in front of it and look at it and know that it belonged to Jardin.

The three injured men were taken into the hospital. That was without question the most patients the place had ever held at one time. All three men were hurt and badly burned, but Colonel Smith had it the worst. Eighty per cent of his body was involved with third-degree burns and he had a fractured jaw and bruises all over him.

Dr. Pelaez and his assistant, a young English-speaking doctor, Dr. Guillermo Uribe, set to work immediately. It was not very long before the last of the tiny cache of medicine was used up. When the people of the village, many of whom were gathered around the little hospital building, heard about this they dug into their own lean pockets and made a collection and sent runners out to nearby villages to buy more. And men came to Dr. Pelaez and offered their blood.

Just before three o'clock that afternoon an SA-16 from Albrook landed at Medellin, the nearest place a plane could get into, carrying Chuck Barnes. Barnes hired a car and started for Jardin. The distance between the two villages is not great but the road connecting them is so primitive that it took eight hours to make the trip. When Barnes got to Jardin around midnight he pitched in with Pelaez and Uribe to try to save the life of Joe Smith, giving him dextran and plasma and more of the medicines brought by Barnes and brought back by the native runners. The other two men were in good shape by then and the only burns Bartlow had were the ones he picked up making his lonely journeys into the fiery plane to get the others. At dawn Smith was still managing to cling to life.

At eight o'clock that morning Mike Ramage, after sending out another Rescue plane to continue the search for the missing Rockwells—who were never found—took off from Albrook in an SC-47 with Major Dick W. Thompson, his squadron commander, and the other Chuck, Dr. Berry. They brought more medical supplies. While in flight, upon being informed of the almost impossible condition of the road between Jardin and Medellin, Thompson radioed to Albrook and ordered out a helicopter to Jardin to carry the injured from there to Medellin.

The chopper took off at ten o'clock. It had to abort because of failure of a servo valve. At ten-forty a second helicopter was on its way. This aircraft also developed trouble and was forced down in Panama. The trouble was tracked to a faulty rotor. Repairs were made and the helicopter got under way again. Because of the time lost it had to come down for the night at Turbo, in Colombia.

As soon as it was known that the second helicopter was encountering difficulties, officers of the Colombian Army stepped in. They sent one of their own ambulances to Jardin. Bayer and Watson were transferred to the ambulance and were brought to Medellin and put aboard the SA-16 that had brought up Chuck Barnes. They were flown directly to a hospital in Albrook.

Colonel Ramage, Thompson, and Berry landed in Medellin in their SC-47 and went up to Jardin immediately by car. Now there were four doctors—two American and two Colombian—sweating out the death that was grabbing Joe Smith. The struggle went on all through the night and into the next morning. It was a losing game and probably one that was lost before it started. Despite everything that could be done for him Colonel Smith died a few minutes before ten o'clock in the morning in the little hospital in the village of Jardin. He was in delirium most of the time, but just before he passed on he had a few lucid moments and he saw that Mike Ramage, one of his closest friends, and the others were with him.

During this time the bodies of the other two men were taken by natives from the wrecked SA-16 and were brought to Jardin. By now there was no one in Jardin who did not know there were three American aviators dead and that they belonged to the part of the United States Air Force dedicated to saving the lives of others.

Without being asked, without saying anything to anybody at the hospital, local carpenters in Jardin began to put together by hand three coffins for the three dead men, and at the same time a group of native women set out to do something else. They went from house to house and collected scraps of silk and they stayed up all through the night. When the sun rose the next morning, they had finished sewing together an American flag.

The bodies of the dead men were placed in the beautiful hand-wrought coffins and the coffins were set side by side and covered by the flag that was made of pieces of skirts and petticoats and blouses. They were carried down the street in Jardin to the church and the people of Jardin walked behind them. And when the coffins were carried into the small house of God it was discovered that while some women had sewn the flag others had spent the night gathering flowers, for the church was filled with all the lovely blossoms that grow high in the Andean village of Jardin. The air smelled sweet as the old priest, in a language none of the dead men would have understood, asked that their souls be received in peace.

The story was related to General Hood, and how Dr. Barnes and Dr. Berry had asked Dr. Pelaez for a reckoning to pay for the medicines that had been used and how Dr. Pelaez and the people of Jardin had been deeply offended that anyone would believe they would charge for what they had done. And how everything in the hospital had been used up, medicines, drugs, bandages, everything down to the last aspirin tablet, and how the medicines for miles around had been used up, too. Whereupon General Hood directed Colonel Richard S. Fixott, chief surgeon for the Caribbean Air Command, to see to it that everything was replaced. Berry and Barnes also mentioned that the hospital needed a proper sterilizer. The Rescue officers and airmen at Albrook chipped in and bought one, the best they could get.

The United States embassy in Bogotá then made arrangements for the medical supplies and sterilizer to be turned over to the people in Jardin, and Medellin was chosen as the place to make the presentation. Mike Ramage thought a dozen or so people might show up and he sent out word that anybody who might want to go through the inside of an SA-16 and look around would be welcome. When the SA-16 arrived from Albrook there were more than four hundred persons gathered at the airfield there. And there, too, to greet the plane was the Jardin Band—twenty-five musicians who had ridden in a bus for nine hours through the night.

As American and Colombian military and civil officials stood at attention the band from Jardin played the Colombian national anthem and after that the "Star-Spangled Banner." And then Willard Barber, United States chargé d'affaires in Bogotá, spoke briefly in Spanish: "The families of these men, their brother officers and friends in the United States Air Force, the Government and the people of the United States will never forget this action by the people of Jardin. It is the spirit exemplified by actions such as this that is the hope and salvation of the world today. . . ."

Then Dr. Pelaez rose and said: "When someone needs help it does not matter what nationality. If we are able to repay in small measure the debt owed by our people we are grateful." It seemed then that Dr. Pelaez had more to say but he was so overcome with emotion that he merely waved his hand a little and sat down.

A banquet had been arranged in Medellin and Dr. Pelaez was supposed to speak again. But he was so drained by what had taken place at the airfield that he could not find the strength even to attend. It was a long banquet with many speeches, and it was good that it took a long time because Mike Ramage had promised the people they could look through the SA-16—and he wanted to keep his word. Everybody who had been waiting at the airfield trooped through the airplane, some of them more than once.

What was done by the people of Jardin of course cannot bring Lieutenant Colonel Joseph C. Smith or Captain Cullen D. Hardin or Staff Sergeant Edgar W. Callaway back to life. But those who grieve for them must feel a certain peace in knowing they died for a purpose, for an ideal, for a reason perhaps more important than any they might possess ever in a war. And after all they won an alien village, which is more than many other soldiers do, and they won it without causing any deaths other than their own.

GREENLAND, ICELAND, ENGLAND

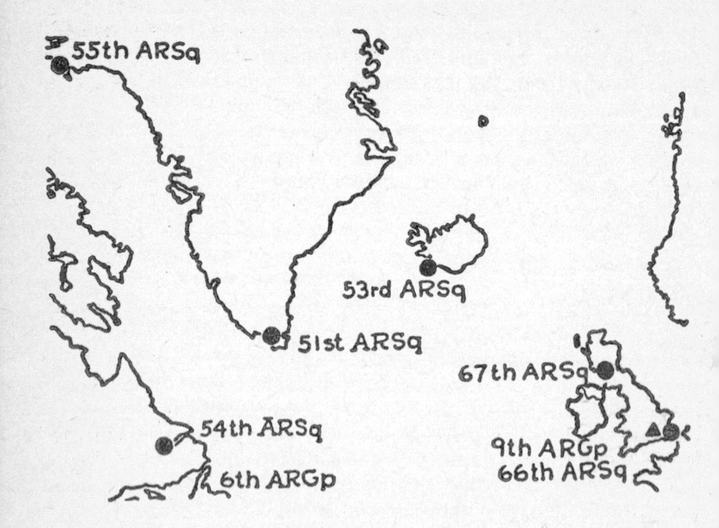

"We Seem to Be Running Out of Petrol . . ."

The air base at Narsarssuak in Greenland is the last stop on a dead-end street called Tunugdliarfik Fjord. This fjord cuts in from the southern tip of the huge island and twists and winds its way inland for more than fifty miles. And the end of the line is Narsarssuak.

It's a real end of the line, a cul-de-sac, a blind pocket with no future, jammed against the bottom of a cliff that walls up like a building half a mile into the sky. There is only one way into this airfield: from the fjord. The landing strip begins where the fjord ends, and it runs in the same direction and when you come in you got to land, period.

There is no traffic pattern, no circling, no instrument let-down procedure. Planes coming in let down over the ocean outside the mouth of the fjord and then the pilot flies on his eyeballs a couple of hundred feet above the water with 2,500-foot palisades smothering him on both sides until he comes to the end and sees the landing strip. Then he has to land. God help him if he is not lined up properly with the strip. He can't turn anywhere. There is no place for him to go but straight up.

At its broadest, just before you come to the base, the fjord is maybe five miles wide. For a distance of twenty miles down its length, the middle part, between Narsak Point and Sugar Loaf Mountain, the fjord is less than two miles wide. A couple of miles may seem like enough elbow room for a small airplane until you remember that the plane is in the middle, which means a mile leeway on either side and at 180 miles an hour that is exactly twenty seconds of flying time—to the right and to the left.

The Narsarssuak squadron is part of the Rescue group that is headquartered at Pepperell Field in St. John's, Newfoundland. I was flown into Narsarssuak by Lieutenant Colonel Ernest Ewan, deputy commander of the group, an urbane gentleman with the appearance and charm of Fred Astaire. The day we came in was brilliant and clear. The range station on the tiny island of Simiutak at the mouth of the fjord let us down, and we proceeded up the corridor at an altitude lower than the smokestack of an ocean liner.

It was July, late July, and the fjord was cluttered with icebergs, breakoffs from the glaciers, colored blue. Some of the bergs were higher than we were. Pilots don't worry about these big ones. They can see them. The ones that give them gray hairs are the little bergs, which they call "bergy-bits," and which, after a while, take on the coloration of the water all through them so that they are almost invisible and when you land in the water you don't know they are there until they bang into the side of your airplane and maybe knock a hole in it.

The cliffs on either side of the fjord were almost vertical, as though the land had been pulled apart just a litle bit to let the water in. And there was plenty of ice anywhere you looked. The trip up the fjord took only a few minutes but it came very close to being the most exciting flight I have ever made. I was glad that I made it and that I could see how it is when it can be seen, because then I understood later what Harold Mechling and Bob Millican did that day when they couldn't see anything at all and they had a plane on their tail that was running out of gas and the guy on the plane was trying to keep them in sight and was asking over his radio in his British accent: "How much farther is it? Where is the field?" And Mechling told him to take it easy, that there was no sweat, that he had done this a hundred times before, except he never had, never once, never when he couldn't see.

Mechling is a pilot and Millican was his navigator when they were stationed at Narsarssuak—which, by the way, some of the boys may identify better as Bluie West 1—the old grim BW 1 of World War II days. In the normal course of earning their pay, mainly intercepting cripples coming in from Iceland or from Labrador, these two young officers, both of whom are captains now, had flown down the fjord and back up again many times.

Going out wasn't so bad. You can climb and get higher than the cliffs and the mountains. Coming in, as I said, was different. You can't stay higher than the cliffs because you can't come down from that altitude to land. So coming into Narsarssuak they were always quite happy when they could see where they were going.

But the weather in Greenland is not the pleasantest in the world, despite the name of the island, which is one of the big misnomers of all time. The place is almost wholly a glacier, or combination of glaciers, and Whiteland or Snowland would be a better name. The only green part is a rim around the coast, like the tonsure of a monk, and then only in the summer, which lasts a few minutes. Most of the year the weather in Greenland is quite dependable. It is bad.

So along with other Rescue fliers stationed there Mechling and Millican practiced a lot getting into the base by radar. They would start at the beginning of Tunugdliarfik and pretend they couldn't see, and Millican would stare into his radar scope and give Mechling directions by interphone—so many degrees to the right, so many to the left. It was quite a job because the radar screen is about eight inches across and everything that appears on it is reduced to that degree, and figuring out a course with those cliffs leaning against them on something as big as an automobile headlight was a nightmare.

But the thing was this: they made these practice radar runs on *clear* days, when Mechling, in his pilot's seat, could look out and check on how Millican was doing. And when Millican was a little off, as he had to be in the beginning, Mechling could still guide the plane visually and tell his navigator he was wrong and by how much.

Millican, a big, husky youth, got better and better. After a while he was able to translate the thousands of feet into pieces of inches on his scope and keep Mechling away from the cliffs. Still, they never attempted it except when Mechling could keep tab with his eyes. They never did it for real, when the weather was closed in. They never had time to work up to that point—in a practice test.

At 0855 on an April morning Rescue Operations at Narsarssuak was jolted by a radio message from the range station at Simiutak: a civilian DC-3 with an American husband and wife flying pilot and copilot and an Englishman navigating was inbound from Keflavik, Iceland. It was experiencing strong head winds but it didn't need any help. Over and out.

It didn't think it needed help, that is, but that was only because the people inside the plane had no idea what the weather was like at Narsarssuak. The weather was already below minimum and forecast to close to zero-zero within ten minutes. It was so bad that none of the Rescue planes that lived there could get *off* the ground. Nobody even wanted to think about a stranger trying to crawl up that fjord, and land.

Rescue at Narsarssuak gave this word to Simiutak and Simiutak gave the word to the Englishman on the radio in the DC-3: turn around and go back to Keflavik. The Englishman replied: "Sorry, old chap, but impossible. You see, we seem to be running out of petrol." They'd had head winds all the way from Iceland, he added, and now he was even beginning to question whether they had enough fuel to make it to Narsarssuak.

The timetable for the next hour or so went like this:

0904: The DC-3 reported over Prince Christian and estimated Simiutak at 0956. By this time the winds at Narsarssuak were reaching gale velocity, fifty knots and more, and all the SA-16's had been trundled into hangars for protection.

1006: The DC-3 arrived over Simiutak. It was instructed to get up to Narsarssuak as fast as it could because the bad weather there was pouring down the fjord and blanketing it rapidly.

1020: At Narsarssuak the weather lowered rapidly. Snow showers. And there was no word from the DC-3, nothing since its 1006 report to Simiutak.

Now Mechling, who is as slim and taut as Millican is beefy and jolly, was on alert that day, and if there was going to be anything it was his baby. Only the way it was then there couldn't be anything: it was, plainly and simply, impossible for an airplane to get off the ground. And, as I mentioned before, there are no facilities at Narsarssuak for an instrument letdown. There was nothing on the base that could help the DC-3 find its way in and down.

Mechling got his airplane out of the hangar and taxied out to the runway. He looked at the snow swirling down and began sweating out a break. All he needed was a hole, something he could get through, if he had to get through. He would worry about getting in again later on. While he was there a word of good news flashed in: the weather down at Simiutak was still clear and the pilot of the DC-3 had spotted a little place where he thought he could land. Not a strip, there was no strip down there, but some flat land.

Mechling tried to figure out where that could be. He had flown over Simiutak scores of times and had never seen any place he could land but the DC-3, the same as the C-47, the dependable gooney bird, that could set down almost anywhere. Maybe there was a place. . . . But then a few minutes later the DC-3 called in that it was all a mistake. There was no place to land. It was going to try to make it up the fjord.

Mechling stared at the weather again. "It was ceiling zero, visibility less than a quarter of a mile," he told me. "The weather at BW 1 was such that we could barely see the end of the runway." For the time being he was glued to the ground. But there was one way he might be able to help, even sitting there. He ran up his engines, tested the radios, and then preflighted the radar. And then he left the auxiliary power unit in the plane turned on so he could use the radar. The idea he had was that maybe he could help the DC-3 in with his own radar, a kind of makeshift Ground Control Aid.

Then he and Millican and the rest of the crew sat and waited. At 1040 they got word from Simiutak that the DC-3 had flown up the fjord as far as Narsak—thirty miles from the base—and that when it got there the fjord was completely socked in, a solid wall of impenetrable snow, and that the DC-3 had made a 180-degree turn and had returned to over Simiutak, and—and this was what made ice crawl down Mechling's back—the pilot now estimated that he had fuel for *one hour* of flying time left in his tanks.

At 1116 Mechling got the break he was praying for, if it can be called a break. "The weather cleared to the point where visibility was two miles and the ceiling ran about five hundred feet." That was enough. He took off.

"We circled in the Big Basin twice, trying to fly visually if we could by following the shore line. I tried the left-hand side of the fjord and got socked in to the point where we could not go on. Then I circled and tried the right side. The same situation. I turned back up toward the field. Millican was on the radar all this time and we lined up with the center of the fjord and he gave us our vector and we started out again."

Mechling's copilot, Lieutenant Kenneth MacCammond,

got on the radio and made contact with the DC-3. He said: "We're coming down. Don't land."

As Mechling probed his way down the fjord the ceiling closed down lower and lower. At ten miles down-fjord from Narsarssuak he was flying 100 feet above the water and he could barely see it below him. Forward visibility was less than seven hundred feet.

Now Millican was doing it for real, almost. There were moments when everything closed in and the plane seemed to be in the middle of a world made of gray cotton. And then there would be a break, briefly, and Mechling could check. Then they came to the narrow part, with Sugar Loaf Mountain on one side and Sawtooth Mountain on the other, the part that was just two miles wide. By now the sweat was running down Millican's face as he stared into his little scope: "Turn five degrees right. . . . Turn ten degrees left. . . . Now ten degrees right. . . ." There were still those momentary break-throughs when Mechling could use his eyes as well as Millican's words. But they were coming less frequently now.

"We went down to about fifty feet over the water," Mechling said. "The visibility was such that from time to time we could see ice cubes in the water. Large amounts of ice will give you a bad radar reading, will give you a reflection almost the same as land. When ice is up against the banks, you can't tell where the ice ends and the land begins."

MacCammond got on the radio again. "Don't try to make a forced landing. We're coming down. Did you read me?"

"Loud and clear," the Englishman said.

Millican guided Mechling with his radar through the soup. It was a ten-minute run. "Then we broke into the clear," Mechling said. "About ten miles from Simiutak. We could fly visually. I told the navigator he could get off the radar. It's hard on the eyes to keep peering into that, and I figured I'd need those eyes some more."

At 1146 MacCammond said: "There they are." He got on the radio again and told the DC-3 that the Rescue plane had them in sight. "We are going to make a 180," he said. "Follow us back up the fjord. Keep us in sight and follow us back up the fjord. Did you read me?"

"Loud and clear, old chap," the English voice said.

Mechling turned his plane around and waited until the DC-3 reported it was in a position to follow and then with the DC-3 behind him like a blind man gripping the harness of a seeing-eye dog, Mechling started back up the fjord. And then he saw that the Narsarssuak weather finally was catching up with them. The fjord was almost wholly obscured. Now, except for the little radar screen and Millican's eyes, it was a case of the blind leading the blind.

At the beginning, Mechling knew, it was not going to be too bad. Here the fjord was wide enough. It was how it was going to be when they hit the narrow part at Narsak Point. Right here Millican could allow himself a slight margin for error. Not much, but a little. But there . . . He shook his head. He'd wait until he came to that.

"Did you read me?" he asked over his radio.

"Loud and clear."

"Then listen carefully. Stay close. Stay close and don't lose us. If you stay close enough you can keep us in sight. Even in this stuff. Keep us in sight. Repeat, *keep us in sight*. Over and out."

The English voice came through immediately. "Yes, old chap, yes." Mechling, who had climbed at Simiutak to make his turn, went down again to 100 feet. "How far is it in, old chap?" the Englishman asked.

"Not too far," Mechling said.

"You know about the petrol situation here?"

"Yes. Don't worry. We'll get you in. Just keep us in sight."

"Don't *you* worry about that, old chap. Just try to lose us."

They got as far as Narsak. Mechling stared ahead into the narrow corridor and he could see nothing up there, nothing at all. Then Millican said suddenly that they were lined up improperly and they had to break away.

Mechling switched to radio immediately. "We will have to turn around and try again."

"Why? Our petrol . . ."

"We're not headed right. You break to the right and take a heading of 270. Toward Simiutak. I'll break to the left and take the same heading on a parallel course."

"Our petrol. The gauges . . ."

"It can't be helped. Break to the right. *Now*."

"Affirmative, old chap."

The two planes broke and turned in opposite directions and then they flew alongside each other back out the fjord. "We were very close," Mechling told me. "We got back into the clear again and flew about five miles, which brought us within five miles of Simiutak. Then we started another 180 and told him to do the same thing right after us, and we started another run up the fjord. I told him to stay right behind us and he did—just about 100 feet behind us, a little above us and to the right."

They came to Narsak Point again and the narrow part

of the fjord. As they entered the corridor the visibility dropped to almost zero, a couple of hundred feet, no more, all the bad weather bottled in the slender passage and stuck there. If the Rescue plane had been alone it hardly would have mattered. Mechling had enough fuel to go upstairs and sit it out or even turn around and make a water landing at Simiutak. But the DC-3 couldn't do any sitting out, not for long, and it couldn't land in water.

Mechling gripped the controls and thought about the gas tanks on the DC-3 and how they were emptying by the second. They had said they had about an hour's fuel, and how long ago had that been? How many minutes were out of that hour and how many more to go? And how accurate were the gas gauges on the DC-3? Maybe what read sixty minutes of fuel was actually only fifty minutes or forty.

Mechling called the DC-3 again. "Listen carefully. The fjord narrows here. It is very narrow. Repeat, very narrow. We are proceeding on radar. My navigator will give me the course and then I will relay it to you. Did you read me?"

"Affirmative."

"Do you understand?"

"I do, old chap."

Millican bent down over his radar scope. He had done it before, but always when Mechling could see, even if only a little. It would be the same way now, only Mechling couldn't see. If he made a mistake, Mechling couldn't tell him. If he made a mistake, nobody would ever be able to tell him anything. Not him nor the five other men in the SA-16 nor the two men and the woman in the DC-3 that was following every move. He had maybe half a minute of space on each side of him. Thirty seconds, maybe only twenty-five seconds, to keep between the cliffs. Thirty seconds to correct any error and two miles of air squeezed down to eight inches on glass in front of him.

"Ten degrees to the right," he said to Mechling.

"Roger," Mechling said. Then he switched to radio. "We are turning ten degrees right."

"Righto."

"Are you still with us?"

"Still have you in sight, old boy."

Millican said: "Five degrees left."

"Roger." Then: "Five degrees left."

"Righto. How much more of this?"

"Not much."

"Good."

"No sweat. We've done this before."

"Very good."

"We've done it often. No sweat. Relax."

"Righto."

"We'll have you down and a drink in your hands real quick."

"Splendid, oh, splendid." Then: "I say, I *could* use one, you know. We all could, I daresay."

"You'll get it. All of you. As much as you can take aboard."

Millican said: "Ten degrees right."

"Roger," Mechling said. Then he heard the voice of the Englishman. "I say, *I've lost you.*"

"Ten degrees right," Mechling said.

"I can only see your shadow on the clouds."

"Never mind that. *Ten degrees right.*"

"Where are you?"

"Change your course."

"Yes, yes. But I can't see you. Oh, *there* you are. I can see you now."

There was a brief opening below them and Mechling could see the water. Mechling knew about that water. The temperature ran about twenty-eight, twenty-nine degrees. Five or six minutes of staying alive if anybody went in. Six minutes, tops.

"Another five degrees right," Millican said.

"Roger." Then: "Five degrees right."

"Affirmative. How much more to go?"

"Not much."

"That's good. I say, do you really do this often?"

"Every day. Even when we don't have to. For kicks."

"I've lost you again."

"Just stay on course."

"Can't see a thing, really, not a thing."

"Just stay on course."

"My God, it's black."

"You'll pick us up again. *Just stay on course.*"

"Oh, *there* you are."

And just then they passed out of the narrow corridor into where the fjord widened again. Mechling knew the weather had indeed stalled inside that bottleneck because when they came out they were in the clear as though blinders had been torn off the windscreen. Millican lifted his head from the radar scope and his big, good-natured face was as wet as though he had been holding it in the rain. He leaned back and rubbed his eyes and his huge body sagged.

And at that moment Mechling heard a great noise from the DC-3. It was a cheer. It was a well-bred English cheer, controlled and restrained, but a cheer. And then the Englishman asked: "How far to the field now?"

"Just ten miles," Mechling said. He grinned. "Old chap . . ."

"Oh, very good. Very, very good." There was a pause. "I say, that was wizard, old boy."

Mechling climbed from where he was to about six hundred feet and he told the DC-3 to follow him. He figured it was a little safer higher up for the DC-3 with its draining tanks. If the DC-3 lost an engine because one of the tanks expired first it would then have a little more altitude, which meant more time, to switch tanks so both engines could draw on the tank that was left. And then at last Mechling was able to give out the big direction of the day: "You're lined up with the field. Drop your gear and go in. Did you read me?"

The Englishman replied: "Very loud and very clear." And as Mechling continued to climb he looked down and saw the DC-3 land safely on the strip at Narsarssuak.

Mechling went up until he was in the clear. Then he circled and flew back down the fjord and turned around again and lined himself up properly with the strip and brought down his own plane.

When the Rescue men climbed out of the SA-16 they found the three people from the DC-3 and almost the whole squadron waiting for them. The DC-3 people were Mr. and Mrs. Raoul V. Cote and the English navigator, Mr. Peter E. Palmer.

Mechling was told that when Mrs. Cote climbed out of the DC-3 and touched the earth she had grabbed the first man she had seen and had held him very tight, which was greatly appreciated by that young man because Mrs. Cote was an exceedingly attractive young woman.

For Mechling and Millican and their crew there were no hugs and not much anyone needed to say or was able to say at the moment. What the Cotes and Palmer had on their faces made a big silent sound. And when an Air Force mechanic strolled over and announced he had checked the tanks on the DC-3 and had found six gallons of gasoline in them the silence seemed to sound even louder. Six gallons of gasoline would have given them exactly four more minutes in the air.

"We Saw a Large Cloud . . ."

When an American military man stationed at Keflavik desires to relieve his feelings he picks up a stone and throws it. There are variations. One of the Air Force officers at this isolated airfield in Iceland keeps a pile of stones and a large hammer outside the front door to his quarters. When he returns home after duty, he always picks up the hammer and smashes one of the stones. Sometimes more than one.

There is another officer who keeps stones in his living room. He has chosen these stones very carefully because their indentations and contours remind him of faces. He has given the stones names and he keeps them in definite places around the room and when he comes back after work he greets them by name. Once, for a rib, some of his friends got into his apartment while he was on duty and they shifted the stones around. They did not remove any, just changed their locations. When the officer came home, he spotted the changes instantly. He became very angry.

He went outside and picked up some other stones and threw them. Then he went to the quarters of the officer with the hammer and he smashed some more stones. He felt better immediately, and he did not neglect to replace the stones he had broken with new stones so the other officer's supply would not be depleted. And then he went back to his own establishment and put his own stones with the faces back where they belonged.

A man must have some security.

If it has been gathered from the above intelligence that duty at Keflavik is a tour of interminable boredom the inference is not incorrect. Keflavik is another of those Air Force bases officially termed a "hardship station," which means, as I have pointed out, a twelve-month stretch without families. It is for the Air Force boys who draw the assignment a year of low-grade, chronic tedium, despite the strategic importance of Iceland and the fact that for the Rescue men their beat covers the North Atlantic which, for the bulk of the year, is a very unpleasant expanse of water.

The Americans stationed at Keflavik are virtually isolated on the base. Reykjavik is only about two hours away but the road is very bad and those few Americans who have cars up there are disinclined to wreck them. Moreover, the weather can close in at any time, stranding motorists. The only other means of transportation between Keflavik and Reykjavik is by bus, which is expensive and infrequent. To add to all this the American military must obtain special passes, which are not easy to get, to go to Reykjavik, and once they get there there is a curfew, a very early curfew, after which they must be off the streets, and that includes officers as well as airmen. Since Reykjavik, by American standards, is not much of a fun town anyway, the Air Force men seldom bother to go there. There are men who put in an entire tour of duty at Keflavik and then go home without ever having visited Reykjavik even once.

The Icelanders have an expression, "Bless." It is short for "God bless you" and it is used in parting, like saying "So long." The Americans have created the institution of "Bless Parties," given when an individual's tour of duty is up and he is homeward bound. The flying men throw their stones and look forward to their "Bless Party" and wait. They can always see the "Bless Party" coming, through the worst of the fogs, and up there the fogs are pretty bad.

All of this is rather sad because there are many places of great and terrible beauty in Iceland. The ancient songs are still on the land, the story of Burnt Njal, the saga of Grettir the Strong. And Reykjavik is a city of culture, interest, and literacy, with a university, libraries, a symphony orchestra, a national theater, museums, and art galleries. And men of great education and women of supreme beauty—the Celtic and Scandinavian blood produces superb physical types.

There is, however, a common meeting ground between Icelanders and Americans. It is the ground that has been hallowed in many places and in many times: coming to the aid of those in distress. Lifesaving is an old business in Iceland. The country has a number of organizations devoted to that task. There is the Life Saving Association of Iceland—ILSA—a volunteer group that goes out in surface vessels when fishing trawlers in the North Atlantic get into trouble. These waters have served for centuries as fishing grounds for people of many nations. A large proportion of the Icelandic people themselves live off the sea. In the last twenty-five years ILSA has been credited with rescuing more than fifteen hundred persons.

There is also a ground-air rescue team, formed of volunteers as well, which stands ready to help out when nature strikes at Iceland itself—people lost in glacial wastes, villages stricken by storm or flood or volcanoes. It was quite natural that the Air Rescue squadron based at Keflavik found itself from the very beginning in complete accord with these native organizations.

From the outset the Rescue men in Keflavik joined with the Icelanders in lending a hand in wresting victims from the violence of nature. But they added something else, something that made the Icelanders, with all their age-old traditions of mercy, open their eyes wide: assistance to people anywhere in the country who encountered private, individual trouble, such as accidents or illness. And the proud, independent people of Iceland have come to accept this help without question or embarrassment.

For instance, there was the time when a country doctor named Rognvaldur Thorleifsson got word to Rescue at 1020 one day that a farmer, Sigurdur Petursson, had got himself mangled up in an accident on his farm near the village of Breidhabolstadhur and that he was in a state of deep shock and was bleeding to death. It wasn't going to be hard to locate the village. By air, Breidhabolstadhur was only about sixty-five miles away, due north on the Hvammsgjördhur, the fjord that cuts in under the great Western Fjords. By road it was just three times that long and not all of it passable. The village was easy—but where was Petursson's farm? It could be anywhere for miles around.

Lieutenant Colonel Frederick Smith, Rescue commander in Keflavik, telephoned his good friend, Björn Jönsson, director of the Reykjavik Oceanic Airways Control, Iceland's CAA, and asked for help. Jönsson, a short, ruddy-faced man known to all airmen in Iceland as BJ, turned up an Icelandic pilot named Pall Palsson who said he knew exactly where Petursson's place was. Smith put the mission together fast.

Lieutenant John Coleman took off at 1132 in a helicopter for Breidhabolstadhur. At the same time an SA-16 flew down to Reykjavik, picked up Palsson, and then went on to Breidhabolstadhur, passing Coleman, in the slower chopper, on the way. When Coleman got to the village the SA-16 was orbiting directly over the farm, practically pointing a finger. Coleman landed right in the pasture just before one o'clock, and Petursson was given a blood transfusion on the spot. Then he was loaded on the helicopter and started back for Reykjavik. The farmer was so far gone, even with the new blood, that Johnny Coleman decided he'd better not waste the time an ambulance would take to transport him from the airport in Reykjavik to the hospital in town.

Coleman sent a radio message down to BJ and BJ notified the police. The police gave BJ an escort to rush a radioman with a portable transmitter over to the hospital. The radioman led Coleman right over the city to the hospital and while the citizens of Reykjavik rushed outdoors to stare upward Coleman brought his chopper down on the hospital lawn, twenty feet from the emergency entrance. Petursson lived to walk out of the hospital and found himself kind of famous, as the only man in the history of Iceland who was brought to the hospital in a flying ambulance.

Iceland has a number of volcanoes that are still quite active, and in June of 1955 one of them, Mt. Katla, near the south coast, burst its seams. This news was enough to frighten everybody in the country. It was eight years before, in 1947, when Mt. Hekla, another volcano in the same general area, erupted after sleeping for more than a century. Its snow and ice went up out of its throat in a fantastic column of steam, smoke, and ashes that reached a height of 60,000 feet. Lava dust and pumice covered all of Iceland and drifted as far as Europe.

BJ telephoned Fred Smith at one o'clock in the morning with the news about Katla. The eruption of the volcano, under the glacier called Myrdalsjokull, was endangering the existence of the little village of Vik with its 300 inhabitants. "He was very excited," Smith said. "He told me Katla was tossing pieces of ice as big as automobiles and that the steam was melting them and the water was beginning to flood Vik."

BJ said he was going to fly as close as he could with a DC-3 with some radio equipment to bring Vik into communication with the world. Trouble was that the closest he could get was a landing strip outside another village called Skojasandur, several miles away. The problem was how to get the radio stuff from Skojasandur to Vik. Smith had an answer.

At two forty-five in the morning Johnny Coleman took off in his helicopter. It was raining heavily and there was a thick fog. Coleman made his way to Skojasandur and landed next to BJ's DC-3 at three fifty-five. He picked up the radio gear, BJ, took off again, flew on in the black storm, and at six o'clock in the morning sat down in Vik.

During that same night Smith ordered that a C-124, a big four-engined transport plane, be made ready, with the idea that he would bring it as close as he could to Vik to evacuate people if that proved necessary. As soon as it was light he took off himself in another helicopter to survey the terrain around Vik, to find out whether there was any place where the C-124 could possibly land. If not, he planned to set up a shuttle operation by helicopter, flying people out of Vik to Skojasandur.

An SA-16 flew cover for Smith in the chopper and the two aircraft felt their way slowly along the southern coast. The weather and visibility worsened by the minute. "We saw a large cloud in front of us and we turned to avoid it. As we passed it we saw it wasn't a cloud but a huge rock on the coast," Smith said. He reached Vik in the early afternoon and found that by some grace of God the flood waters had shifted and that Vik and its isolated people were in no immediate danger.

The natives of Vik paused in their efforts of salvaging their possessions and walked over to where the two helicopters, Coleman's and Smith's, were parked side by side. They stared at them for a long time. BJ explained to them what Smith had prepared to do in the event they had to be evacuated, and then they turned their eyes from the helicopters to Smith and looked at him silently. "I have never forgotten the expressions in those faces," Colonel Smith said.

"Lady, Take a Bow . . ."

Every time Joe Kusy looks at a helicopter a strange light appears in his eyes. He walks around it with pursed lips and knit brow, his glasses gleaming like low-voltage headlights, staring, staring, until surely the clumsy potbellied thing must be blushing with embarrassment and wanting to pull in its rotors and hide. For to Joe the helicopter is a comical bird, a pelican among flying creatures, capable of feats of hilarity. He does not depreciate one bit its capabilities for serious work and has exploited these capabilities to the fullest on many occasions. But the wingless machine with the droopy blades has another dimension for him, a dimension in a world of laughter.

Joe was born with his own offbeat sense of humor and in the whirlybird he knows he has found a playmate. Like Mel Ayau, the Hawaiian chopper wizard, he is a supreme virtuoso, only he approaches his recitals with the puckish manners of one of the Marx brothers.

Joe Kusy is Major Willis B. Kusy. He works in Rescue in Manston, in southeastern England. Where the "Joe" came from is long forgotten but nobody calls him anything else. He is a tall, thin youth from Jennings, Kansas, speaks with a Midwestern twang, and looks more like an accountant or bank clerk than chopper pilot. His glasses are rimless. His sandy hair is brushed straight back. He speaks soberly, deadpanned—only once in a while a kind of manic light flashes and his grave words spill over in silent chuckles.

In Manston the helicopters were greeted heartily as giving Rescue a new kind of tool. Kusy helped check out other pilots and under his guidance they underwent the strange metamorphosis from conventional flying men to chopper jockeys. Helicopter pilots are a new breed of aviator, with language, thinking, and attitudes all their own. They look with mild amusement even upon the arrogant jet brats. After all, they reason, flying jets is the same as before, only faster. Helicopters are something entirely new.

And, for some odd reason, the helicopters went straight into the hearts of the people of Manston, as they were, eventually, to strike a chord of affection in the hearts of everybody in England, right up to and including the Queen and her Royal Consort, the Duke of Edinburgh. Joe found himself a favorite in the local pubs. Men would stop their games of darts and gather around him when he appeared and ask him all kinds of questions about the strange bird he was flying. Was it true helicopters could go straight up? Was it true they could stay still in the air, in one place? Joe became a sort of oracle.

The first big military test came when the helicopters were called upon to join with the Royal Air Force in complicated maneuvers. "It added a new quality to the show," Joe said. "They never had choppers before. And it did us a lot of good, working with them."

And then Joe was summoned at last for some serious business when two small freighters ran together off Dungeness Point and he went out to look for survivors. "We spotted five of them in the water for the boats to pick up. And then my engine quit right over the water. I didn't know it but I had broken a piston. I had an explosion in the induction system and it blew the cowling off. I dropped almost to the water and then the thing started running again. We were about ten miles out when it happened but we made it to the beach at Dungeness."

Joe climbed down and looked at the helicopter that had brought him back, damaged as it was. He looked at it from all sides, and what had started as a love affair, good-humored and light, became a marriage on the spot.

The helicopter, he understood perfectly, was a utility machine, able to do things no other aerial vehicle could do. But he brought to the pilot's seat a new bemusement and curiosity. It was not what special things had been manufactured into the helicopter that interested him but what special things could be done only by him. Slowly, carefully, like an Indian mahout who has an elephant for heavy labor but who tries to teach it tricks in his spare time, Joe explored the possibilities of his flying windmill. And his friends and neighbors at Manston and Margate and Ramsgate watched him with enchantment.

It surprised no one at all when it was announced that one of the features of the great Searchlight Tattoo at Woolwich

Arsenal in London would be a helicopter demonstration, and it surprised the people in the local pubs even less when they heard Joe would give it. The only question was: what would he dream up?

Joe did a lot of dreaming. He dreamed and tinkered and he took out his favorite helicopter and fooled around in the air and then he came up with his answer. "The Queen was supposed to attend this tattoo," he said. "What we were going to do was fill a kind of tennis marker with luminous powder. A technician was going to hold the marker out of the door of the helicopter and I was going to fly 'ER 2' over the ground and he would let the marker trail out.

"I rigged up a bank of ultra-violet lights on the underside of the chopper. We had 110 volts accessible to us and, together with a small auxiliary power unit, that would be enough to light up the bank of lights. The way we had it arranged, after I completed writing, the people were going to turn out the lights in the stadium and then I would hover and light up what we had written. We worked it out a couple of times at the base so we could do it."

Joe's friends were delighted. That was something, they chortled, that only Joe would think of, to write the insigne of the Queen with a helicopter. And then the blow fell. It couldn't be done. "The seats at the stadium were flat," Joe said. "The arrangement didn't provide enough height for the people to see it, so it was washed out. We had to scratch around for something else."

It was decided to stage a mock rescue instead. A man would be put in a life raft in the middle of the field. Joe would fly in, lower a sling, and "rescue" him. The men in the pubs grumbled that it all sounded flat, after the dye-marker idea, even when they heard Joe had added a little something: after picking up the man he would deposit him on the front seat of a jeep parked before the royal box. That was a little better, but still . . .

But Joe's sense of the comic had provided him with another thought, which he kept to himself.

On the night of the tattoo he flew into the stadium, as scheduled. "They had searchlights. They were searchlight happy. It was marvelous for everybody except us who had to fly. We came down in the small stadium with these powerful beams shining on us all the time. They blinded us and kept us blinded. We couldn't read the instruments. Our eyes couldn't see anything. But after we put the 'survivor' in the jeep, he detached himself from the sling—and then we went over to where all the dignitaries were sitting and we *bowed* the helicopter. You can make it bow by grossly overcontrolling the ship momentarily. It will bow quite nicely."

The dart players were satisfied, after all. Joe had not let them down.

If Joe's tricks with the helicopter had not been enough to win over the people in the southeastern coastal towns, his passion for speedboats would have done it. Everybody there is boat mad and Joe is one of the maddest of all. When he is not in the air he is on the water, and the more time he spends with other boat lovers the more he finds it helps him in this primary job, rescue.

"I got to be pretty friendly with the Margate Coast Guard and the Pilot Boat people. Once we got a call that a pilot had bailed out of a jet plane and had been picked up by a freighter. They needed a doctor. We picked up the base doctor and I took him out.

"When we got there I found I couldn't let him down on the ship because it was dark and the weather was very bad. So I turned around and headed back for Margate. I knew from hanging around there that the message for help must have been relayed through the Coast Guard and so I brought the helicopter to the Margate Pilot Boat and lowered the doctor. He stepped from the sling onto the pier and from the pier onto the Pilot Boat, and they took him out to where the freighter was. The pilot was in bad shape—he had a gash in his head and was suffering from shock. We stayed, hovering over the town, in case they needed us again. The whole town fell out to watch."

He also got to know the men connected with the Margate Boat of the Royal National Lifeboat Association. With these men, who do on the surface of the sea what Rescue does from the air, Kusy, informally, without red tape, helped straighten out a knotty problem that had bothered everybody for a long time.

"We established an elaborate and very efficient coordination system by radio from aircraft to surface vessels. The helicopter was VHF—very high-frequency radio. The boats have HF—high frequency. There is no way for them to communicate. But the SA-16 has both, so we worked out a procedure by which the SA-16 acts as liaison between helicopters and surface vessels."

It is a historic cliché that the British are cold and without feeling and that their native chilliness drops even a few more degrees when they encounter members of their lost tribe from America. This is a premise that brings Joe Kusy as close to rage as it is possible for that cheerful man to get. The men and women in his part of England have made him feel as much at home as he could in Jennings, Kansas. And this bond was not something that took many years to develop. It happened almost from the very beginning.

Every year at Christmas the mayor of Ramsgate and other important persons in the community participate in a moving and very British ceremony. They board the Margate Boat and go out to the Tongue Lightship, anchored nine miles from shore, and spend a few hours in Yuletide communion with the men who maintain the lonely vigil at sea.

These lightships are stationed around the British coast in places of danger where ordinary lighthouses cannot be built. They are, actually, floating lighthouses, designed to illuminate dangerous areas—shifting shoals, sandy estuaries, rocks. They are anchored in one position. They are not part of the Coast Guard but come under operation of Trinity House, an organization that is separate from but under the control of the British Government.

Because space on the little Margate Boat and on the Tongue Lightship itself is very limited, only a few persons may join in the annual Christmas event. Through the years it has become a highly sought-after social prize. There are people who have waited twenty-five years for an invitation and who are still waiting.

On the first Christmas Joe Kusy and his wife, Mildred, were stationed at Manston—less than six months after they arrived there—they were both asked to attend. "They take food and gifts to the people on the lightship," Joe said. "They hold church services and sing songs and then they conduct a tour of the ship."

Joe was deeply touched by this sign of affection and esteem from people who still were strangers to him. He and Mildred were invited to the ceremony every Christmas thereafter except one year when he was down in Tripoli conducting a helicopter school for the Rescue group there. It is nice to know that nobody, not even among those who have been waiting for a quarter of a century for their invitation, protested, or would have it any other way.

Joe got to know the lightship well and to know the men who spend barren weeks manning it. It became a very personal thing to him when he reported for duty one morning in November 1954, and learned that another lightship, the one at South Goodwin, had slipped its moorings and was aground in sand.

There is only one person alive today who can tell the tragic story of the South Goodwin Lightship. He is a young man named Ronald Keir Murton, twenty-two, an ornithologist connected with the Ministry of Agriculture and Fisheries and Food. I went to see Murton in his office on the outskirts of London. I found him a slight, pale, almost frail-looking youth. He told me he was sent aboard the South Goodwin Lightship on the first day of November to make a study of bird migration over the water during that month.

"We were anchored approximately three and a half miles off St. Margaret's Bay," he said. "There were eight men aboard, including the master, Mr. Skipp." Skipp was a short, plump, jolly man and an amateur painter of considerable skill who spent much of his spare time before his canvas, recording the bleak emptiness of the sea. "The first few days I studied the migration of starlings, skylarks, and so on, counting them, studying the direction from which they came and to which they went, and other interesting facts."

A couple of weeks later a shackle on the mooring cable that held the vessel fast went bad. Skipp, with some concern, radioed Trinity House and reported it. A repair ship arrived the next day and tried several times to lower a boat to get at the cable but the seas were too rough and the repair ship departed. Skipp hauled in the cable himself, removed the faulty pin, heated it red hot over the galley stove, and fixed it up as best he could. A few days later another repair ship showed up. An inspection was made and the pin was said to be all right.

A week later the weather turned bad. "The wireless gave us gale warnings," Murton said. "In the afternoon, about three o'clock, there was a strong wind that built up gradually into a great force by evening. It continued like that throughout the whole evening. We carried on exactly as normal, except a little bit of extra watch was kept and we got the normal discomfort of bad weather.

"I shared a cabin with the master and, as usual, I went to bed at seven o'clock, but I couldn't sleep very well owing to the movement of the ship and the fact that the radio was going most of the time. I did manage to doze off occasionally. I was awakened about eight o'clock, I should say, by the wireless telling us about a ship that had gone aground on the Shipwash Sands, off the coast of East Anglia, and we listened to the wireless between her and two ships going to her rescue. I listened to that for some little while and then dozed off again. Then the next thing that woke me was the intercommunication telephone going from the bridge. They reported seeing a flare going up over Dover and the master was being informed, you see.

"Then I managed to go to sleep again. I was awakened by a very heavy sea we took and the water splashed down into the room where I was sleeping. At the same time there was a very heavy bang on the deck above us. The master ran up to see what the trouble was and he found that one of the lead sounding weights that are normally fastened to the gunwale of the ship had been washed out of its hanging on the hook and had thumped on the deck.

"The master was not in the cabin at the time and I decided I was not going to stay there, so I put an overcoat over my pajamas, slipped on a pair of shoes without lacing them, and went up to the wheelhouse where there were two men on watch and the master. We stayed there keeping a lookout and drinking coffee and in general discussing the state of the weather. We couldn't tell much where our position was because very heavy seas were breaking over the ship and spray was continually being dashed across the wheelhouse and occasionally over the lantern as well. The result of this was that we got only occasional glimpses of shore lights. We stayed like that for something like three quarters of an hour during which time the master showed concern as to whether we were still in our position.

"On the last occasion the master had taken a check on deck. He came in and questioned the two men on watch as to whether we were still on position and they stated that they thought we were. One of them walked to the back of the wheelhouse and looked out of the window. He exclaimed immediately that we were on top of the East Goodwin Lightship. We all looked around and at that moment the light from the other ship flooded the whole of the wheelhouse and we all realized simultaneously we were adrift.

"We had drifted about three and a half miles along the east coast of the Goodwin Sands, missing all the sands, and then close to and parallel with the other lightship, and when both ships went up on a swell the light flooded through.

"We then had to warn the rest. The master immediately led the way down into the hull of the ship from the wheelhouse. We went along a companionway to the galley from where a flight of stairs led down to the men's berths. On the way he intimated that he wanted to get them up but I realized that he also wanted to get out the rescue apparatus and the wireless that is kept in his cabin and isolated from the rest of the ship. I therefore told him to carry on and I'd get the men up from their beds.

"We came along the companionway in the following

order: the master leading, myself second, followed by two other men, leaving the last one in the wheelhouse to maintain a watch. I went down into the men's quarters while the skipper went aft. I shouted as I went down the ladder: 'We're adrift! We're adrift!' I stayed at the bottom just long enough to make sure they had all heard and were out of bed and immediately rushed back into the galley.

"A man was following me and he managed to get into the galley as well. The other two were still on their way. At this point we felt a jar as the bottom of the ship ran aground. We lurched to about forty-five degrees. The master appeared from aft into the galley again but he'd only just stepped inside when we turned completely over on our side.

"Everybody was thrown down. Loose pots and pans that were on shelves fell down and water flooded in immediately through the door leading from the galley and from the skylight on top of the galley. The water filled up very quickly, and in a matter of minutes everybody was out of their depths in water, trying to keep afloat and being slopped around by the movement of the water inside.

"All this time more water was coming in through the skylight and I realized I had to get out. I made for the skylight but got washed back again by the rush of water. I tried several times, and after about five or ten minutes managed to get my fingers on the outside of the skylight and pull myself through. After the exertion I hung on, trying to prevent myself from being washed in again or washed off the boat. One man attempted to follow me and I took hold of his shoulder and tried to pull him through. The next moment a bad sea hit us. I nearly got washed completely off the boat itself and I lost my grip on him and he washed inside again.

"I realized I couldn't stay there indefinitely. For long periods I was completely under water during the swells. I hung on by twisting my legs around the built-up part of the skylight and hanging on with my fingers as best I could. There was nothing to get a firm grip on. A piece of rope was hanging across the skylight and I tried to pull this around me to make myself fast but the next moment, owing to a swell, I found it around my neck, nearly strangling me, so I had to let go of that.

"Hanging directly above me was one of the ship's lifeboats that swung out from its davits, and I could see that the support was weakened and that it was liable to fall down on my head at any moment. I realized I'd better get up on the side of the boat if I was going to last, so making use of a ventilator shaft which was about three feet above me, when a lull occurred I half-scrambled and half-sprang onto this, hung on for a little while as we took the next big sea, and then grabbed hold of the chimney that was about two feet above this, and from there up the side of the ship where I wedged myself in the rails.

"I made one rail come across my stomach and I was able to grip it as well with my hands so that as the seas broke over the hull of the ship they hit me in the back and I was prevented from being washed over by the rail across my stomach, and if I lost my grip that held me back. After about two hours of this the seas gradually got less and I was able to relax my grip. As the tide went down I was able to turn around and lie on the side of the ship.

"I pulled my overcoat over my head and breathed into the space formed. This helped keep me warm. I had lost my shoes in getting onto the side and my feet were completely bare. They were painful at first but as the life left them because of the coldness I didn't notice. They just seemed like a couple of pieces of lead."

Murton remained there through the night, huddled in his coat. During the early hours of the morning the winds reached hurricane force. The vessel shuddered on its sandy trap and from time to time a particularly heavy sea rolled it violently so that he had to grab hold of the side to keep from being washed off.

"When daybreak arrived I thought it was a bad fog—I couldn't see. But it wasn't fog. The salt and sand had scratched the corneas of my eyes, I found out later, and I was almost blind. At first I could only see my hand twelve inches from my eyes. Then I gradually got so I could see about fifteen or twenty feet away. I just thought the fog was lifting.

"About that time I heard planes and then a Sunderland came very low and most often and I waved and waved but they didn't see me. I thought it was because of the fog I imagined was around me."

And then Murton heard a knocking from inside the boat. He saw a thick glass porthole. He scrambled over to it. He tried to open it. It opened from the outside and was secured by wing nuts that had rusted and been painted over. He tried to force the wing nuts until his fingers ached and then he tried to smash the glass with his fists. He couldn't work the nuts open or break the glass. He put his face close to the glass and tried to look inside but he was unable to see.

"We shouted back and forth, and I was told there were three men alive inside, resting right then in an air pocket above the water, that they had survived the night, and that two of the men—the master was one of them—were in bad shape. I shouted to them that planes were flying around, not to lose hope. Planes were making low flights, and after a while I was able to make out their lines as they flew over. I stayed there, sitting on the side of the ship or making little walks back and forth, and I talked to the men inside."

The first thing Joe Kusy thought when they told him about the lightship was that maybe there were men trapped inside and he could close his eyes and see the inside, just like the inside of the Tongue Lightship, and he could see the faces of the men as well, just like the weather-beaten faces he had seen so often raised in Christmas song.

He was told that an SA-16 was already out, searching for a lifeboat that appeared to be missing from the capsized lightship and in which there might be survivors. He was also told that other planes, RAF planes, had flown over the vessel and had reported no sign of life, inside or out.

The more Joe heard the more he knew he had to go out, so he grabbed another chopper pilot, Captain Curtis E. Parkins, because he had a plan and the plan called for another pilot. He didn't want to do the flying himself. He wanted to go out as a passenger in the cabin and then lower himself down to the grounded vessel on the hoist and try to get inside it. Even if it were dark inside, half-filled with water, he knew he would remember the layout well enough to get around.

Parkins said he was ready, able, and more than willing, and the two of them went in to see the assistant Operations officer, Major Paul L. Parks, and they told him of their scheme. "Because the wind was so high it took a little consultation," Joe said. "Then Major Parks said he would get the chopper out of the barn. I went out to round up any special equipment I thought we might need—flashlights, extra batteries, two coils of nylon rope, and a grappling hook to toss aboard as I crawled up the side by rope, if that was necessary.

"Then Major Parks said he'd go along as copilot. That way the helicopter would have a full crew aboard while setting on the sands in case it had to fly off and leave me there, or needed manpower with the stretchers. Airman First Class Elmer H. Vollman was taken as medical technician and the four of us took off.

"It was about eight-thirty in the morning. The weather was still blowing a gale but the wind velocity was fairly steady—it would build up to about forty-five knots and then slack off to about thirty-five. The difficulty Parkins was trying to avoid was engaging the rotors of the helicopter in high winds. You can get yourself in trouble. The blades could start flapping and one of the blades might strike the tail boom and knock the tail off. The blades are very flexible. Parkins was an exceptionally well-qualified man and he had no hesitation.

"We stayed rather low and flew over land to Deal and left the coast there. It was possibly just twelve miles east of there that we saw the ship and in just a few minutes after we left the mainland, but instead of being high and dry the tide had come in and the water was breaking completely over the ship. And that definitely eliminated any chance of landing or even me going down on a hoist cable to see if anybody was aboard.

"As long as we were out there we decided to circle the thing and take a look and then head back. We made a right bank around it at about a hundred-foot altitude and just as we got abeam of the lightship we saw a man crouched down in the superstructure."

Murton heard the sound of the helicopter and he looked up and tried to see it but the brine and the wind had been working in his eyes again and he was almost blind and he could make out only a vague shape. He waved his hand feebly, and then he had to close his eyes because it felt as if the wind and the salt were burning them out. But he kept waving, and he thought that soon the sound would go away again, the way the other plane sounds had gone away, and it would be the same as before. He was under water most of the time now, each time the sea washed over him, and he thought that maybe this was getting close to the finish because his hands were numbed with the cold and the sea was getting higher and more demanding.

"Parkins slowed the ship down and came to a high hover, at possibly thirty to forty feet above the ship," Joe said. "When the man started to wave, I motioned to him to give hand signals to see whether he wanted aboard. He didn't seem to be excited to see us there. We didn't know he could hardly see us at all.

"I considered the possibility of him being a member of a salvage crew or something, but I could hardly believe that. The financial value of a lightship couldn't be too great and I knew definitely there couldn't be any cargo, so we decided to lower the sling.

"We let down the sling and actually it was three quarters of the way down and he was still waving at us as he had at first. I don't think he saw the sling until it was on him."

And by "on him" Joe Kusy means exactly that. For the

incredible thing that Parkins did on that day was to bring his helicopter directly over Murton and hold it there with such exquisite precision in that battering gale that when the hoist was lowered the harness went down until it *came to rest on Murton's chest*. "Murton just took hold of the two sides of the sling, stuck his feet into it, and sat down in the sling, and we hauled him up," Joe said.

The first thing Kusy asked Murton was whether there were other men inside the lightship and if so were they alive. "He said there were three men aft of the galley who were alive early that morning and that while they had talked to each other he couldn't understand them through the closed porthole. He said the only way we could get to them was with a cutting torch because they were trapped in there.

"He said there was a man on the bridge and three or four in the galley but he didn't know what happened to them after he had crawled out of the ventilator. He told me he had tried to help one of them out and how he had been washed back."

Parkins started back for Manston and radioed this information en route. It took just a few minutes for the helicopter to fly from the Goodwin Sands to the air base but in that brief time Major Charles Lowe, the Operations officer, had located some portable welding equipment, and when the chopper touched down the equipment was on its way to the strip along with volunteers to use it.

"Where they got it I'll never know," Joe said.

Lowe had also radioed to the SA-16 out on search that a survivor had been taken off the vessel and that the other men had not gotten away in a lifeboat but were still trapped inside. The SA-16 returned to the Goodwin Sands immediately. As the helicopter landed and Murton was transferred to an ambulance and the cutting torches were brought out to the chopper, the SA-16 called back and reported that the vessel now was wholly submerged and that just a small piece of it could be seen between swells.

Lowe told the volunteers to stand by with their cutting torches and then he got a call from the Ramsgate Coast Guard relaying a request from the Trinity vessel *Patricia* asking if it were possible for a helicopter to go to the navy yard at Sheerness and pick up some diving equipment and take it to the *Patricia*.

"Captain Parkins, Major Parks, and Airman Vollman took off, landed in the navy yard, located equipment, loaded it, and went back out to sea," Joe said. "They found the *Patricia* but they couldn't get in close enough because there were too many masts. So they set it down on a small launch that was with the *Patricia*."

Kusy looked up. "That was a great piece of work Parkins did—setting that equipment right on a tiny launch in that wind. It was the greatest feat of the whole thing. This was winter, remember, and we got beat out because of the darkness. It gets dark about four or four-thirty in the afternoon then. There was nothing we could do until morning. Meanwhile the *Patricia* requested that the helicopter assist in putting some frogmen aboard the lightship at dawn the next morning. The *Patricia* used the procedure we had set up—using an SA-16 as an intermediary in talking to the helicopter."

At dawn the following day Kusy and another helicopter pilot, Captain Harold Welch, took off again. "We were supposed to go out to a small launch to pick the frogmen up," Kusy said. "We found the launch but they didn't seem to like the idea of a chopper ride and they signaled they would swim to the lightship, which was above water again. We landed on the sands about fifty feet from the lightship and they swam over. We met on the sands and they told us their plans and they went to work on the lightship."

Kusy chafed to go inside the lightship with them but they were experts at this business and he knew there was nothing he could do to help and that he would only be in the way in those constricted quarters. He stood by his chopper, the only transportation between the surface vessels gathered around and the sands, ready to use it as a shuttle for anything that was needed.

"We received code from one of the small launches that was in the nearby water and thanks to our training with the British we were able to read the blinker. It was the chief officer of the *Patricia* requesting that he be delivered to the lightship. We went out and picked him up from the little launch and landed him near the lightship. He was wearing ordinary seaman's clothes and we were very careful not to get him wet. Just then one of the frogmen came out of the lightship and said he needed special tools. We took him out to the launch, lowered him by sling, he got his tools, and we picked him up again and brought him back to the lightship."

The three frogmen worked desperately inside the vessel and Kusy stood by his chopper and watched the tide slowly rise again.

"We stayed there until the tide just about ran us out. The helicopter started to sink into the sand. The frogmen couldn't make it—there just wasn't enough time. Then it reached a point where we had just ten feet of sand around us, that was all, and the water started to cover the lightship again. We took off and hovered—we didn't dare leave the frogmen and the chief officer there.

"Then one of the frogmen ran out and said he needed different tools. We took him back to the launch, waited for him, and brought him back and landed again."

By now the helicopter was resting on a patch of sand scarcely wider than its wheels and the ground was beginning to slip away from under it. At low tide the sand is as hard as concrete. Footsteps of men, tires of the helicopter, make no impression upon it. As the water creeps in it turns into something close to quicksand.

Kusy realized that he was going to have a problem getting off from that treacherous floor with four grown men adding their weight. It would be better, he thought, to climb up light, hover, and then haul the frogmen and the chief officer in by the sling. Before he went up he tested the hoist. "The hoist was fouled," he said. "I told them that I would wait there and take off with all aboard."

The frogmen worked until the last possible minute. Then at last the chief officer from the *Patricia* walked slowly toward the helicopter. The water came up to his neck before he reached the aircraft. He climbed aboard. He said that every possible compartment had been investigated. "There is no chance of any survivors," he said.

The frogmen emerged from the lightship just as the water closed over it. They still wanted no part of the helicopter and they plunged into the sea and swam to their launch. Kusy lifted his chopper and hovered over them until they were safely aboard, and then with the officer from the *Patricia* in the cabin he flew back to Manston. By the next low tide the South Goodwin Lightship was buried deeper in the sand, and after that it vanished.

The tragedy that befell the lightship and the valiant efforts that were made to get to the unfortunate men who were held prisoner in its water-filled hull stirred the people of Britain the length and breadth of the land. On a raw January day the four men who had snatched Ronald Murton from death were summoned to Westminster Hall in London. There the Duchess of Kent, widow of the Duke of Kent, brother to the late King George VI and feudal lord of Kent, in which Manston is situated—who had himself died a hero's death in the air in World War II—awaited them.

In the name of the Royal National Lifeboat Institute the Duchess presented to Captain Parkins, as the pilot of the helicopter, a bronze lifesaving medal, and then she gave to each of the four men a document of honor.

But the people who knew them and who saw them on the street and played darts and drank beer with them had to say something, too, something more personal and closer to home. And so, a month later, the mayor of the Borough of Ramsgate, Edward G. Butcher, invited the four men to his office. When they got there they found the mayor dressed in his ancient raiment of office—satin knee breeches, robe, and silvery wig—and around him were all the aldermen and burgesses of the borough. Mayor Butcher raised his gold mace for silence and then he read from another scroll of honor:

"We, the mayor, aldermen and burgesses of the Borough of Ramsgate, hereby record our appreciation of the services rendered by the aircraft of the 66th Air Rescue Squadron, United States Air Force, based at Manston, near Ramsgate, when the South Goodwin Lightvessel was wrecked during a severe gale on 27 November 1954, and in particular by the undermentioned members of the crew of the helicopter, who at considerable hazard rescued the sole survivor, Mr. Ronald Murton."

Then Mayor Butcher slowly read off the names of the four men.

That evening at the pubs the dart players were content. The widow of their duke had spoken in London. And their own mayor had spoken in Ramsgate. All was well.

AUSTRIA, HOLLAND AND "SIR ROBERT" RIZON

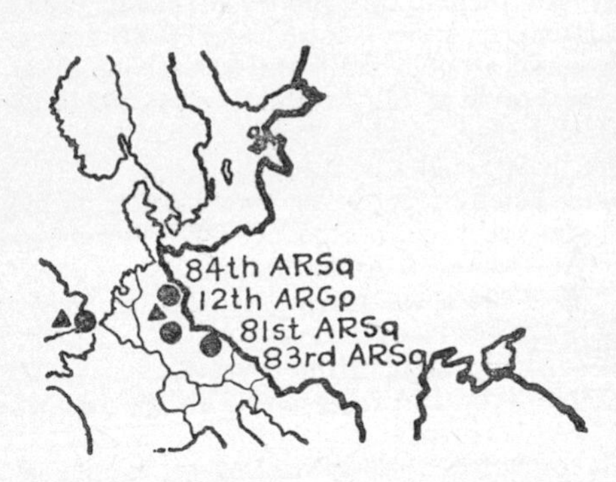

"The Hand of God—or the Devil . . ."

For almost three hundred years the people of the Walser Valley in western Austria have remembered the Great Avalanche of 1670. There have been wars, and dynasties have changed and the world has moved from one century to another, but nothing that happened anywhere was so important in the Grosses Walsertal as that time when the snow slid down the mountains. That was theirs alone, the personal catastrophe of the dwellers in the valley, and in the winters, when the new snow fell, they held close to their fires and repeated the stories they had heard from their fathers. And each detail remained sharp and clear as though it had happened not almost three centuries ago but the year before or the year before that. It was even easy to remember exact names—in this remote valley near the borders of Lichtenstein and Switzerland family names have not changed in 300 years.

The Grosses Walsertal, in Voralberg Province, is called a valley but it is more of a giant gorge, a great cleft, a narrow-angled V without even a flat floor, the sharp, steep sides meeting at a trickling stream. There are little villages along the hillsides where men have to lean almost sideways to keep erect—Blons is closest to the mouth, Sonntag, Fontanello,

Buchboden, others—and so precipitous are the slopes that even in midsummer one side of the valley is in twilight from early afternoon on.

There have been other avalanches, many of them, some great and some small, but none could measure up to the Great Avalanche. The danger was always there in the winter when the snow gathered on the roofs of the hills and men always asked themselves why they lived there under the hanging blanket of death, but there was no answer. None was needed. It was their home. Even though there were those who said it should not be called Walser Valley but Death Valley.

On the afternoon of Thursday, January 7, 1954, snow began to fall upon Grosses Walsertal. The men and women noted that it was the dreaded *Staublawinen*—the dry snow. There are two kinds of avalanches, the wet and the dry. In the wet avalanche the snow packs as it falls and it destroys by brute force, by weight and impact. It is bad but it is a physical thing that can be seen and understood and perhaps with luck even be avoided.

The dry avalanche is different. The snow remains a powder, a fine dust almost. It builds up a solid wall of *air pressure* in front of it, invisible and deadly, and it destroys houses it never touches directly, and it strangles people standing in the open air. Because people smother and homes crumble from something that is unseen and many yards from them the people look upon the *Staublawinen* as something supernatural, something strange and mystic that belongs to the powers of darkness.

The dry snow continued to fall through the night and through that Friday and Saturday. On Sunday morning it was still falling. And on that day Maria Tuertscher, a husky, unmarried woman of thirty-two who worked with her father on his farm, dressed in her warmest clothes and left her home in Blons to go to church. It was a time to pray to Saint Nikolaus.

"Two of my sisters and my cousin went with me," Fräulein Tuertscher told me many months later when I visited her in Blons. "The church was a mile from our house and the snow was very high but we were able to go there and return. On the way back I saw several smaller snowfalls started from their deep pathway above. We spent all Sunday and all that night in our house and on Monday morning my sister, Adelheid, looked out through the window and saw that a thick blanket of snow was blown along the house and at the same moment we heard a loud crack and the house moved."

There was sudden darkness, as though night had sprung upon them, and then the house wrenched itself from its foundations and toppled over on its side, the way a tree might fall. Then there was a great smashing sound, and heavy timbers broke through and the air filled with dust and snow and the people inside began to choke. Then there was silence. After a little while the people called out to each other.

"We were all laid out, more or less covered by wooden beams from the barn that had been driven into the house. The ceiling and the floor of the room were almost vertical. My sisters and my cousin could get out by themselves but they had to carry me out because I had a terrible pain in my neck.

"When we were all outside, we saw that the whole house had moved down about a hundred yards and that the barn with the hay was on top of the building where we had been. The roof of the barn and the cattle in it were all thrown over the roof of the house and were wiped down to the river.

"They carried me, and then we noticed that the house of another sister of mine, a sister with ten children, which had been about a hundred yards from our house, was now about ten yards away. In that ruined house we heard voices calling: 'Mamma! Mamma!' They put me down for a minute and went over there and they found my sister lying upside down, all broken from falling beams, and five of her children. They could not find the others. Then men came down and they took us all into the village."

For a little while it seemed as though the village itself might escape the full force of the *Staublawinen,* Frau Maria Schiebel, wife of Rudolf Schiebel, an engineer in Blons, told me. "The electric lights went out on Sunday," she said. "The telephone connection with the main valley was interrupted by avalanches. On Monday morning our house was snowed in almost completely. They tried to dig a pathway up to the church but they could not do it until the afternoon. It was not until that afternoon that the avalanche alarm was given.

"The first big avalanche had come down already at Esch, a mile farther up the valley. Ten houses were hit and wiped away there completely. There were deaths in every family living there and all those who were not killed were injured. Some of them managed to escape. All who could move came to Blons and gathered in a house near the dairy which was believed to be safe. The injured people who could be rescued from nearby were also brought out to that place and to the Inn Kroner close to the church of Blons.

"At seven o'clock on Monday the whole hillside of Blons moved down in a huge avalanche and also the people who were thought to be safe in the house near the dairy were wiped away with the house and most of them were killed. It was still snowing heavily through the night and nobody could leave the few houses and spots that were a little safe on the edges of the gorges. On Tuesday morning two men went out to Thüringen to give the word on what had happened."

By then twenty of the twenty-three buildings in Blons were swept away by the powder snow. Debris was scattered 1,000 feet down the mountainside. Standing were only the old church with its image of Saint Nikolaus, the inn, and one dwelling.

The snow fell almost everywhere across Austria, on Bludenz, just outside the Grosses Walsertal, down the long Klostertal, on Alberg and St. Christoph's Pass, on St. Anton and Landeck, on all the valleys and mountains and villages that look like pictures in a storybook or settings on a stage, on Innsbruck, the lovely city on the river Inn. Innsbruck is a popular skiing center. The snow that fell upon it was dry snow, too, which was excellent for the runs. Those who had come to holiday were joyful.

From his office window in the University Hospital in Innsbruck—a hospital that treats many skiers when they break an arm or a leg—Dr. Haid stared at the falling snow. Dr. Haid is a skier himself—he has won many prizes in championship competitions—but on that morning he was not thinking of the ecstasy of skimming swiftly down a slope. The reports from Grosses Walsertal had just come in.

Bruno Haid is a young, tall, blue-eyed, flaxen-haired man of great charm, a doctor and surgeon, and more recently a specialist in anesthesiology. He is regarded as one of the finest anesthesiologists in Austria, perhaps in all Europe. He was born in Oetz, a little village in a valley near Innsbruck, where his father runs a resort hotel, the Drei Mohren—Three Moors. A skillful mountain climber, hunter, fisherman, Haid served as a lieutenant physician in the Austrian Army, first in Russia and then in the Rhineland and Holland.

He was taken prisoner by the Canadians in Leeuwarden, North Holland, in April 1945, but was permitted to continue working as a doctor—only his patients became Americans, Canadians, and Englishmen. At one time he was responsible for the care of no less than 350 Allied wounded.

From his patients Dr. Haid learned to speak English and

for them he was able to put to good use his family's hotel connections. He made friends with a Dutch hotel proprietor who knew his father and from him managed to scrounge many delicacies to supplement the dreary hospital fare of his charges.

After the war he studied anesthesiology for two years on a scholarship at Iowa State University. In 1950 he was team physician for the Austrian ski team at Aspen, Colorado, and in March 1951, he was asked to lecture on mountain rescue at the University of Boulder—to pass along the techniques and skills that had been developed for centuries in his native land. He also lectured on the same subject at the Air Force school for mountain rescue at Camp Carson, Colorado Springs. One of the officers who attended his lectures was a lieutenant colonel named Robert Rizon. You shall hear more about Rizon.

When the full extent of the disaster that had befallen the Walser Valley became known in Innsbruck on that January morning, Dr. Haid consulted immediately with his chief, Professor Burghard Breitner, director of the Department of Surgery at University Hospital and head of the Austrian Red Cross. "Professor Breitner instantly started to investigate the possibility of getting a helicopter into Blons," Dr. Haid told me. "There was no possibility of an airplane in the situation. He telephoned the United States Army Headquarters at Salzburg and asked for help." The appeal went direct to the Air Rescue group in Sembach, Germany, the commanding officer of which was Bob Rizon.

To the north the falling snow was swept by high winds as a Rescue pilot, Captain Bill K. Sayers, carefully flew a new-model helicopter he was ferrying from England toward his base at Fürstenfeldbruck, near Munich. The helicopter was a model "B" of the H-19 and there were several important modifications in it with which Bill was not yet too familiar. He felt a great sense of relief when he brought the chopper down on a snowbank at Fursty.

The base was closed down because of the blizzard. Nothing was moving. The helicopter was hauled off into a hangar and mechanics got to work on checking it out, a three-day process required for all newly arrived helicopters during which everything on it is tested and inspected. Bill, a sturdy young veteran of the Korean war, now half-dead with weariness, wondered how he was going to get home—snow had closed the road between the base and his quarters. Somebody found a weasel and Bill climbed in. A path was broken to his house. Bill took a hot bath and fell into bed. That was the night of Monday the eleventh.

The next day word about Blons came down from Bob Rizon to the Rescue squadron at Fursty. "The helicopter was still in inspection," Sayers said. "But the man in charge of maintenance, Master Sergeant Bill Tostanoski, and the aircraft inspector, Master Sergeant George Arndt, went to work fast. They headed up a crew of fifteen mechanics and inspectors who worked without rest, all that day and night and part of the next day. I got out on Wednesday, in the first helicopter, the one I had brought from England."

Bill was off the ground at 1100. With him was his copilot, Lieutenant Harold Cooley, and two crew members, Staff Sergeant John Harwood, a mechanic, and Staff Sergeant John Lowe, a medical technician. "They told us to fly to Innsbruck and pick up some doctors and then fly them to Bludenz," Sayers said. "At that time I didn't think I was going to participate in Rescue work—I thought we were just flying the doctors in. The weather was horrible all the way. We were down in the deep valleys of the Alps. I flew down to Rosenheim and up the valley to Innsbruck. It was snowing terrifically, with a low ceiling. The visibility was about half a mile.

"We had to fly right on the treetops. There were lots of high telephone wires across the valleys. We had to duck under them or over them. The whole thing was nip and tuck. When you're cruising along you can't see but just a few hundred yards and you are going sixty or seventy knots. If something should happen up ahead you're in real trouble. When we got to Innsbruck they had to stamp the snow out—a square about ten or twelve feet—so we could land."

Dr. Haid spent that morning with his colleague, Dr. Wolfgang Baumgartner, and with Professor Breitner, discussing every possible way to help the people in the Grosses Walsertal and assembling what they would need. "I remember thinking at the time how they use sticks to look for people under the snow," Haid said. "They poke them down wherever the snow is deep. I had an idea of linking together hollow tubes to shoot oxygen under the snow to trapped people. We tried to think of all kinds of things.

"Then we heard the helicopter was on its way. We went out to the airfield in an ambulance with equipment for surgery and resuscitation. We also took two dog leaders and two avalanche dogs. These dogs are trained by special men to find human beings under the snow. They train them in the early wintertime up at the mountain huts. They bury somebody under the snow and let the dog find the person. They then pet the dog and feed him.

"One of the dogs was a *riesen schnauzer,* a giant schnauzer. The other was a *schaefer hund,* a shepherd dog. We were all waiting when the helicopter came in about one-thirty. I think it was the first time I ever saw this kind of helicopter. It looked to me like a giant bumblebee. Then Captain Sayers and Lieutenant Cooley climbed down from the cockpit."

Professor Breitner, a tall, white-haired man with a very distinguished appearance, listened with sparkling eyes as Dr. Haid was speaking to me. Now he interrupted, pounding his fist excitedly on his desk. "I have only one impression. They came here not to ask questions, not to speak, but to *do!* The only thing they asked was: 'Who is coming with us?' Not 'Can we get there?' but 'Who is coming with us?'

"And when we told them two doctors and two dogs and two trainers they said: 'It can be done.' And they started to throw out all their luggage. They were in such a hurry! Not 'Where can we store this?' but 'Out it comes!' And then they said they would have to leave their two enlisted men here because of the weight crossing the pass. And off they went! What an impression—work! work! And for our poorest people. Not for a rich and famous person, but for our poorest, poorest people."

Sergeant Lowe, a Negro raised in the British West Indies, briefed Dr. Haid on how to use the intercommunication system in the helicopter so that Haid, riding in the cabin, could speak to Sayers while in flight. "After we took off we kept the cabin door open and I navigated," Haid said. "Although I know the area very well I noticed it was not so easy to say at any place exactly where you were. We saw where we had been but not where we were going. At one place we had to turn around because we went up a wrong valley."

The two dogs became restive in the small cabin and the trainers had difficulty controlling them.

Sayers: "We had to cross this 6,000-foot St. Christoph's Pass. When we got up there the valley got so narrow that we couldn't have turned around in case we couldn't get over the pass. We didn't know whether we could make it or not. It was snowing all the time and there was a strong wind.

"We finally got over the top. When we hit the top we hit an extreme amount of turbulence. We thought we lost control completely for a while. On the way down from the top of the pass we saw a snow slide where it took out a railroad station and a train and everything and killed six people. Later on we went in there and helped evacuate."

Haid: "We arrived at Bludenz where we were supposed to

land. There were about 200 people at the railroad station there, pointing toward Ludesch, which was closer to Blons."

Sayers: "When we got to Ludesch, about four o'clock in the afternoon, they marked a place for us to land. And we set down."

The equipment for surgery and resuscitation was taken out at Ludesch, loaded in a small truck, and rushed off to Bludenz with Dr. Baumgartner, who set up shop in the small hospital there. A couple of Austrian rescue experts climbed into the cabin of the helicopter and Sayers took off again for Blons.

Sayers: "We flew up the valley with the help of an Austrian map that cost twenty cents and showed the mountains. It was far better for our purpose than our own flight map. We got about a mile and a half in the mouth of the Walsertal. There was a kind of three-cornered place there. Blons sets in a corner. We had to approach it from one side, against the wind."

Haid: "On the way up we saw on top of the hills where the snow broke away deep, deep crevasses. People were digging everywhere. There were ruins of houses—just parts of them above the snow. It was a complete scene of desolation and catastrophe. When they saw the helicopter coming they waved and directed us toward Blons. And when we first saw Blons it looked like the hand of God—or the Devil—had swept down across the mountain and the valley."

Sayers: "When we went in the whole town had been wiped out. The only possible place to land was where there had been a building and part of the floor was still there. But I couldn't really land there—I couldn't get on the platform because the hill rose too steeply in front of it and my rotors would have hit the ground in front."

And so Bill Sayers, at the controls of a helicopter that was still largely unfamiliar to him, set down on the edge of the floor of the ruined house with his two *front* wheels and the two rear wheels *off the ground*, and he held the helicopter in a hover in that position against a maddening wind that smote the aircraft as though in anger at its defying the destruction of the elements.

"I had the feeling," said Dr. Haid, "as if a swallow had set down at its nest. The rotors were two feet from the hillside." The dogs and their trainers and the Austrian rescue experts and the remaining equipment were off-loaded and then the first patient was taken aboard. She was Maria Tuertscher.

Haid: "She had a displacement of the seventh vertebra at the neck. We had to move her very carefully so she would not get paralyzed and be unable to breathe. We put others in the helicopter, a girl who was frozen up to her waist, she was black all the way to her waist, and there was another woman. And all the time we all kept watching the mountainside and we wondered whether the sound vibrations from the helicopter would start a new avalanche."

While they loaded on the patients Bill Sayers watched the hover and Cooley, who, as it happened, was fresh out of helicopter school and on his first mission, watched the instruments. And when there were as many persons aboard as the helicopter could carry Bill made his take off—by just falling off the side of the hill and then backing away.

Sayers brought his patients to Ludesch where they were moved on to Bludenz and put under the care of Dr. Baumgartner. Sayers got some more gasoline from a representative of the Swiss Red Cross, loaded his helicopter with more rescue experts, and returned to Blons. In all, that first night, during constant snowfall, he made three round trips, bringing in volunteers and carrying out patients, four or five each time. The last trip was made in almost total darkness. Each time he set down in Blons on just two front wheels.

Sayers: "We have a landing light that shines on a fixed spot and we have a searchlight that you can swing in a 360-degree arc. You can go into a place at maybe ten or fifteen miles an hour and check for wires and posts and trees. We tried usually to cruise between twenty-five and thirty knots, but it varied. If I got into a tight spot I would slow down. Dr. Haid flew with me and he loaded and unloaded patients and then between trips, whenever he got free time, he would run up to the hospital in Bludenz and treat people. After the last trip we couldn't make it any more that night. They gave us a hot dinner—wiener schnitzel, I think—and they gave us a place to sleep. They were extremely nice. They wouldn't let us pay for anything, room or food."

But Bill wouldn't permit himself the luxury of sleep, not just yet, although he had flown that day from Fürstenfeldbruck to Innsbruck to Ludesch and then three times back and forth in the snow-swept Walsertal. He drove over to the hospital in Bludenz and asked Dr. Baumgartner what additional medical supplies he needed and then he telephoned his commanding officer, Major Edward J. Ontko, up at Fursty, and he told him how bad it was and what Haid and Baumgartner had to have.

At Fürstenfeldbruck maintenance men were working tirelessly getting other newly arrived helicopters in commission. Ontko went out to the hangars and urged them to work even harder, and then he called Bob Rizon at Sembach. He related the facts that Sayers had given him and Rizon, a full colonel now, immediately turned over almost the entire facilities of his group to the suffering people in the Grosses Walsertal. The group surgeon, Major Rufus Hessberg, took off from Sembach the next morning and went to Fürstenfeldbruck to get together the supplies Sayers had pleaded for.

A word about Doc Hessberg. He is a deceptive-looking little man. He is quiet, small, hardly ever speaks above a whisper. As I mentioned earlier in this book he is a jumper and has helped develop many new types of chutes now in use, always trying them out himself first. In the 1949 blizzard in the United States he flew day and night in temperatures reaching twenty-six below zero in the memorable Operation Snowbound, bringing medicines and food to people isolated in the Midwest. In February 1953 he worked indefatigably with Bob Rizon in flood-ravaged Holland. Later in the year 1954 he jumped into the mountains of Italy when a C-47 crashed there, killing twenty-one Air Force boys.

As soon as he landed at Fürstenfeldbruck he set to work with para-rescue personnel and the base hospital commander collecting the medical equipment and supplies—plasma, bandages, antibiotics. By four o'clock the next morning he had everything loaded on a plane and a couple of hours later he took off for Austria.

He arrived at Ludesch about the same time Bob Rizon pulled in from Sembach. There was time for only the briefest greetings between Dr. Haid and Rizon, and then Haid filled in Hessberg on the medical situation and Bill Sayers gave Rizon the Rescue picture. And then the four of them piled into Sayers' chopper and went up to Blons. When Rizon saw how dangerous was the flight into "Death Valley" he issued an order: no helicopter pilot was to make the trip up the Walsertal without going first with a pilot who had already been there.

Sayers and Cooley split up and checked out two pilots who came down later that day, and when the new arrivals had their initiation they in turn checked out others. And then Rizon set up a shuttle with his fleet of helicopters, taking in Red Cross workers, Austrian rescue experts, and food, bringing out the sick, frozen, and maimed.

During the day Haid and Hessberg flew with the choppers, gave first aid on the spot in the valley, loaded the seriously injured and frostbitten aboard the aircraft and delivered them to Baumgartner. At night, when the flights had to stop, Haid and Hessberg went to the hospital and worked there until the small hours of the morning—the former Austrian Army doctor and the American Air Force doctor laboring side by side to make whole the broken and gangrenous bodies of the people from the Walsertal Valley. For a four-day period neither Haid nor Hessberg nor Baumgartner got more than three hours' sleep a night. And the avalanche was not the only emergency.

Hessberg: "In the midst of all this we got an SOS call for a *maternity* case up another valley. The local doctor who called Bruno said it was a matter of life and death. One of the chopper pilots resting between trips to the Walsertal offered to take Bruno up to this other valley. The doctor who had called in was not at the place where he was supposed to meet Bruno. Night was falling and the helicopter had to return.

"Bruno remained up the valley. When the chopper returned for him the next day he had not one but *two* women —both pregnant with complications. They were brought to the hospital and on top of everything else Dr. Haid delivered the two babies."

Now that the other helicopters were making the round trip to Blons, Sayers and Cooley began to probe deeper into the Walsertal, to the remote villages, Sonntag, Buchboden, Fontanello, seeking out people who needed help. They were almost booby-trapped.

Sayers: "The valley itself is extremely narrow, much narrower than the section below Blons. They have cables strung across it where they go up and cut hay and let it slide across the cables.

"I was driving through there the first time and it was snowing and visibility was very poor and I came to one of these cables. It was about a thousand feet above the bottom of the valley. I threw the plane into a quick stop and started falling straight down on auto-rotation. I thought I would go under it. I thought there was just one strand. But there was another cable about a hundred feet under the first one and a third just under that and a fourth under that. Just like a wall. I got down to the bottom one and still had to go down.

"I was about thirty or forty feet off the ground. I did not have much room from there. If I had hit one of those cables I wouldn't be here. The top one that I saw was almost in the clouds and I didn't know if there was any above that. I managed to slip under the bottom one and I had to be pretty careful going up the rest of the valley. They had cables strung across at different altitudes and you'd never see them until you were right on them and then you'd never know whether to try to go over them or under them. We were lucky."

And they saw how the hand that was either God's or the Devil's had smitten the entire length of the Grosses Walsertal. It was a white hell. Houses uprooted and tumbled over on their sides, some of them a mile or more from their foundations. The stream that coursed along the valley bed choked with bodies of human beings and animals. Solitary dark figures of men and women and dogs burrowing in the snow like moles seeking out those who had been engulfed and buried. And the sudden cessation of digging and the raising of heads and hands beseechingly as the helicopter passed slowly with its shadow dark on the sparkling snow, and then the hysterical rush when the aircraft came down.

Sayers: "People fought to get on the helicopter, and we were loaded up so much we were in danger in getting off the snow. People would just have to be pushed off."

For three days Sayers and Cooley flew up and down the length of the Walsertal, dodging cables in the continuing snow.

Sayers: "I guess we flew about forty or fifty round trips. All the villages were wiped out to a great extent. The people would stamp out in the snow what they needed and we would put it down and then bring them what they asked for. Some of them needed bread and they would stamp out 'brot.' Others wanted potatoes and others wanted meat. So many people wanted onions. They would ask specifically for onions. We would drop fifty-pound sacks out. I will never forget one place where we couldn't land and people had 'brot' stamped out and I picked up a big sack of bread and kicked it out the side. It fell right in the middle of the 'o' of the word 'brot.' And on each trip we would land somewhere and bring out the injured.

"One thing they kept talking about was the 'white death.' It is a complete lack of oxygen from these avalanches. It must be a vacuum because there is a white mist and they cannot breathe. Lots of people smothered without being under the snow. People kept muttering about it all the time.

"I didn't have any trouble with the helicopter until the second day and then it scared me half to death because I was on my way up the valley at a pretty low altitude and I was losing my fuel and oil pressure. I thought I was going to drop into that valley. There was no place to land and there was just this stream at the bottom.

"I just made it to the mouth of the valley when my fuel and oil pressure hit zero. But it turned out there was no trouble at all. It was just that my instrument had gone out but I didn't know it at the time. Remember, I was brand new to that airplane. I was just new to the airplane and I didn't know what was wrong.

"We got out at a place one day and walked into the church and they had all the people laid out there. All the dead. I think there were thirty dead adults and fifteen children. They had all the children on the pulpit. It was terrible.

"Another time we took one fellow out who had been pinned on top of a stove by the snowslide. The whole front of him was burned. The back of him was frozen. Burned on one side, frozen on the other! Dr. Haid told me how another fellow was buried while he was milking a cow. The avalanche came and hit him and he was buried under the snow in the hay with the cow for three days. He was real snug and warm and both of them were pulled out all right.

"I caught a terrific cold from tramping around in that snow. I had boots on but they got wet and never did get dry. Once in a while I got a stiff shot of cognac from Dr. Haid. I was as nervous as a cat. Toward the end of the day I would get tense and short-tempered. I would yell on the radio. It was a terrific strain.

"Then next to the last day they got in some more helicopters and Colonel Rizon told me to take a rest. He said I looked like I needed one. I remember it was raining then. I went over to the helicopter and climbed into it. It was leaking. I wrapped up in some blankets. One of the boys brought along a bottle of scotch. He said: 'You're not going to fly any more, take a drink.' "

Bill had himself a stiff shot and was just starting to warm up a little when Rizon came over and told him a new pilot had just arrived and had to be taken up the valley for his first trip. Bill said nothing about the drink. He threw off his blankets and told the newcomer to hop in, and he flew him to Blons.

Bill Sayers from Lubbock, Texas, told me of these things on a sunny afternoon in Sembach. He did not speak of the impact the Rescue operation had upon the people of Grosses Walsertal because Bill's mind doesn't work that way. He did tell me the impact it had upon him. "You realize how completely cut off they were, these people. There was no way they could get in or out. I can't imagine what would have happened to them if we did not have helicopters. They were just about frozen to death and you could not get to them from the ground.

"This was my first major mission for Air Rescue. To me, it sold me on Air Rescue. I kept thinking that a few years ago these people would have blown me out of the sky and now we were saving their lives. It gives you a very funny feeling when you are risking your own life and the lives of your crew." Bill paused. His forehead wrinkled. "I would do it again."

During the entire operation there was only one serious helicopter accident. It was the time when Major Ontko was flying Doc Hessberg into Blons to pick up some more survivors. Hessberg: "We came in once and because of a tricky wind we had to go around again in emergency flight. In the second approach for a landing we sheared off the tail rudder shaft."

The tail rudder shaft is what operates the rotor on the rear of the helicopter and that rotor is what keeps the chopper from spinning in circles. With it out of commission Ontko struggled with his controls and kept the aircraft aloft although it turned around and around, faster and faster. He dropped it as gently as he could, revolving like a whirling dervish, in deep snow on a steep incline. The men inside sat there for a little while waiting to see whether the chopper was going to slide down, then they cautiously crept out.

Hessberg: "We were not sick from the spinning. We were more scared. But we almost did get sick when we got out. Just about fifty feet from where we had set down there was a sheer drop of about fifteen hundred feet—straight down."

Major Ontko's comment later was this: "We set a lot of records on this mission and we almost set another. If we'd hit about twenty yards farther down we'd have become the biggest snowball ever seen in Austria."

By Saturday, the sixteenth of January, Austrian ground rescue workers broke a trail through to Blons and some two thousand ski-borne volunteers poured into the valley and shuttling by air no longer was necessary. Bob Rizon's gang were able to leave for their bases in Germany, leaving behind them as a memento a helicopter crashed into the side of a hill. They also left behind a memory.

The number of men and women and children close to death who were brought out of the Grosses Walsertal by helicopter ran well into the hundreds—Bill Sayers alone brought out between seventy and eighty persons. Rescue workers with equipment and dogs were brought into the valley by the same helicopters—which also hauled in almost four tons of food, giving life to people, many of whom quite possibly would have starved to death before succor could reach them on the ground.

A year and a half later, on a beautiful Saturday in June,

Bill Sayers and I flew down from Sembach to Innsbruck. We were met at the airport by Dr. Haid. We visited for a little while with Professor Breitner at the University Hospital and they told me many of the things you have just read. And then Bill and I got into Dr. Haid's little car and we drove almost a hundred miles, over St. Christoph's Pass, to the village of Blons. It was the first time since the avalanche that Bill Sayers had gone back to the people who exist, in a certain degree, due to him.

Word had gone ahead that the American helicopter pilot was coming to visit them and when we arrived the people of Blons and of other communities up the valleys were gathered in front of the church. They were scrubbed clean and they wore their best clothes and as Dr. Haid stopped the car and Bill got out they walked slowly toward him, their faces radiant. Bill began to look uncomfortable.

They stopped a few feet from him and just looked at him, and then a plump woman rushed up to him, paused, and reached out and touched him slowly on the face. "Do you remember me?" she asked. "I am Frau Schiebel." Her eyes filled with tears. She smoothed her green dress. "That morning, do you not remember?"

Maria Tuertscher spoke: "I was the one with the neck injury."

Another woman, in her early thirties, her blond hair braided elaborately over her ears, cried out: "I am Annamarie Metzler. Do you not remember me?" At Frau Metzler's side was her husband, Hermann, a soldier in the German Army during the war. He shifted self-consciously and then he straightened and raised his hand in salute to Captain Sayers. Frau Metzler seized Bill's hand and pressed it to her bosom and began to talk rapidly. Dr. Haid translated her words.

"How I remember! I was five months with child at the time. I was working so hard those days and nights and I didn't get anything to eat and I could not stand any more to see all the people getting hurt around me and some of them dying in front of me. I broke down, and I had the feeling it was the end of my life and I lay there for days almost out of my mind. Then they told me that an American helicopter is coming to fly me away. I was never in a helicopter before.

"I remember how they put me in Captain Sayers' helicopter and I was crying for my children and how Captain Sayers would not leave until they found the children and put them in the cabin with me. And then Captain Sayers took us out—to think he did it, without knowing any of us, or the danger of the area! How dangerous it was for him!

"I know he rescued me risking his own life. I thank my life and good health only to him. A rescue group in an air force is almost a holy thing. It was only through their help so many people were saved."

Now all the people pressed closer to Bill Sayers, all talking at once, Dr. Haid trying to translate what everybody was saying as they reminded Bill of the things he had done for them. The burgomaster of Blons, Herr Josef Bischof, spoke a few words in the name of his people, and Bill got redder and redder, and he ran his fingers around his collar. When Herr Bischof was finished Bill said to Dr. Haid: "Tell them I'd like to see how they are rebuilding their village."

When Dr. Haid translated this the people swept Bill away, struggling to get close to him, to be nearest to him, to touch some part of his clothing, and they led him around Blons and showed him the new homes and barns that had been built and were being built.

Bruno Haid bit his lip and lowered his eyes. Herr Bischof shook his head slowly. "They will never forget him. This was our greatest avalanche since the one of 1670. They will not talk of that one any more but of the one of 1954. We have never been able to find out how many lives were lost. In Blons alone it was well over a hundred—dead and missing. We still find bodies. But we do not think of the dead, only of those who were given back to us by men like Captain Sayers and the others who came after him."

Late that night we drove back through the mountains to the little town of Oetz where Bruno Haid was born. Although it was well after three o'clock in the morning Dr. Haid's father was waiting for us in the Drei Mohren and he led us to the dining room. A table was laden with a cold buffet and bottles of rare Austrian wine from Herr Haid's private stock. We lingered until after dawn that Sunday morning. The Oetz church bell began to toll slowly.

Bruno Haid stared at his glass. "You saw them in Blons, the way they feel, even now, after all this time. But you should have seen them then. I had the opportunity to listen closely to them.

"I saw people crying in gratitude and happiness when your people brought in injured relatives whom they thought were dead. And they knew this was not for money or for reward, even not for the expectation of gratitude."

Dr. Haid looked up. "Today you have seen for yourself. I do not have anything to add, except that on that day when your people left, I wept when I said farewell to Colonel Rizon and Dr. Hessberg and Captain Sayers. I never experienced such generosity as this was."

"Sir Robert . . ."

The blue United States Air Force sedan drew up in front of the Royal Netherlands embassy on Koblenzerstrasse, 96, in Bonn, the capital of West Germany. A tall, striking-looking Air Force officer wearing the eagles of a colonel on the shoulders of his summer uniform stepped out of the car. He was followed by his beautiful young wife. The two of them entered the austere brown building.

Inside, the Netherlands Ambassador to Bonn, His Excellency, Arnold Theodore Lamping, greeted them warmly. And then Ambassador Lamping performed a solemn rite: in the name of Her Majesty Juliana, Queen of the Netherlands and Princess of Oranje-Nassau, he invested Colonel Robert Lewis Rizon with the Queen's Order of Knighthood of the Oranje-Nassau with Swords, in the grade of Commander.

As he hung the brilliant blue-and-white medal around Bob Rizon's neck, the Ambassador said very slowly in English: "This award is in token of Her Majesty's gratitude for your assistance in the darkest hour ever experienced outside of the war in Holland."

The "darkest hour" to which the Ambassador referred were the 1953 floods, the worst in almost a thousand years of Dutch history. Nearly two thousand men, women, and children perished—from drowning, exposure, disease, and injuries. The whole civilized world responded immediately to the cataclysm that struck the tiny lowland country. The entire United States Air Rescue effort, which included aircraft from the Air Force, Army, and Navy, was placed under the direction of Bob Rizon.

The most important factor was the speed with which the Rescue planes, from England and Germany, responded, according to Dr. Willem Drees, the Netherlands Prime Minister. "We were very grateful for the immediate help," Dr. Drees told me. "Certainly it saved many lives. Casualties would have been much higher if help had not come that way. The people of the United States were ready to help in any way. They asked: 'What can we do?' But it was so important that the *immediate* help was made by the Air Rescue Service. They came so quickly—the people of Holland will never forget."

The fliers, who themselves went sleepless, who existed on field rations and lived in tents that could barely be warmed against the bitter cold, who flew in the freezing weather and snow and wind—weather that was so bad that again and again they were forced down in mid-flight and had to wait out a gale or sudden blizzard—left their impression not only upon those who were directly affected and who could witness their actions with their own eyes but also upon those more fortunate Dutch men and women who escaped the unprecedented invasion of the sea.

Among those men Bob Rizon was just one man. His was the responsibility for putting it all together and making it work, for seeing that the most was gotten out of what he had to work with, for keeping duplication, waste, and confusion, all inherent in such times of chaos, to a minimum. But he was no more than any other airman who kicked a bundle of food out of a chopper, or who went down on a hoist to pick up a child from a piece of floating debris, or who worked through the night in bitter cold so that an aircraft could fly again the next day. Rizon will argue that he was less. And feeling that way and because he is a man of modesty with a high sense of duty, he accepted the decoration and the rare honor that went with it not for himself but for all his men. And the gang that did the job, by then scattered all over the world, knew that no one was more qualified than Bob Rizon to hold the award in trust for all of them.

For many years now throughout the Air Rescue Service, which is a close-knit affair, a kind of inner brotherhood within the Air Force, Bob Rizon has been known as "Mr. Air Rescue."

There are some towering names in the ARS: Colonel Richard T. Kight, whose dream it was originally and who carried that dream through to fruition with messianic passion; Brigadier General Thomas Jefferson Du Bose, who took over where Dick Kight left off and with driving force and energy developed Rescue to its present efficiency; Colonel Lloyd H. Humphreys, Colonel Theodore Tatum, the Korean hero, others, the pioneers, the builders of Rescue.

But with the exception of Lloyd Humphreys, who is Tommy Du Bose's chief of staff, Bob Rizon was in the Rescue business longer than anybody else. And he had it in his head and in his heart long before there was a Rescue business. The monkey climbed on his back before the service ever was invented and it has never climbed off. His career, his thinking, his experiences all over the world might be said to concentrate in one man the whole concept and history of Rescue. His friends rib him and call him "Sir Robert" because of the Dutch knighthood, and Bob's big grin has to get him out of that when it pops up. But no matter what titles and honors they hang on his wide shoulders and no matter whatever else he may do in the Air Force or anywhere else, he always will remain Mr. Air Rescue.

Bob Rizon started flying airplanes when he was thirteen years old. He started jumping from airplanes at the same time. It began in 1924 when Bob was twelve. He was going to Los Angeles Junior High School at the time and a neighbor, Howard Kimbal, bought a wrecked "Jenny" and tinkered at rebuilding it in his garage. On his way home from school one afternoon Bob stopped to watch. A strange, new excitement filled the boy. He asked Kimbal if he could help. Kimbal said sure.

"From then on I went over after school and on weekends and helped him fix it up," Bob said. "After a year we finally patched the thing together and we made our first flight. As a reward for my assistance he taught me how to fly." Without a license and just past his thirteenth birthday, Bob hedgehopped over the fields of southern California, despite the natural objections of his parents, Homer and Cladie.

"My mother always knew when I was flying because I had goggles and a helmet. She would go to my room and see they were missing and then she knew I was in the air. That was bad enough, but then she found I was making jumps as well. I knew she was violently opposed to my flying and in those days I guess she was right. When she found out I was doing parachute jumps she would try to find out where, and then she would call the police department and have them come down.

"There was an old movie stunt man named Herbert McClellan. His hobby was parachute jumping. Youngsters would take his homemade parachutes and jump and he would go around and take up a collection and we would split the money. With that money I used to pay for my flying time. Flying in a Jenny was around twenty-four dollars an hour. That was an awful lot of money. Normally a fifteen-minute flight was a good, long flight. I think we would get as high as fifteen dollars for an exhibition parachute jump."

The technique was slightly different from that used today. The homemade chutes were strapped to the wings of the plane. "It was in a package. A shroud line would hang out of the package. You would climb out on the wing, attach the package to your harness, straddle, and then jump out backwards. We called it the 'push-off.' "

Bob made more than thirty jumps in that fashion before he was fifteen. Then in 1928 he decided he wanted to make a career out of flying and the most logical place for that, it seemed to him, was the Army Air Corps. He added a couple of years to his age and enlisted. When his parents saw him in uniform they abandoned the struggle and gave their consent. He was sent to Nichols Field in the Philippines.

In a way he was a kind of problem child. He was not yet sixteen. He was rated officially as a private first class and first class air mechanic. But he also had about two hundred hours of flying time, which was a lot of time then for anybody. It made for rather uncomfortable relations with bright young second lieutenants fresh from flying school.

There was the time, for example, a few months after he got to Nichols, when he was flying as crew chief in a Douglas C-1C, a transport with an open cockpit and a cabin that seated ten. The flight from Clark Field to Nichols and there were some very important persons aboard, including Henry L Stimson, who was then serving as governor general of the Philippines.

"The C-1C had several gas tanks and when you switched from one to the other you had to use the wobble pump—the old name for the fuel pump—to maintain the prime. I was flying with a smart young pilot. I had placarded the instrument panel with a warning that you had to use this wobble pump. We were about two thousand feet over the Philippine jungle when this pilot reached down and switched the tanks. The wobble was on the pilot's side. The engine quit. We were headed no place but down."

Bob ripped off his safety belt and dived for the pump. The plane was just about two hundred feet over the treetops when the engine caught. "When we landed at Nichols after this little incident this young second lieutenant stood me in a brace and read me the riot act about interfering with the duties of a pilot. He said he had known what he was doing all the time. He was very, very embarrassed. He said he was going to take disciplinary action against me."

When the pilot cooled off a little, however, he decided it might be better not to bring up the subject at all. Rizon never heard any more about it—but he thought of that near-fatal moment many times afterward, particularly as he followed the subsequent career of Mr. Stimson, who became President Hoover's Secretary of State and then Secretary of War under Presidents Roosevelt and Truman. And that experience, being in a helpless plane that was plunging into a dense jungle, did something else to him. It was then that the little monkey took its perch on his shoulders.

"The idea of crashing and getting lost and the fact that there were no facilities for rescue stuck in my mind. I kept thinking how hopeless it would be—even if you survived the crash. In those days if you went down in the jungle you were gone. The jungle is a terrible, terrible thing. It's easier to cut through a wall with a penknife than to cut through some parts of the jungle. In many of our experiences since then we have had to take native cutters and just cut a tunnel through the undergrowth—and then a few days later we would have to recut to get back."

Soon after that Rizon had another kind of experience in a Loening amphibian, the first plane of that type the Air Corps had. "We were towing targets for a coast artillery unit stationed at Corregidor. One day they put a 37-mm. shell right through the engine and we went down into Manila Bay. We were rescued by a launch. The airplane did not sink." That was the thing that stuck: the amphibian did not sink. If it had been a conventional plane, the chances for survival would have been almost nil. The need for rescue, the need for planes that would stay afloat—these things Rizon never forgot.

In 1930 Rizon returned from the Philippines and was assigned to the 11th Heavy Bombardment Squadron at Rockwell Field in California, the outfit in which George McManus, creator of "Jiggs and Maggie," had served during World War I and for which he had drawn the insigne. The base commander at Rockwell at the time was a lieutenant colonel named Henry H. Arnold.

"We had Curtis B-2 bombers, Keystone LB-5's and LB-7's. We had a dawn patrol of three old De Havillands and my job was crewing the De Havillands. I worked on the ground and flew also. The crew chief at that time maintained and flew with his airplane."

Over the long water flights the thought of how helpless fliers were if they crashed kept nagging at him. "Our only source of rescue there was an old crash boat. It was an old boat in which we had installed a Liberty engine. It took quite a long time to get to the scene of a ditching out in the Pacific or in the waterways in San Diego."

And then one day the need for organized rescue suddenly ceased to be an abstract thought and was brought home with sickening reality. "When I was in the Philippines, thank God I had some wonderful guidance from some of the people assigned to the unit. One in particular was a sergeant named Robert G. Blunden. He realized how young I was, I guess, and he used to talk to me quite often, just like a father.

He rotated a year before I did and was sent to Panama and he went out of his way to stop off and see my parents and assure them I was all right. That was the kind of man he was.

"Then after I was stationed at Rockwell I received word one day that he had been killed in an airplane accident. His plane crashed into the Atlantic. I'll never know, of course, but I have never stopped thinking that maybe if there had been a proper rescue outfit at Panama at the time Bob Blunden might have been saved."

In 1931, his three-year tour up, Rizon was discharged and for the next eight years he flew commercially. For a time he ran his own charter service out of Monrovia, California. "I always wondered what would happen if we had to go down in the mountains. In the early days of aviation when we flew from one cow pasture to another you never made a flight of over sixty miles that you did not have a forced landing. I would always look out the side or the rear of the airplane for a place to put the plane down. You just flew from one forced landing to another—we took them as a matter of course."

With the outbreak of World War II in 1939 Bob joined the Clayton Knight Committee, ferrying Lockheed bombers across the Atlantic. He made two such flights and when the project was dissolved and was taken over by the Royal Air Force he went back into uniform—a Canadian uniform. "I took a commission in the RCAF as a flying officer, the equivalent of our first lieutenant. I was assigned to the Coast Patrol Squadron at Patricia Bay. It was there that I began to have some real experience with flying boats. Our mission was to escort British troopships en route to Hong Kong to the maximum range of our aircraft and to patrol the western Canadian coast to the tip of Alaska for submarines."

And one day the monkey reached over and pinched his ear. "I was flying a Stranier bomber, a twin-engine biplane on a subpatrol mission. We had a crew of thirteen. Shortly after becoming airborne, at approximately two thousand feet, I lost power out of my port engine. I looked out. The engine was in flames. I tried all the normal emergency procedures to extinguish the blaze but nothing helped. I realized that in a few minutes the airplane might explode. It had linen wings and I knew they would just burn completely. We were about fifteen miles out over the Pacific. I radioed my distressed condition back to the base and started bailing out the crew."

When he believed everyone was out he left his seat and made ready to jump—and then he saw that the engineer was still aboard and that the man had apparently lost his head and had failed to put on his chute. By then the aircraft had lost too much altitude and there was not enough time for the man to get rigged up. Rizon ran back to the cockpit and got into his seat again and brought the plane down on the water with the power he had in the remaining engine. Upon impact the upper and lower wings exploded and tore themselves off.

"We were trapped. The plane was due to blow up any minute and we would never be able to swim far enough away in time. I told the engineer to get a sea bucket and got down on the spray fins and filled the bucket with water. We kept throwing the water on the engine and by the grace of God we put it out. The metal part of the plane was quite hot and when the salt water hit it it would make steam and the steam smothered the fire.

"Then we just sat there and waited and wondered how long what was left of the plane would float. There was another flying boat that came out but it couldn't do any good. He kept passing around in wide circles. I thought how useful it would be if he could have been trained to land in the open sea.

"A crash boat finally came along and picked us all up. They gave us a shot of rum and then brought us back to the base. I was met by the base commander, Johnny Plant—he later became deputy commander of Allied Air Forces in Central Europe—and his comment to me was: 'That was a nice job, Rizon. I'm going to make you base fire marshal.' "

Plant's comment for the records was something else. For his actions that day in keeping the flaming plane aloft until his crew were out, and for returning to the cockpit to remain with the plane when he saw the engineer could not jump, Flying Officer Rizon was awarded the British Air Force Cross, the first American, it was said, ever to receive that decoration. The medal was presented to him personally by the governor general of Canada and his wife, the Earl of Athlone and Princess Alice. The pattern was taking shape now. The monkey was beginning to grin, a little smugly.

"We had many, many little fishing villages, lumber camps, and Indian villages on up the coast of British Columbia where we would cache supplies and gasoline and go in for refueling. As a result we became well acquainted with a lot of the fishermen, lumbermen, and Indians, and of course we depended upon them on many occasions for weather reports. They would send us these reports through little amateur radio setups. That was early in 1940, prior to the establishment of the big land and seaplane bases that they have now.

"We were quite frequently called in to evacuate a miner or an Indian or a fisherman who was seriously injured. It added a new dimension to rescue for me—the civilian, the man who is in bad trouble and only an airplane can get him to where he can be helped properly and only too often the only airplane around is a military plane. I'll never forget the faces of some of those people when we came down to get them.

"We had many unusual experiences getting back into those little isolated places and picking up the injured and getting them back to the Queen Charlotte Islands or even back to Vancouver. But it was not organized. We did it when we could, but it was always by chance and by luck and there was no system. There was no search and rescue facility as such.

"And as far as we were concerned, the military pilots, the amount of flying we had to do over water gave us a lot to think about, too. We were always concerned as to what would happen should we go down. I know that when I was on coast patrol in conventional-type aircraft I expended a lot of time wondering what would happen if I had to ditch.

"I was completely unfamiliar with any aspect of the sea. I didn't know what was going on. Like many other conventional airplane pilots I didn't have any idea of what I would do. I am quite certain that if I had been required to ditch I would have done everything exactly the opposite of what should have been done. My point is that I spent a lot of time worrying and fretting about just that—and not devoting myself to the mission at hand. When I started flying seaplanes those worries just never occurred to me. The mental hazard was completely relieved."

In 1941 Air Marshal Lloyd Samuel Breadner, chief of the RCAF, appointed Rizon his personal pilot, no small honor in any case and a distinct compliment in this instance since Rizon was an American. Rizon spent the year flying Breadner and other high British and Canadian military and political officials around the Dominion. As he droned for hours over the vast forests and spectacular mountains it was borne upon him more and more how helpless they would be if they were forced down. The sky would soon be black with search planes—but they would be searching without coordinated system, without designated plan, almost impromptu.

He was in his quarters on a Sunday in December mulling over these ideas which had become an obsesssion with him when he learned of the Japanese attack on Pearl Harbor. Flight Lieutenant Rizon changed his uniform as rapidly as he could and became Captain Rizon. Since he had long civilian and military experience with multi-engined aircraft he was sent to the four-engine school at Sebring, Florida, checked out in the B-17, and then assigned to Hobbs Air Force Base, New Mexico, as an instructor. It appeared now that all thoughts about the rescue thing would have to be helved in favor of the more immediate job of fighting a war.

Henry H. Arnold now was boss of the Army Air Corps and on one of his trips to the United Kingdom he had seen omething that interested him keenly. Many RAF fliers and, as our own 8th Air Force built up in Great Britain many American fliers as well, were getting their bombers and ighters shot up over the Continent. Often they were able o keep their cripples airborne until they got over the English Channel where they ditched. The RAF had begun to develop a procedure for rescuing these men from the water and many a flier who had seemed destined for a prison camp or worse was soon back in the air again. General Arnold was deeply mpressed with the work of this rescue branch of the RAF and in 1944 he issued an order that a similar service be established in the Army Air Corps.

A rescue school was established at Keesler Field, Biloxi, Mississippi, and the record of every pilot in the Air Corps was screened to locate pilots with seaplane experience. By this time Rizon was director of flying training at Hobbs. Then, along with others, he was ordered down to Keesler. His own commanding officer at Hobbs protested, arguing, with some logic, that the training of B-17 crews was pretty important, too. It was resolved that Rizon would go down to Keesler for just a few days to check out some of the instructors there and then return to Hobbs and his duties there. He never returned to Hobbs. Rizon, a major now, was made commandant of the school at Keesler and for the next ten years he was in Air Rescue and nothing else. The monkey on his back relaxed, for good.

"The Rescue school consisted of an Air arm and a Marine arm. The Air arm at Keesler conducted training in the PBY, the Catalina. It consisted of 105 instructors and we would train an entire squadron at a time. It was a two months' course. When one squadron was fully trained we would equip them and they would go overseas. During the course of the war we trained seven full squadrons and 150 replacement crews for those squadrons. In the Marine arm we trained the crash-boat crews. We took over a yacht club at Gulfport and made it our crash-boat training school. After completion of training the crews went out into the various theaters of operation."

And now Bob Rizon had at last come into his own. Rescue —this personal thing that had pestered at him for so long, from the beginning in the Philippines, over jungle and forest and mountain—now was a reality. Ideas that had teased his mind for so long now could be tested and, if proven feasible developed. For example, working with the Higgins Ship building people in New Orleans, Rizon developed the air borne lifeboat, a thirty-foot affair that was attached to the bottom of a B-17 and dropped to survivors at sea.

To this day, more than a decade later, in a business where ten years is a lifetime and World War II is two wars away and its equipment obsolete, B-17's, now called SB-17's, the "S" meaning "Search," still carry these boats on over-water missions. Improved over the years, equipped with food and medicines and clothing and radios, they have saved countless lives all over the world.

In Gulfport at the time there was also a transition school for the new B-29's that were coming off the assembly lines. This school had nothing at all to do with the Rescue school, but as Rizon observed the men being trained to use the Super Fortress he could not rid himself of his memories of the old gnawing worries that had beset him when he had been flying land planes himself over water. He knew the B-29's were designed for the bombing of Japan and he knew there was going to be a lot of water between wherever they would take off and where they were going and water again on the long journey back. It was not difficult for him to know what must be going on in the minds of the men who were learning to fly the new aircraft.

"I asked to run a test of a hundred aircraft commanders to see what their reactions would be to ditching an airplane. And I studied Navy statistics and I found that the Navy was considerably more successful under the same circumstances than we were. Their ditched B-29 would float for two days. We would ditch one under the same conditions and it would sink in fifteen seconds.

"I felt a basic reason was that the Navy man had his training in water. I took the 100 B-29 pilots and gave them a very short orientation in the PBY. I would put them in the copilot's seat and go out over the water and tell them to land. Practically all would have killed themselves. The first thing they would think of was to get the nose down. Again, they didn't realize the various sea complexes and would land against a heavy running swell."

And so in addition to his own work at the school Rizon undertook the self-assumed task of communicating to these B-29 pilots some of the basic principles of making open-sea ditchings. There are no statistics, but it is reasonable to assume that of the stream of pilots who were given this instruction some of them found the knowledge invaluable in the months that followed when they made their long, lonely passages over the Pacific, welcomed by Japanese flak, and sent off with more of the same when they departed.

During the months he commanded the school at Keesler, Bob Rizon was a more or less contented man, even though he could not escape feeling twinges now and then as he saw his students take off for the various zones of combat, knowing that such overseas duty could not be for him. He managed to get out for an inspection of the first squadron he had trained and which was operating in the Mediterranean. He spent two months flying missions into Yugoslavia, picking up bomber crews who had bailed out or had forced landed. It was a rewarding two months. It was one thing to imagine it back on the Gulf of Mexico and another thing to see how well it worked where the shooting was.

And when the great conflict finally was at an end and the figures were assembled for the records, Major Robert Rizon could feel perhaps even a little more gladness. "The squadrons and the crash-boat crews that we trained during the life of the emergency rescue school rescued about six thousand men—Americans, our Allies, and in some cases enemies."

With the close of the war came the inevitable shrinkage of the armed services, and one of the first things to be eliminated was the Rescue school at Keesler. "They felt that we had trained enough squadrons and that it was not necessary to maintain a school strictly for that purpose. That was not my point of view. I envisioned that there would be vastly increased air travel after the war and there would be a much greater need for Rescue than ever."

But Major Rizon's voice was a very small voice, and the ax was swinging, and better-known enterprises than a little Rescue school in Mississippi were being chopped down. After all, nobody was getting shot at any more, so why Rescue? Bob Rizon had answers to that. Bullets were not the only things that brought aircraft down, and, as he said, there were going to be more planes than ever before, flying oceans they never had flown before the war, but in any branch of the military junior officers do not argue against policy, especially when it comes from the very top and it is formulated under the sacred name of economy.

Major Rizon made his reports, dissented in the cold, rigid military terminology, spoke strongly and passionately when he could, and then when the law was laid down, obeyed. But when the school went there was something that somehow stayed. Lost as it was in the greater dramatics of the war, when the stories were all of the destructions and kills, the idea of Rescue had left its mark on people who were a little higher up on the ladder than Bob Rizon.

He was overjoyed one day when he was ordered to gather together those men from the first squadron he had trained at Keesler who were still in uniform, and when he got them all in one piece again they were sent down to Panama. There they were given a name that they wore with very great pride: 1st Air Rescue Squadron. Its commander: Major Robert Rizon. The 1st has grown up now, as you have seen, and now is the 1st Air Rescue Group with three squadrons of its own. But it is still the 1st.

Other stray Rescue veterans were collected from here and there and were formed into small units that were not dignified with even the modest name of squadrons. They were called detachments, which meant they were pieces of squadrons. They were stuck in airbases all over the United States wherever there was any spare room and were fastened onto other organizations like warts. Nobody knew what they would ever be any good for and with the cutbacks all up and down the line the military dollar had to be stretched until it snapped and a lot of intelligent people insisted in all sincerity that they were sheer waste—if you got to pay a salary to a pilot to let him fly a combat plane or even a transport, who the devil needs Rescue? For want of a better roof the Rescue men were all put under the Air Transport Command. Then, for the most part, they were quietly forgotten.

It was about at this point that Colonel Richard T. Kight walked on the scene, and that was a very happy thing for everybody, from the Rescue people all the way up to the wide world. There was Bob Rizon when there never was Rescue, and there was Dick Kight when Rescue was fallen apart, and there would be Tommy Du Bose when Rescue was breathing a little better and looked like it was going to live, after all.

Each time, by some incredible grace, it was exactly the right man—the right personality and mind and thinking and way of doing things. Americans who perhaps never heard about the Air Rescue Service before they read these pages might do well to offer a little sound of thanks to whatever they believe in for these three men. There are many Americans and many people all over the world who are not Americans, as you have seen, who have already done so.

In December of 1946 Dick Kight was named boss of the scattered Rescue units and he found out fast he was more in the position of executor of a bankrupt estate than he was in the position of military commander. Major General Gordon Saville, then deputy commander of the Air Transport Command, ordered Dick to take a good look at Rescue and if it was as useless and wasteful as many persons believed it to be, to put it out of business.

Kight went to his new office and got out the files to see what he had. He didn't have much. Some eight hundred officers and men divided up into one squadron and eleven detachments. For airplanes he had obsolete stuff that had long outlived its original purpose. It appeared that when anybody had anything anywhere he didn't want he shoved it over to Rescue, like old clothes to a poor relative.

He saw, too, that some of the brass at his West Palm Beach headquarters was somewhat less than top drawer. For just as a lot of old equipment had been dumped on Rescue so had been officers who had failed somehow to impress their superiors as fireballs. The idea seemed to be that if they had to stay in uniform they could do the least harm in Rescue which wasn't doing anything anyway.

"My first reaction was to wash it out," Dick told me. Dick Kight is a tall, thin man with the passion and strength of a dreamer of dreams. He is something of an anachronism, I guess. His proper uniform is chain mail and his natural habitat is the saddle of a charger, and whatever weapon he carries it is always really a lance. He never has hesitated to tilt at anything, including the swinging arms of windmills. Only to get that glow in his eyes he's got to believe.

From his point of view there was not much to believe in and being stuck in a back alley such as Rescue appeared for a career officer to be the kiss of death. But before he scrubbed Rescue out of existence he felt he had to make a survey not of paper but of people. He went out on a tour of his units. It began like hail and farewell. What he saw and heard was a revelation.

He found physical conditions as bad as he thought they would be. His boys were the orphans everywhere, the scrubs on the benches, the players who never were called into the game, always with secondary assignments, such as mess officer. They had nothing, no decent airplanes to fly—there was not in existence one single type airplane designed specifically for Rescue work. Wherever they were stationed they were looked down on by the hot-shot fly boys in their shiny new aircraft, and their wives had to do a lot of explaining and blushing when they got together with the other officers' wives. They were a kind of horse cavalry of the air, dealers in antiques.

But he also found that despite all this his Rescue kids owned a collective morale that was high and wide and screaming. They acted as if they had got hold of something big and fat and round and they were hugging it close as though they knew something nobody else in the world knew. It was a kind of religion.

There was a kid named Major Tom Thorne, who commanded the detachment at Selfridge Field, Michigan, a tall, good-looking, exuberant boy who took Kight into his pitiful shop and said cheerfully: "It's good—and it's getting better." There was Major James Keck, who ran the outfit at Hill Field, at Ogden, Utah, a short baby-faced officer who acted as though his moth-eaten warplanes were just fresh out of the factory, who talked all day and all night about Rescue. There were others, all over.

"I couldn't understand it," Kight said. "They were all ready to whip the world with nothing." It didn't make any sense at all until one day at the bar of an officers' club a young lieutenant said it: "Sir, I'd rather save people than kill them."

At that moment Kight got the religion, too. And it came to the right man, for as I have tried to explain, Dick Kight always wears an invisible plume. He hotfooted it back to West Palm Beach and the light in his eyes was blazing brighter than the sun over the palm trees. Kight had found his own mission in the Air Force.

The first thing he did was clean his own house and rid himself of the dead wood. He was in the midst of replacing eightballs with converts when he got a call one day from one of his commanders in the field: could the commander send a plane out to rescue a civilian who was in trouble? "What the hell do you have to ask me that for?" Kight asked. When the commander informed him there was an Air Force policy letter restricting Rescue activity to the military, Kight said: "Go ahead anyway."

Then he checked. He looked high and low but could find nothing that forbade in so many words military aircraft from being used to save the lives of civilians. It had never been forbidden because the question had never come up. That was only half good enough for Kight. The book didn't say no but it didn't say yes either. He sat down and rewrote the regulations so that they said yes, an emphatic yes. From that time on anybody who needed help, whether he wore a United States uniform or any other uniform or no uniform at all, would get that help if Rescue could deliver it.

Moreover, nobody out in the field had to ask through channels for permission—while maybe people died. Local commanders, wherever they were, were authorized to make the decision themselves—if they felt help was needed they could order the wheels to roll, on their own. As Kight enlarged upon this concept of Rescue he began to know he had something special in his hands, something so basically American—as he understood his country—that it sang. Something a little larger size than Air Rescue or even the Air Force itself: mercy for human beings in distress.

"And it makes practical sense, too," he said. "Rescue was an Air Force public instrument that would give the taxpayer a return for his money in time of peace. Flying all kinds of missions also was an excellent way of training our people. But most of all when people are in trouble and you can help you have to help. That's an ingrained part of American life. It's impossible not to do so."

Some of Kight's fervor stuck to his official reports that went up through the channels, even though those reports had to be phrased in the emotionless military language. The new face of Rescue was a revolutionary face, but it was bought, all up the line, up to and including the star-studded brass in the Pentagon. It was bought cautiously and with reservations but it was bought, as Kight saw it.

It was necessary, Kight next felt, to give Rescue a credo, something that would sum up the things he had heard from his kids in the field and had added to as his own concept had emerged. He worked out the following:

CODE OF AN AIR RESCUE MAN

It is my duty as a member of the Air Rescue Service to save life and to aid the injured.

I will be prepared at all times to perform my assigned duties quickly and efficiently, placing these duties before personal desires and comforts.

These things I do that others may live.

He printed those lines on cards and distributed them throughout the Rescue Service for his men to read and carry with them, and then he designed an emblem that would symbolize Rescue: a blue sky streaked with a golden ray of hope and on it an angel with his arms around the world. And on the bottom of the insigne the last line of the code: "That Others May Live."

"Americans get embarrassed when they talk of moral things," Kight said to me, embarrassed. "But even in the Crusades men had to have a banner." That statement, I submit, tells a lot about Rescue, and even more about Dick Kight.

And now Kight worked as a man possessed by a vision. He talked Rescue everywhere, in all military halls, and since he was a full colonel his words made a little more sound than those that Major Robert Rizon had shouted up his chimney. I should like to make it clear that there is no villain in this piece. Nobody had tried to fight Rizon and nobody was trying to fight Kight. It was a simple question of economics. The military theme was economy, more now than ever before, and even Strategic Air Command and Tactical Air Command were tightening belts.

Kight was still a small voice against the trumpeting of these giants and the missions of SAC and TAC were plain enough to be read out to any taxpayer: they had to have the money to be ready, in case. Rescue had yet to prove it was entitled to even a decimal point and half-a-dozen zeros and then a very small digit of the defense dollar.

It was nice to have St. Bernards flying around so they could pull a fisherman out of the Gulf of Mexico when his boat swamped, but after all that was a luxury, and the Air Force was eating low enough off the hog and was that really Air Force business anyway? As Dick Kight pleaded his case he got a series of big assists from his number-one pro in the field, Bob Rizon.

In the latter part of February 1947 the Mamoré River in Bolivia burst its banks and flooded the section of the country known as the Green Hell. Rizon flew down from Panama, across the Andes, to see what Rescue could do to help. "We landed at La Paz, which has an elevation of 14,000 feet, right next to Lake Titicaca, and picked up the American Ambassador to Bolivia, Joseph Flack, and some Bolivian officials, and flew over to Trinidad where the flood was at its worst. When we arrived we found that a 100-square-mile area was completely under water and all the small villages were washed away. The natives were living in trees and hollowed-out log boats."

Rizon landed the plane on a strip that was several inches under water and got out and looked around. The strip was on a rise, above the surrounding terrain, and he said he would gamble that it would not get any worse there and that if people were brought to that strip he could get planes in to take them out. They returned to La Paz and Rizon reported to the newly elected President of Bolivia, Enrique Hertzog, whose term had started only a few weeks before. Mr. Hertzog agreed the evacuations should be made.

The only kind of airplane available to Rizon that could get down on the short underwater strip was a C-47 and he radioed back to Panama asking for as many as could be spared. Eight of them landed in La Paz before dark. "We started the next morning. We would land on this little strip and when the plane was full of people we would fly to a village called Kochabomba, high in the Andes. To get there we had to go through one of the cordilleras at an elevation of 18,000 feet. The flight lasted only thirty-five minutes, but with the natives and children on board it was rather tricky."

To start with none of the natives had ever been in an airplane before and many of them got hysterical in the air. And then, as the planes climbed up more than three miles, they suffered from lack of oxygen, especially the children, and turned blue. The Rescue crews moved among them constantly with oxygen bottles, soothing their terror and helping them to breathe.

It was on this mission, incidentally, that Bob Rizon established a world's record for the number of passengers carried in a C-47. "When we landed we would be met by Bolivian Red Cross relief workers and they would take over our survivors and make a head count. One time it totaled ninety-seven." Bob grinned. "Of course about ninety of them were small babies, anywhere from three to seven months old."

In a period of five days Rizon and his men evacuated 2,300 natives from the submerged strip in Trinidad, and on return trips brought in fifteen tons of food for the people who remained, plus medical supplies, doctors, nurses, and volunteer workers. When the waters receded and Rizon returned to La Paz he was informed by President Hertzog that the first official act of his new administration was to award Rizon the highest decoration of the Republic of Bolivia —the Condor of the Andes, in the grade of Commander, equivalent to the United States Congressional Medal of Honor.

The award was presented in rather bizarre surroundings. "I was invested with this decoration in a palace that had just recently undergone the revolution that had put President Hertzog in power, and it gave me an unusual feeling to see all these bullet holes in the walls. I was told they had driven a Sherman tank right into the front of the palace and had cut loose with the machine guns. While waiting for the President to arrive for the investiture I was standing in the lobby and leaning against a beautiful marble-top table that had a large crack in the center of it and was chipped on one side. The officer who was conducting the ceremony told me it was the table the last president fell over when they shot him."

The effect of this Rescue operation, conducted by less than fifty men in eight airplanes, upon the Bolivian people and their government and the people of other South American countries, made a profound impression in Washington, not only in the Air Force and other military circles, but within the State Department as well. Men who had never heard of the Air Rescue Service before began to ask questions. And then less than three months later, while the beneficent political results of this mercy operation were still being analyzed by the experts, Rizon came up with something else.

On an evening in May of that year of 1947 a B-17 took off from Albrook Field in the Canal Zone for Kelly Field, Texas. A few hours later the number-two engine caught fire and sixteen men bailed out into the Nicaraguan jungle—a dense, uncharted area with trees that stuck up 200 feet in the air and there was no trail of any kind because a trail would last for perhaps half a day and then the growing things would take over again. By all the rules these men were goners, from injuries, from starvation, from aboriginal, hostile Indians.

Rizon went into action immediately, triggering off what was probably the largest-scale and most intensive peacetime search and rescue operation up to that time. Within *twelve* hours all but one of the survivors were located by the fifteen search planes Rizon sent out, and then there started six weeks of complicated and backbreaking effort to get them out of their jungle trap. "The men who had jumped out were not equipped at all," Rizon said. "In those days they still didn't understand the value of Rescue and as a result they had a very difficult time. They had little or no survival equipment, used incorrect emergency procedures in getting out of the aircraft, and were scattered all over the jungle."

Several chutes had been spotted near the village of Alamicamba, on the Prinzapolca River, about one hundred and seventy miles east of Managua. There were gold mines in the hills around Alamicamba and a 1,900-foot strip had been built near the village so the mines could be supplied. The strip, incidentally, was made out of ballast taken from the mines and was supposed to have some five million dollars' worth of gold dust in it. Rizon made the strip his advanced base.

A survey of the jungle convinced him that he was going to need more than conventional airplanes for the job and he sent a request to Dick Kight for some helicopters. Kight had three of them dismantled, loaded on cargo planes, and transported down from the States. Within thirty-six hours after the B-17 went down the choppers were in operation at Alamicamba. The jungle was too dense for the helicopters to get into the trees and pick up the survivors by hoist. Instead, Rizon used them to haul jungle-trained Army troops to places as close as possible to where the survivors were waiting. Then the ground parties hacked their way in and brought the men out to where the choppers waited to take them away.

After his years in the Philippines and Panama Rizon knew better than anyone else how important morale was to a man lost in the jungle—how he had to be convinced that help was on its way, how he had to will himself to remain alive. "We would keep an airplane over each survivor from dawn to dark. We would drop him camping equipment and radios —we even rigged it up for some of them to speak over the radios and the planes overhead would relay their voices back to their families in the States. Their families actually would hear them. We dropped them mail from home. We tried to keep them like kings. We were afraid we might lose some of them from shock. In many cases the survivors were in better shape than the rescue teams when they got to them."

One of the search planes maintaining a vigil over the pilot of the B-17, an officer named Rich, noticed that he was not recovering the supply kits that were being dropped to him. A Rescue paradoctor, Captain Pope B. Holliday, made a spectacular jump into the jungle to find out why. Holliday found Rich half-dead. The lieutenant had suffered from shock and had been without food and water for five days. Holliday went to work on him and when the ground party broke through six days later Rich was able to walk out.

Nine days after the B-17 had gone down another ground party reached one of the crewmen, a sergeant named Wylie. They found Wylie had fractured his leg in the jump and had been unable to retrieve any of the supplies dropped to him. He was too weak to be carried the six miles through the jungle to where the helicopter was waiting. The ground team spent the next three days cutting down enough of the trees—with the help of forty natives—to make room for a chopper to come down right there and then they radioed out a summons. Dave Andersen, helicopter pilot, took off and brought his chopper into the hole in the jungle with extraordinary coolness and skill. The whole effort was too late, however. Sergeant Wylie died as he was being loaded on the helicopter.

Other than Wylie, and one other crewman who never was located, every single man on the B-17 was rescued and brought safely out of the jungle. And when Rizon went back to Managua, when it was all over, he was handed an interesting piece of intelligence. "The American consul and the military attaché came out to greet us and they told us we had stopped a revolution. The people were all ready to pull off this thing and then they saw all this equipment and about fifteen airplanes and soldiers with packs and they thought the Americans were interceding and they called the whole thing off."

The Bolivian floods affected only South Americans. The B-17 crash affected only airmen from the United States. There followed an episode that linked North Americans and South Americans in tragedy, when, not long after the fliers were taken out of the jungle, a C-47 crashed in the Andes. On board were Brigadier General John R. Hawkins, chief of the United States Military Mission to Peru, and members of his staff, and also a number of Peruvian officials, including the son-in-law of the President of Peru. The search for these men gave Rizon his weirdest experience of all.

"After a long search of five or six days which was hampered by extreme turbulence and violent weather conditions we located the crashed airplane on the last range of the Andes before the Peruvian jungle area started. It had, according to reports given by the natives, been flying low through a violent rainstorm and apparently had crashed head on and had killed everybody instantly.

"The point of impact was in an inaccessible area inhabited by Inca Indians who speak a language that hasn't yet been deciphered. We conferred with Peruvian officials at Talara and were told the Indians were headhunters and very hostile. Even the Peruvian military never went down there.

"After getting these facts I decided the best approach was to soften up the area, and I obtained the counsel of a young lad who had been a former sergeant in the Air Force and who was now studying for the ministry. He was down there on a university grant trying to decipher the Inca language.

"At the missionary's suggestion we fixed up little bundles of cloth and needles and thread and various things he thought an Inca Indian would be interested in. He also suggested we include a can of gun-powder in each bundle. He told us the Indians had some old Spanish muskets. We got together about fifty or sixty of these little bundles and dropped them all around the area of the crash. We did this for about two or three days, and then finally selected a level area that was about ten miles from the crash and three of us went in with this missionary in his small plane.

"After about an hour the natives came out of the bush and the missionary tried to speak with them. After considerable difficulty he let them know our purpose for being there, that we were Americans, not Spanish, and then he asked if they would recruit about thirty people to carry our gear to the crash site so we could recover the remains and the military documents aboard. While they were getting ready I visited the chief's hut and found the tribe still practiced the art of headhunting and they showed me how they shrank heads and mummified them. They did this by removing the bony structure and filling the head with hot sand which would shrink it down to the size of a fist and still have all the features.

"The chief also demonstrated the art of using the blowgun with poison darts. They carried a little pouch attached to their G-strings and kept it filled with curare. They dipped the dart in the curare and put it in the blowgun and could knock off a bird at fifty feet with the greatest of ease."

It was with natives with these talents and habits that Rizon and the others started out for the wrecked C-47. "It took three and a half days to reach the scene of the crash. It was about eight miles up the bed of a difficult dry stream filled with huge rocks that had tumbled down from the side of the range of the Andes—almost an avalanche of them. We had a C-47 supply airplane that kept in contact with us daily and dropped food and other provisions—including an occasional beer. The natives would have nothing to do with the beer but once we emptied the contents they would fight for the cans. We finally recovered the bodies and the documents and brought them back to Lima."

These missions and similar ones conducted in other places slowly did the job of establishing Rescue, and Dick Kight found that he was having it a little easier selling his command—Rizon and other field commanders were selling it for him in a way that nobody could argue against. Kight saw Rescue grow and win respect. Detachments began to be reclassified as squadrons and squadrons developed into groups and Rescue units were sent out to other places in the world.

In the latter part of 1948 Rizon, a lieutenant colonel now, was rotated out of Panama and was assigned to the 5th Rescue Group, based at Lowry Field, Denver, at the time, and which now mothered four squadrons of its own. In very short order it was demonstrated that regional disasters were not limited to strange foreign countries and that Rescue was as effective and useful in the United States as it was in Bolivia.

For that was the period of the operations "Hay Lift" and "Snowbound" when blizzards struck at Colorado and Nebraska and Wyoming, and Americans found they were as helpless in the face of the fury of the elements as were natives on the Mamoré River. "We evacuated many people by helicopter and snow weasel," Rizon said. "They were completely stranded by snowdrifts and deep snow. We supplied five or six intercontinental trains that were stranded, dropped food and blankets. Initially it was exclusively Air Rescue. Then the Army came into the picture and of course the Civil Air Patrol and the Red Cross and other relief agencies. It was cut down so fine that we supplied individual Indian huts by air drop.

"There was a village that had been isolated for three or four days and we were requested to drop some radium to save the life of a sick woman. The Fitzsimmons General Hospital in Denver supplied the radium. I flew this mission myself. Just before we were ready to depart they arrived with the radium. It was a very small package but when I tried to lift it it almost pulled me through the floor. It was a great thrill to kick off three quarter of a million dollars' worth of radium into a big snowbank. It was recovered, and I was told later it saved the life of the woman."

Among others who benefited were ranchers whose cattle were stranded on the range without food. "One of my pilots told me he had talked to one rancher who had been out attempting to help his stock and it was so cold that he had on an old bearskin coat. He was making his way through the heavy snow when all of a sudden an airplane comes overhead and drops him a bale of hay."

With Rescue looking at last as though it might be here to stay, it became more and more apparent that if its job was to be done with maximum efficiency it was going to need its own special-type airplane to work with, something more than old bombers. Toward the end of 1949 Dick Kight was considering the possibilities of a new plane, the Grumman Albatross, and he sent one of the amphibians out to Rizon to be tested.

"About three weeks after it arrived we had a B-36 crash off Vancouver Island. We were returning to Denver from the search mission when I lost my right engine over the Rockies at 17,000 feet. There was a range of mountains behind me at 13,000 feet and another in front at 14,000.

"I was heavily loaded with Rescue people—there were twelve aboard—and equipment, and with that weight my single-engine ceiling was about forty-five hundred feet. There was no place to go but down, and I was descending at the rate of 500 feet a minute. It was one of the tightest situations I have ever found myself in. It was just starting to get dark and I didn't want to bail out my crew except as a last resort because the temperatures were so low.

"I remembered that a little strip of Highway 40 ran between Granby and Frazier in Colorado and I thought I might make it so I headed that way. When I arrived over Granby I was about four hundred feet in the air and I picked up this strip of highway. I landed on the highway and the landing was successful except on the approach I saw a truck that had stopped. The driver had apparently become so excited at seeing a plane land on the highway that he just stopped the truck and jumped into a snowbank.

"I kept trying to slow the plane down without skidding into a snowbank myself and I also tried to pull the right wheel over on the shoulder of the highway so the float on the plane would miss the truck. Finally, just before coming to the truck, going about fifteen miles an hour, I managed to get the right wheel into the snowbank and did a forty-five degree turn into the truck and came to a stop. We were about three inches from the truck.

"As soon as we stopped the truck driver dashed out of the snowbank and climbed back into his truck and before we knew it he had raced off. About ten minutes later a highway patrol car came along and the officer happened to be a man I had met before in a rescue in the mountains. I was furious, naturally, that the truck driver hadn't driven his truck off the road when he saw us coming. The officer took off after him and caught him. He gave him a ticket—for parking on the highway."

The reason for the engine failure proved to be a minor bug, easily rectified. The Albatross was taken over as a Rescue plane and given the identification SA-16, the initials standing for "search aircraft." The plane went on to make a little history for itself, as you have seen.

Dick Kight's original thesis that going out on any job anywhere would prove invaluable as training was strikingly borne out during the destructive Kansas floods. Rizon and his men assisted in that disaster, along with other military and civilian relief agencies, and American lives were saved because of the experience Rizon had gained in the Bolivian floods.

Soon afterward Rescue headquarters was moved from West Palm Beach to Washington. Rizon was taken out of his group and was assigned to the new headquarters as director of Operations. Now the two men who had believed, Dick Kight and Bob Rizon, were working hand in hand. And they had something to work with.

Rescue now was international. It had its own type plane—one that would set down on land and water, and, as the boys up in Alaska got to fooling around, on ice as well. It was learning to know more every day about the peculiar merits of another kind of flying machine, the helicopter. It was developing scientific techniques for reading the sea to make hitherto impossible water landings simple routine. It was training its own doctors and jumpers and medical technicians. The flying St. Bernards had come a long way in a short time and now Rescue was destined to take its giant step. Three months after Rizon took up his new duties in Washington the "police action" started in Korea. Rescue now was to come of age.

When the Communists began hostilities in Korea, the Air Rescue Service had its 3rd Group in Japan, with group headquarters in Johnson Air Base, just outside of Tokyo, and another in Hokkaido, northernmost of the four main Japanese islands, and two others in Nagoya and Ashiya in the south. The initial mission given Rescue was to fly aerial reconnaissance and to furnish B-29 orbits for the fighters and bombers going out on strikes. It was a respectable job but it wasn't exactly Rescue. With SA-16's and helicopters sitting all around Japan something more than that seemed called for. But what? General Hoyt Vandenberg, Air Force chief of staff, sent Kight and Rizon over to see.

The two men prowled around Korea for a week, talking to Army commanders and then they visited their own bases in Japan and talked to their own officers. From these conferences one step forward was taken: helicopters would be tried out as aerial taxis to fly behind lines and pick up downed airmen. Nobody knew how it would work—the helicopters were without protective armor of any kind against enemy fire and they carried no armament. It was suggested that a single bullet from an enemy rifle might put one out of commission. But the chopper kids were eager to find out.

Kight had to return to Washington to run his command there but General George E. Stratemeyer, commander of the

Far East Air Forces, directed Rizon to remain until he was satisfied Rescue was doing all it was capable of doing. "We knew there was a major mission for Rescue but we didn't exactly know what it was yet," Rizon said. "Rescue, as it was then, had never had a war to find out. After Colonel Kight left I went down to Ashiya and worked there, setting up the effort we would put forth in Korea, as Colonel Kight and I had planned it.

"I then went over to Taegu and contacted General Earl E. Partridge, commander of the 5th Air Force, who had moved his headquarters to Taegu, which was right on the front line. The lines were very fluid. The entire American force occupied a very small corner and we were getting pushed back fast. General Partridge and General Walton H. Walker, the 8th Army commander who was killed later, elected personally to remain there. I elected to retain our small helicopter effort there, too.

"We were using H-5's to retrieve the air crews from behind the line. A full load was four: paramedic, pilot, and two passengers. Normally we would take only one passenger at a time. We also used the SA-16's to pick up ditched crews from the water and as a logistical airplane to get into our advanced strip at Taegu. But that was still not enough. There was still some special mission for Rescue, something only Rescue could and should do, but we couldn't put our finger on it."

And then one blessed day Bob Rizon slapped his whole big hand on it. He was sitting outside his tent one night, racking his brains as usual for the clue to the real mission of Rescue in Korea. He got up and wandered over to the air strip where wounded soldiers were being loaded on C-47's for evacuation to hospitals in Japan.

These wounded men had been picked up from front-line positions and had been carted by ambulance, busses, trucks, anything on wheels, to Taegu. The job of getting them to the strip had been accomplished as rapidly and as efficiently as possible under the circumstances. Only one thing was wrong. About one man out of four was dead when he got to Taegu. These men had been alive when they were loaded on the vehicles, but they had died during the long, harrowing ride.

"The thought occurred to me then," Rizon said. "I turned around and looked at our helicopters doing nothing. I thought: why don't we use the *helicopters* to bring these people out? That was what was killing them—the long ride on the road." On that noisy and harassed air strip it seemed to Bob Rizon that bells had started to ring. He jumped into his jeep and drove to headquarters and spilled out to General

Partridge. "I told him I wanted every helicopter in Korea that we could get and that I had six more of them in Japan committed to local areas and that I wanted to order all of them to Korea."

As Rizon spoke, General Partridge rose slowly to his feet and when Rizon was finished the general took him over to the headquarters of General Walker and asked him to say it all over again. The two generals looked at each other silently. Then Walker brought Rizon to the office of his surgeon general. "When I told the surgeon about it he stood with tears in his eyes," Rizon said.

The doctor and the Rescue expert sat down and worked out a front-line evacuation plan that is still standard operating procedure today and that constitutes one of the great revolutionary developments to emerge from the Korean war. "We set up a front-line aid station, collecting station in back of that, and then a receiving station. They would evacuate to the collecting station and then we would pick up the ones with the more critical injuries and fly them to the receiving station where the hospital was set up. It was no more than twenty or thirty minutes' flight by helicopter—but by truck it took twenty-four to thirty hours."

Rizon went out on the first missions himself, to the front lines and behind the front lines. The big question—the ability of the helicopter to stand up under enemy fire—soon was answered. "It turned out that the chopper was not so vulnerable as we thought it might be. We thought a small shell through the blade would disintegrate the thing. But we would come back many times with holes through the blades. Once we came back with about a foot of one of the blades gone."

As the pilots gained confidence in the ruggedness of their little aircraft they went in deeper and deeper, penetrating far into enemy territory, landing often in isolated pockets under heavy fire from enemy troops. One of the immortal tableaus of that war, repeated on scores of occasions, was that of a chopper coming down in an area ringed by the enemy, a medical technician jumping out and giving a wounded man first aid or plasma or drugs to ease his pain, loading him on a helicopter, and then the aircraft taking off again under a furious hail of Communist bullets. After a while the Rescue men didn't even bother to patch up the bullet holes.

And during all this the Rescue fliers carried nothing more than side-arms. The helicopter picked up a lot of nicknames as the grim weeks wore on, names given in thanks and affection in the heat of battle. The boys called it the "whirly bird" and the "flying windmill" and the "egg beater." By whatever name it was called, the gawky, slow-moving, defenseless aircraft became the symbol of life in Korea. For its work the 3rd Air Rescue Group was awarded the first Presidential Unit Citation given in the Korean war.

Two months after he had got his inspired brainstorm on the air strip at Taegu Rizon went to Tokyo to report to General Stratemeyer. He could now say he believed Rescue was doing all it was possible for it to do. He didn't have to tell the general much. The word had got to Tokyo from Korea. He briefed Stratemeyer on the details and in his turn Stratemeyer briefed General MacArthur. Rizon then was summoned to MacArthur's headquarters and was directed to sit down with Army people to explain the methods he had worked out so that they might establish a similar system. Rizon then turned over the job to Lieutenant Colonel Theodore Tatum, Operations officer for the 3rd Group, and he headed back for the States.

"Tatum was almost entirely responsible for the success of the group from there on out," Rizon said. It was not a small success. In the end, when the deadly "police action" was over, the record was put together: a total of 9,680 critically wounded men—from all the United Nations who had joined to resist Communist aggression—were evacuated from the front lines. At the mortality rate that had prevailed before the choppers went into action, more than two thousand of these would have died before they could get to hospitals. In addition, 996 men were picked up from *behind* enemy lines.

After he returned from Korea, Rizon was sent over to the headquarters of the Strategic Air Command to assist SAC in its own rescue and survival program. While he was there Rescue got itself a new boss. The puny little baby Dick Kight had been handed now was a healthy boy. The 800 men in their little detachments had become almost ten thousand men in eleven groups and forty-five squadrons. Kight had done his job for four and a half years, longer than commanders normally remain with a command. In August 1952 Brigadier General Thomas Jefferson Du Bose was named commanding general.

There could be no greater contrast between men than between Dick Kight and Tommy Du Bose. Kight was a visionary, a crusader, a man who imagined how things could be before they were. Du Bose was a forceful, driving, tireless executive, an officer who set up impossibly high standards and then made his men make them possible. Where Dick Kight appealed, and got—Du Bose demanded, and got. As I said before, both came along at exactly the right time. When nobody knew Rescue and it didn't even know itself, Rescue needed Kight. And now that it knew, it needed Du Bose.

One of the big problems that confronted the new commander at the outset was the high accident rate. There was plenty of reason for it—new-type airplanes, new-type missions, new-type techniques that had to be learned from scratch, and the nature of Rescue work itself. Du Bose ignored all these justifications. He hammered safety into the heads of all his commanders until it came out their ears. There was not the slightest slackening of effort, anybody anywhere could call on Rescue, but the time for hell-for-leather experimenting was ended. And the accident graph started to fall.

Tommy Du Bose's enthusiasm and drive kept building. On the tenth anniversary of the founding of the Air Rescue Service, in May of 1956, he said with great emotion: "To me it has always been a source of wonder and pride that the most potent and destructive military force ever known should create a special service dedicated to saving life. Its concept is typically American. All over the world Air Rescue affords daily proof that as Americans we hold human life to be the most precious commodity on earth. To the people of foreign lands who see Rescue in action it serves as a constant rebuttal to those who propagandize against us."

And Du Bose had some pretty impressive figures to go with his statement. In those ten years Rescue men have flown more than 173,351 hours on search and rescue missions alone. That doesn't include escort and orbit jobs which they do every day of the year, just to be on the scene in case of trouble. During those thousands of hours Rescue came to the aid of 44,520 human beings—in almost every part of the world outside the Iron Curtain.

When Bob Rizon finished his tour with SAC in March 1952, he was given command of the new 12th Air Rescue Group, which existed only on paper. He spent the next eight months activating, training, and equipping the group and its four squadrons and then in November of that year the group was deployed to Europe. The headquarters and three of the squadrons were based in an old bombed-out airfield at Bordeaux and the fourth squadron was established at Fürstenfeldbruck, near Munich. Rizon, promoted to colonel, now had a different kind of task on his hands. The techniques of Rescue were pretty well set. His main job was a diplomatic one—he had to make the military and political leaders of the European nations understand what he was there for.

"It was our number-one mission on arrival to establish

relationships with the various governments and become acquainted with the existing rescue agencies belonging to those governments. For instance, the French Air Force had a rescue service—however, it had very little equipment beyond a communications system. We had to establish a method of cooperation."

He had to proceed with infinite tact. The French, then as always, were touchy and proud. If they were going to accept help it must not appear to be charity. Rizon worked out a plan in which the French monitoring system was combined with American airplanes and crews. The French were given an important function to perform and they responded with grace and dignity.

"We had many, many conferences elsewhere. With the Italians—who have one of the finest rescue setups in Europe—with the Spaniards, Norwegians, Danes. I went to Madrid, Rome, Oslo, Copenhagen. Our relationships became extremely cordial and we were able to effect many rescue operations jointly with these national agencies.

"I think one of the highlights was our association with the Spanish. The Spanish have always had a small rescue arm but only recently started to develop it. They sent several of their crews to the United States and they were trained at West Palm Beach at our school. The Spanish Air Force obtained, through the military assistance program, the same type of equipment that we use—SA-16's and SH-19's. Early in 1954 we offered, through the Joint United States Military Advisers Group in Madrid, to help in the transition from the type they had been using to the new equipment.

"They accepted this offer and we went to Madrid and then on to the island of Majorca and worked with the people in command of the Spanish Air Rescue Service. We gave them all of our operating procedures and we also gave them advanced open-sea training in the SA-16, using our instructor pilots. As a result the present Spanish Air Rescue Service is modeled on our own."

In February 1953, a few months after Rizon arrived with his group in France, he received a telephone call at his headquarters in Bordeaux from General Lauris Norstad, commanding general of the United States Air Forces in Europe, informing him that the dykes had burst in Holland. Norstad directed him to go to the Dutch airfield of Gilze 'Rijen and take command of the United States air rescue effort.

Rizon was at Gilze 'Rijen less than two and a half hours after he hung up, and he conferred with Dutch and American authorities there. Time, he realized, was of the essence. Help had to be fast or it would be useless. He chose Gilze 'Rijen as his command post and picked another airfield closer to the disaster area for the helicopters to work out of. He selected a third field to be used by the transports that were bringing in supplies donated from everywhere.

He rounded up a fleet of twenty-six helicopters, pulling them in from his own squadrons and from the group in England and from other American units. He got twenty more helicopters from European countries. He brought together six SA-16's, twelve C-119 transports, a couple of C-47's, and ten L-20's, lightplanes. It was the greatest peacetime Rescue operation in history and the greatest concentration of helicopters outside of Korea.

His work fell into two parts: first was the direct assistance to the people in the flooded areas, the men and women and little children who were sitting on rooftops and floating in water. Then there was the no-less-important task of coordinating the supplies coming in on cargo ships and transferring those supplies to choppers and smaller planes and getting them to where they were needed.

"On a Rescue mission such as this you are going full steam all day long and when you had to stop, after dark, you spent until about four o'clock the next morning going over what took place that day and what you intended to do the next day and briefing the people involved." Somewhere in that hour Rizon got his night's sleep. In the week he was there he got all of eleven hours on his cot. He lost twenty pounds. But there was plenty all around to keep him and his exhausted flying men going, sleep or no sleep.

"I have seen lots of disasters but nothing like these floods. There was one little village we flew over and the entire village was drowned. There were 300 people in this village. All over buildings were just pulverized from the water. An entire village would look like a row of sugar cubes that had been saturated and just melted away.

"Debris was floating on the surface—including thousands of dead cattle and other animals, making a sanitation problem of some size. It struck so quickly, and before it was realized how extensive a disaster it was and rescue facilities were alerted many lives were lost that could have been saved if we had earlier warning."

The majority of lives were saved in the first couple of days. Then the work settled down to small, individual missions with the choppers often setting down on the dykes themselves to pick up the stranded. "I feel that our people turned in a terrific performance. The entire operation was conducted under extremely adverse weather conditions—blinding snowstorms, freezing rains changing to thawing conditions. Nothing seemed beyond those men. Once a helicopter was very heavily loaded, it had picked up everyone it could carry. It was forced down by a storm and had to wait it out, then took off again. They saw a basket floating in the water and they saw a baby in it. They came down and hovered and one of the men went down on the hoist and took the baby aboard."

Queen Juliana and Prince Bernhard joined personally in rescue work. "They participated from sunrise to sunset doing everything they could do to assist us, and I think they helped us most by encouraging people to leave their floating homes. That was the big difficulty we had. We would go into an area and had to argue with the people to let us take them out. Even though they knew there was a strong chance they would drown, they didn't want to leave their possessions.

"We took the Queen and the Prince out into various areas and we would land on a dyke and the Queen and the Prince would get out and they would talk to the people and tell them they must allow us to evacuate them. In some cases they had to order them out.

"At the end of each day the Prince would come to our headquarters and review the day's activities and make suggestions as to what he thought we should do the next day. Each time I saw him he praised the effort we were making. You know he is a pilot but he had never flown a helicopter before. Afterward, when it was all over, he invited all the chopper pilots to the palace and gave them his thanks."

After a week the job was done and the people of Holland settled down to the heartbreaking task of recovery. Rizon returned to his headquarters at Bordeaux, but he left his units in Holland, still on alert. "We were afraid we would have a repetition. We were still having fairly high tides and if the surface winds built up we would have had an even worse disaster because the big dyke around Rotterdam was just ready to go. The Army had several thousand ground people reinforcing the dykes. If they had let go, they would have wiped Rotterdam right off the map." The winds and the tides held back, however, and the dykes remained firm. A week later the Rescue effort officially was terminated. What had been done by the fliers would never be terminated, not to any person in Holland.

That September Rizon's group headquarters was moved to the new air base in Sembach, Germany. The primary mission of the group was to support the 12th Air Force, but the civilian emergencies kept coming along—big things like the avalanches in Austria, the floods in Bavaria and the Po Valley in Italy, and little things in endless stream, children who fell off a mountain ledge in France and had to be rescued by helicopter, American pilots who crashed, a Swiss pilot who got lost in the Alps.

And then in June 1955 it came time for Colonel Robert Rizon to rotate back to the States. It was then that he received word from the Netherlands Government that he had been honored with a knighthood by Queen Juliana.

Colonel Rizon received other honors from his superiors in Germany and then he wound up his affairs and turned over his group to his successor. After more than ten years in Rescue Bob was then given a new assignment elsewhere in the Air Force. But he hopes that will not be for long.

Dick Kight said it this way: "Once you're a Rescue man you're a missionary for the rest of your life. If it could be done on a voluntary basis, Air Rescue could be manned three times over."

Tommy Du Bose said it this way: "I figure I've got the best job in the Air Force. Air Rescue is an instrument of national policy—not only in the lives we save all over the world but in the lives we don't have to save. I hope they lose my papers in the Pentagon and leave me here from now on."

And Bob Rizon, in his new post, still watching Rescue and what Rescue men are doing everywhere, asks: "When can I get back in?"